FOURTH EDITION

The
Modern
Conductor

A college text on conducting based on
the technical principles of Nicolai Malko
as set forth in his *The Conductor and His Baton*

Elizabeth A. H. Green
Professor Emeritus, The University of Michigan

PRENTICE-HALL, INC.
Englewood Cliffs, New Jersey 07632

Library of Congress Cataloging-in-Publication Data

Green, Elizabeth A. H.
  The modern conductor.

  Bibliography: p.
  Includes indexes.
  1. Conducting.   I. Malko, Nicolai, 1883–1961.
Conductor and his baton.   II. Title.
MT85.G785   1987   781.6'35   86-15054
ISBN 0-13-590183-9

Editorial/production supervision and
  interior design: Barbara Alexander
Manufacturing buyer: Ray Keating

Printed in the United States of America

10   9   8   7   6   5   4   3   2

ISBN   0-13-590183-9   01

Prentice-Hall International (UK) Limited, *London*
Prentice-Hall of Australia Pty. Limited, *Sydney*
Editora Prentice-Hall do Brasil, Ltda., *Rio de Janeiro*
Prentice-Hall Canada Inc., *Toronto*
Prentice-Hall Hispanoamericana, S.A., *Mexico*
Prentice-Hall of India Private Limited, *New Delhi*
Prentice-Hall of Japan, Inc., *Tokyo*
Prentice-Hall of Southeast Asia Pte. Ltd., *Singapore*

Contents

13

Interpreting the Vocal Score   191

14

Interpreting the Instrumental Score: Band and Orchestra   202

15

Memorizing the Score: Performing the Score   218

Appendix A

Seating Charts   229

Appendix B

Instrumentation   236

The Art of Conducting

by Eugene Ormandy

The art of conducting, one of the most complex and demanding activities in the realm of music, comprises both the visual public performance and the constant application of technique. Although they are inseparable in performance, they can be analyzed in the light of the unique problems which each presents. Similarly, the conductor himself functions on three levels, each dependent upon the other, all culminating in the performance itself.

Personal Study. On the first level, his period of study, the conductor prepares himself both technically and artistically. On this level he must be musician, historian, stylist, orchestrator, and listener. He must study the score so that he "hears" it in his mind. As he does this he evaluates the music and makes a beginning toward balancing the many strands of musical line. He must understand the historical context in which a particular work is conceived, and bring to bear upon the growing interpretive edifice a thorough knowledge of the stylistic requirements inherent in the work. To study such a masterwork as Beethoven's *Eroica* Symphony without some knowledge of the composer's response to the ideals of the French Revolution and Napoleon's unique political position in 1806 is to study music in a vacuum. Needless to say, it was not created in a vacuum. Among the elements of stylistic validity are tempi and dynamics. A Mozart allegro differs by far from a Tchaikovsky allegro. Similarly, a forte in Haydn is an entirely different matter from a Wagner forte.

A thorough knowledge of the orchestral colors and timbres enables the studying conductor to "hear" the orchestral sound while he studies. When conducting older composers he must sometimes compensate for the technical inadequacies of the times by delicately rewriting certain passages in terms of today's more complete orchestras and more highly skilled players. Present-day performances of such works as the Fifth Symphony of Beethoven, the Great C Major Symphony of Schubert, the symphonies of Schumann, to mention but a few, are rarely given without many instrumental changes. Even so "pure" a conductor as Toscanini did not deny the composer the benefit of today's heightened instrumental resources.

Finally, while he studies, the conductor must "listen" objectively to the work, pacing its progress, spacing its climaxes, deriving a general aural concept of the musical architecture, and evaluating its merit as it will be heard by the public. He must recall Richard Strauss's dictum: "Remember that you are making music not for your own pleasure but for the joy of your listeners."

Rehearsal. The second level upon which the conductor functions is the rehearsal, in which he prepares the orchestra both technically and

Reprinted from *Encyclopedia International* by permission of the publishers, Lexicon Publications, New York.

artistically. It is on this level that he acts as a guide to the orchestra, building up in their minds a concept of the work parallel to his own, for the eventual public performance requires an enlightened and sensitive orchestra playing not "under" a conductor, but rather "with" him.

During the rehearsals he must clarify all problems of metrics and tempi, elucidating his own pacing of the work. He must temper all dynamic markings so that the instrumental "sound" is balanced in all its components. The older composers always wrote the same dynamics vertically for each simultaneous part, straight down the page in their scores. It was only composer-conductors like Mahler or Wagner, who realized the pitfalls of dynamics incautiously marked.

As he rehearses, the conductor, surrounded by the physical sound of the work, checks his own concept of the music, comparing it with the actual music. In those particular instances where the two do not fit, he must alter one or the other. It is essential that the two, the concept and the actuality, run amicably along. In addition, there are instances, such as the lengthy oboe solo in Strauss's *Don Juan*, where the prudent conductor who is fortunate enough to possess a highly sensitive oboe player permits him to "have his head," acting almost as an accompanist rather than a leader.

Performance. It is in performance that the conductor operates upon the highest and most demanding level. Here the work is finished technically; the orchestra is fully prepared for all of its demands; the conductor, his study and preparation behind him, now immerses himself in the music, identifying himself with it both emotionally and mentally. But it is at this crucial time that the most difficult function of the conductor comes into full play. He must, while identifying himself with the music, keep a constant watch upon the progress of the work, allowing a portion of his analytical mind to constantly evaluate the sound and pace of the performance. He must be prepared to instantaneously make any adjustments, large or small, in the actual performance required for the fullest realization of his inner concept. Many factors make this necessary: a different hall, a player's momentary inattention, the effect of several thousand persons upon the acoustics, even the understandable enthusiasm of performance which might affect the tempo. At such a moment the conductor meets his greatest challenge, for the progress of the work must not suffer in the slightest; there must be no detectable "hitch." At such moments the experience of a conductor tells, for the young conductor, new to such emergencies, tends to do one thing at a time. Music does not permit this, for it flows in time, and all adjustments must be superimposed upon the uninterrupted continuum.

In the extent to which he succeeds on any or all of these levels lies the measure of the conductor's merit, both as a musician and as an artist. In his study he can separate the art from the technique, but in performance he must strive fully and constantly for a total artistic experience. Otherwise he can never fulfill his high calling: creating the reality of the work itself.

Preface

This fourth edition of *The Modern Conductor* is the result of some gentle streamlining, with the goal of achieving still more clarity through brevity and of saving time for everyone concerned.

Where chapters from the previous edition have been deleted, their content will be found elsewhere in the book. All technique now resides in Part I, all score study in Part II. The chapter on clefs and transpositions has been largely rewritten. Some small and necessary additions have been made here and there.

It is our firm belief that all conducting students should be required to sing. Singing is the quickest and most secure way to develop the inner hearing so necessary in score study. The vocal cords respond *only* to what has first been *imagined in the mind* (the inner ear). Welcome additions to the text are the eight new excerpts to be sung or played—five of them drawn from George Frederick Handel's Op. 1—for the very first classes where time-beating is introduced.

The technical materials—physical exercises and manual techniques—are those originated by Nicolai Malko, whose impact as a conductor and teacher was felt around the world during his lifetime. There was scarcely a great orchestra anywhere in Europe, the Soviet Union, North America, South America, Israel, or Japan that he had not conducted, and he was knighted by the King of Denmark for his contributions to the musical life of that country. Malko died in 1961 while he was resident Musical Director of the Sydney (Australia) Symphony Orchestra. The Nicolai Malko International Competition for Young Orchestra Conductors originated in Copenhagen in 1965 and continues to be held at three-year intervals. During the last year of his life, Malko read the manuscript of the first edition of *The Modern Conductor* and gave it his blessing. The author pays respectful tribute to this great teacher and superb conductor.

While no two mature conductors conduct exactly alike, there exists a basic clarity of technique that is instantly—and universally—recognized. When this clarity shows in the conductor's gestures, it signifies that he or she has acquired a secure understanding of the principles upon which it is founded and the reasons for its existence, and that this thorough knowledge has been accompanied by careful, regular, and dedicated practice.

Students who have patiently *mastered* the material presented herein have proven its worth by the appreciative responses they have received from professional musicians and by the contracts they have been awarded.

The author extends sincere appreciation to the many publishers who have again permitted duplication of their copyrighted materials in this new edition. Appreciation also goes to Mr. Norwell Therien, Jr., Senior Editor in the College Humanities Department at Prentice-Hall; his most helpful assistant, Jean Wachter; and Barbara Alexander and Mark Stevens, production editors of this fourth edition. All of us have tried to make it the best of the four.

Elizabeth A. H. Green
Ann Arbor, Michigan

1

So You Want
To Be a Conductor?

To stand in front of an orchestra, band, or chorus and beat time does not make one a conductor.

But to bring forth thrilling music from a group of singers or players, to inspire them (through one's own personal magnetism) to excel, to train them (through one's own musicianship) to become musicians themselves, personally to feel the power of music so deeply that the audience is lifted to new heights emotionally—or gently persuaded, through music, to forget momentarily the dust of earth and to spend a little time in another world—yes, *this* can be called conducting.

A fine conductor is, first of all, a fine musician. He must be a sincere and inspiring leader. He must have integrity where the music is concerned. He knows his score thoroughly and can convey its meaning to the players through superbly trained hands. He has developed his sense of pitch not only to be able to sing any part of the score, but to be able to hear it in the mind (the inner ear) so loudly that when the actual rendition does not come up to the standard fixed in the musical imagination he will set about attaining that ideal during the rehearsal. He *knows* theory, harmony, counterpoint, musical history, form, and analysis. He has reached a professional performance level himself on some one instrument (or with his voice), and he is eternally interested to learn more and more about the problems of each instrument of his ensemble. He has, somewhere along the way, taken a thorough course in orchestration; and all transpositions have become second nature.

The best conductors are innately endowed with musicality—a term that need not be defined because those who have it know what it means and those who do not will never understand it through definition. Finally, any conductor worth his salt must have a mind trained to work as fast as lightning and a thousand times more continuously.

The art of conducting is the highest, most complete synthesis of all facets of the musical activity, and it should be so regarded by anyone dedicating himself to the profession of the baton.

PRELIMINARY OBSERVATIONS

The student of conducting should remember that, whether he is practicing exercises for skill with his hands and baton, or whether he is studying repertoire, *he should constantly carry in his mind a musical sound.*

Early in his career, the student will learn that there is *never* enough rehearsal time. It is a most precious commodity and must not be wasted. *The goal for each rehearsal should be set in the conductor's mind before he steps on the podium.* He should have thought through what he wishes to accomplish, and then he should proceed to do it confidently and enthusiastically. Things will not always go as he has planned, but he will not be so inclined to waste his opportunities *if* he has planned.

In the school-music field, a pleasing personality is a great help. In the professional field it will also help provided the young conductor is modest, sincere, and knows his business. If he respects the musicians of the orchestra, he will start out with at least a chance of winning their respect in return.

No conductor can disassociate himself completely from the teaching facet of his trade. Knowing how to teach, how to suggest changes, without prejudicing the members of the ensemble, is a valuable asset.

A conductor does not "conduct" every note of the score-page, even though he must *know* every note. Learning what to conduct is a process of continuous growth. Gradually the score will tell him, beforehand, that this or that is going to cause trouble. Such things as the very first sound at the beginning of the composition, the indicating of cues when the players need them, showing changes of tempo, the isolated cymbal crash (Heaven help the conductor who forgets to show them!),* sudden pianos (*piano subito*), dangerous cut-offs and subsequent entrances, difficult tutti chords that come on irregular beats—for these and similar hazards the conductor *must* be there when he is needed.

---

*Cue the first one in a series. The player will carry on thereafter.

As the conductor works with his own organization he will come to know his players individually as musicians. He will find that this one needs to be reminded (by the conductor's gestures) of certain things that transpired during the rehearsal; that that one must be kept under control dynamically; that this wind-melody-line must be encouraged to project; that the strings will not use the necessary sweep of bow-stroke in certain passages unless the conductor's gestures show that sweep; and that the pianissimo will always be too loud if the conductor does not control his own hands with infinite care. All of this knowledge comes with experience. But during the conductor's student days, he must build the *skill in his gestures* that will give him the control and the interpretative technique he will need as he gains experience.

Above all else every conductor must remember that he is there for the purpose of making music. He makes this music through the medium of his ensemble, the human beings in it. He himself must be inspired by the music; but he must also be able to translate that inspiration into readable signs for the musicians in front of him. He should be dynamically conscious, should have a vital sound-concept of the grandeur of a double-forte or the intensity of the most breathtaking of triple pianos. Every phrase should glow and diminish as the music requires. His gestures should show these things. He must be vital and excited when the music is vital and exciting. He must be able to change instantly to utter calm when the music demands it. Always it is the music and the musical sound that must assume pre-eminence over everything else. After all, that is what made Toscanini Toscanini.

EXERCISES FOR PRACTICE

1. Take with you to a piano any full score. Establish the key of the composition. Then proceed to sing each part, horizontally, skipping octaves as necessary to keep it within your range. Check your pitch often against the piano. If you find that mistakes are creeping in, then sing softly all notes that are skipped between the terminal ends of the intervals. Be sure that you sing them in the given key.

2. Drill your sense of "inner hearing" by playing any note on the piano and then, *without singing that note, imagine* the sound of the next higher half-step and sing *that* pitch. Do the same with the lower half-step; then with whole tones. When the *correct pitch forms in the imagination*, it will come out of your throat. Your vocal chords can produce only what you imagine, nothing else.

3. Further drill your musical imagination by memorizing several lines of one part and then writing them from memory.

2

The Baton

The baton is the conductor's technical instrument as distinguished from his sounding instrument, the orchestra, band, or chorus. The manual technique should be mastered both with and without the baton, and both hands should become skilled. Whether or not to use the stick should be the inspiration of the moment, not the result of insecurity in working either way.

The baton in its present form is the end result of hundreds of years of experimentation in the leading of massed musical performances. The earliest conducting was done with gestures of the hands alone, describing melodic contour, pitches, lengths of notes and phrases. Passing through stages where the leader sat at the organ or piano (often with his figured bass part) and made signs now and then to the singers and players, progressing through the thumping-out of an audible beat, to the silent waving of the concertmaster's bow, and finally resulting in the use of the baton and patterned rhythmic designs, conducting has grown into the most refined sign language we know today. The conductor's slightest gesture has an impact on players who have been trained to watch. And the baton has emerged (especially for the instrumental ensembles) as the *most efficient means of conveying a precise message to the players, if its technique has been mastered.* The tip of the stick gives the clearest possible definition of the exact instant of the beat (the rhythmic pulse called the **takt**), and the cleanest outline of the beat-pattern as such. A skilled baton technique is a great time saver in rehearsals.

To be read easily, the conductor's gestures should be projected to the tip of the stick. The conductor and the members of the ensemble meet at the tip of the baton. When the baton is used, the projection to the tip takes place through the medium of a slightly flexible wrist. The wrist and hand respond to the motions of the arm with a natural ease, and the baton, in turn, to the hand and wrist.* Gestures initiated from the elbow, but accompanied by an inflexible wrist, can be clear, but they are rigid in appearance and do not depict the *musical* aspect of the sound.

EASE WITH THE BATON

The manner in which the baton is held can contribute greatly to the subsequent development of a facile and comfortable technique. Over the years a certain basic grip of the hand on the stick has emerged, subscribed to by such internationally recognized conductors as Sir Thomas Beecham, Wilhelm Furtwängler, Nicolai Malko, Pierre Monteux, Yevgeny Alexandrovich Mravinsky of the Leningrad Philharmonic, Charles Munch, Eugene Ormandy, Herbert von Karajan, Bruno Walter, George Szell, and others.

The basic grip is a fundamental way of holding the stick (Figure 1). As such it should be made the point of departure. This grip, however, is not an eternal attribute. It is often interchanged with the "light grip" (Figures 2 and 6) during the performance in order to show some particular quality dictated by the music itself. George Szell, for example, often resorted to the light grip in his greatly admired interpretations of Mozart.

When the baton is used, it is of utmost importance that it be held so that the tip is clearly visible to all members of the performing group. There is a current tendency to grasp it so that it points too much toward the left. This handicaps the players on the conductor's right and is caused by the faulty grip shown in Figures 9 and 10.

1. The stick is held, fundamentally, between the *tip* of the thumb and the *side* of the index finger. The stick contacts the finger somewhere between the middle joint of the finger and the nail. Just where the contact is made depends upon the relative length of the individual's thumb and finger. It varies among the great conductors. Experimentation will result in a proper and comfortable adjustment. (Figure 1.) Use the baton in the right hand.

2. It is most important that the thumb should bend outward at its knuckle. This bent knuckle contributes to a more relaxed wrist and relieves

---

*The wrist, as such, is only a link between the hand and arm. When the hand is curved upward, the wrist appears to be low; when the hand hangs downward, the wrist appears to be high. What actually happens is simply an adjustment of angle between hand and arm.

a certain amount of muscular tension in the wrist and lower arm. (Figures 1, 2, and 3.) An open space should form between the thumb and the side of the first finger. (Figure 6.)

3. The heel of the stick rests in the fleshy hollow near the base of the thumb. (Figure 2.) This spot shows up well as a dark shadow in Figure 8.

4. The ring finger lightly contacts the heel of the baton, completing a three-point grip: tip of thumb, side of first finger, and ball of ring finger. This grip is both flexible and secure.

5. In time-beating with the baton, the palm of the hand should face the floor. (Figure 4.) This permits the hand to move freely up and down in the wrist joint. In performing the time-beating patterns, the student should feel as if he is tapping each beat with the *tip* of the stick.

6. The tip of the baton should point forward, not leftward. (Figures 4 and 5.) Keep the heel of the stick near the base of the thumb.

7. The light grip is shown in Figure 6. It is used for delicate passages in the music, but lacks intensity in the fortes of a broader character such as in Wagner and Brahms. Both grips should become functional, instantly interchangeable, and used interpretatively as the music demands. Figures 1, 3 and 4 give the basic grip.

Avoid the following:

8. When the first finger presses on top of the stick (Figure 7), a certain stiffness shows in the other fingers and this is inclined to transfer itself to the wrist. Further, such a placing of the first finger often results in a "low" wrist that becomes quite inflexible. Thereafter, the beat-point, instead of being projected to the tip of the stick, actually lies beneath the wrist itself. In passing, notice the rigidity of the ring and the little finger in Figure 7.

9. When the heel of the stick does not contact the palm of the hand, but is allowed to "float," the wrist flexibility tends to become exaggerated; the tip becomes uncontrollably free and precision is lost. (Figure 8.)

10. One should guard constantly against letting the heel of the baton slide to a position under the base of the little finger. (Figures 9 and 11.) Such a position causes the stick to point far left and presents it broadside to the players in the center of the ensemble. Readjust as given in No. 2 above.

11. When the stick slides under the little finger, it sometimes protrudes beyond the palm of the hand thus resulting in "two conductors." (Figure 10.) When the tip is downward on the beat-point, the heel is upward—a difficult situation for the players on the conductor's right.

RECOMMENDED

Figure 1.   The basic grip. Note bent thumb.

Figure 2.   The light grip.

Figure 3.   Contact of the ring finger.

Figure 4.   The basic grip: palm toward floor. Little finger relaxed.

Figure 5.   Baton pointing forward.

Figure 6.   The light grip. Second finger replaces first.

NOT RECOMMENDED

Figure 7.   First finger on top. Ring and little fingers stiff.

Figure 8.   Heel of stick not contacting palm of hand. Thumb stiff and flat.

Figure 9.   Heel of stick under little finger.

Figure 10.   Heel of stick protruding beyond hand. Baton points left.

Figure 11.   Inefficient wrist position, palm not facing floor.

Figure 12.   Strained wrist position: heel of stick is under little finger.

12. The leftward pointing of the stick (Figure 10) can be corrected by holding the hand thumb upward when conducting. (Figure 11.) But now the wrist cannot bend in its natural up-down direction and therefore cannot deliver the conductor's intentions to the tip of the baton. A real tenuto gesture becomes almost impossible.

13. In an effort to make the baton "line up with the arm," certain overly conscientious students have sometimes put an ungainly turn toward the right with the hand in the wrist joint. (Figure 12.) This is unnatural, feels uncomfortable and looks clumsy. Make a straight line from the elbow to the base joint of the middle finger and adjust the stick properly under the thumb.

VISIBILITY OF THE BATON

The natural motions of the arm are circular in character. Any bending of the elbow or wrist causes the fingers to describe a section of a circle. In spite of this, the baton should not be allowed to make circles around the conductor's body, nor should it make arclike vertical lines in its up-and-down motions, swinging back over the shoulder or dropping below the music stand. The tip of the stick should move in a perpendicular plane opposite the conductor's body, and should be clearly visible to all members of the ensemble. The basic (and so important!) etudes for acquiring good arm motions are given below in the Exercises for Practice. They should be practiced daily until the circular motion is eliminated and the desired results achieved. Ten minutes a day will show progress.

What type of baton to use? While personal preference colors one's decision, there are several factors that should be considered. First, is the baton clearly visible, without strain, to the players who are farthest from the conductor? Second, does the stick have a feel of good *balance* in the hand? Third, is the heel of the stick so constructed that the standard grip is easily acquired? The answer seems to indicate a stick that is about twelve inches long, made of light wood (holly wood is often used) properly tapered for effective balance, and with a pear-shaped handle of a size that fits the particular hand and allows the thumb and first finger to contact the shaft. A white baton is easiest seen by the performers.

EXERCISES FOR PRACTICE: CORRECTING
THE CIRCULAR MOTION OF THE ARM

1. Stand rather close to a wall, facing it. Cross the hands in a horizontal position on your diaphragm, palms toward the body, right hand fingertips opposite left wrist. Run the hands outward in a straight line, right hand to the right, left hand to the left. Go about two-thirds as far as your limit of reach. Keep the

hands pointing toward each other all the way and the backs of the hands about two inches from the wall *throughout the motion.* At the terminal ends of the outward motion, turn the hands so that the palms are toward the wall and bring them slowly back to the diaphragm. Keep the fingers pointing outward as nearly as possible until the wrists cross in front of the body. Flip the hands into their original position and continue the exercise. **Warning:** Do not shrug shoulders, especially in the return gesture. Keep the elbows at the side of the body, not resting against the front of the rib cage. The arms hang freely from the shoulders.

2. Let the arms hang full length at the sides, palms facing backward. Gradually raise the arms in a perpendicularly straight line to eyebrow level. Maintain the hanging position (fingers downward) of the hands throughout. At the top of the line flip the hands upward, palms to the front. Bring arms downward to the starting point, retaining the position of the hands (fingers upward) as nearly as possible throughout. Gradually the arms will acquire the feel of the vertical-plane motion, noncircular in character. Wrist flexibility will also have begun its development.

3. Take the baton in hand using the basic grip. Stand so that the tip of the stick is about two inches away from the wall. Repeat the gesture of Exercise 2, keeping the baton about two inches from the wall throughout. Check particularly on the terminal ends of the gesture, that the baton is still two inches from the wall. A similar exercise may be adapted to the horizontal lines of Exercise 1, the palm of the hand facing the floor. In all of these exercises, keep the shoulders relaxed, no shrugging. The arms hang freely from the shoulders.

   Note: The preceding exercises form the basis for the later development of *independent* action in the two hands. Take them seriously at this time so that the foundation is well laid. The results will provide ample reward.

4. Practice holding the baton with the basic grip while you are reading a book or studying. This will help the hand to acquire a feeling of ease and familiarity with the stick. Be sure that you check accurately on the directions as given in the text. It is a waste of time to form an incorrect habit.

5. Practice flicking imaginary drops of water from the tip of the stick. This produces a "crack-the-whip" motion in the wrist and hand and begins the motion needed later on for a good staccato gesture.

6. Study the time-beating patterns for three and four beats per measure (pp. 25 and 26). Perform them with an easy, natural freedom in the arm. Check on the appearance of the time-beating by looking in a mirror. Is the beat-point clearly defined? Can the performers see the stick clearly? Does the tip of the stick make a good connective arc between beat-points?

7. Without the baton, try to acquire the feel of bouncing a ball by tapping it with the tips of the fingers. Then repeat with baton in hand.

   Note: One last word: Too much flexibility in the wrist is as bad as none at all. Keep the wrist motion small.

3

Time-Beating 1: The Basic Techniques (Traditional)

Time-beating is chiefly the business of the right hand, i.e., of the baton. Since a complete conducting technique entails the eventual development of each hand, working independently, students who are naturally left-handed are urged, right from the beginning, to place the baton in the right hand.

For the introductory work in conducting, each hand is trained in time-beating, individually and the two together. The perpendicular motions are similar, but the horizontal gestures move in opposite directions in the two hands. As skills gradually improve, the left hand will replace time-beating with interpretative gestures that are independent of the right hand but correlated with it. This "advanced" facet of the technique will be dealt with in Chapter 5, The Development of the Left Hand.

The mind of the conductor must be trained simultaneously with the hands. The Exercises for Practice at the end of this chapter cannot be done with a static mind. They are designed to challenge the mind to transfer its commands to the hands. In conducting, controls are built first from the mind to the hands, then from the hands to the performers, and finally the music proceeds from the performers to the audience. It is vitally important that the first step, mind to hands, be given the necessary attention while habits are being formed. To attempt to retrain the hands later on, when the mind is giving its active attention to the interpretation of the music, is a difficult and easily neglected process.

When you are on the podium, ready to conduct, stand up straight. Make your appearance as commanding as possible. Feel that you are balanced on the ball of each foot, heels relatively *close together*. A wide stance is ungainly and undignified. Do not stretch your arms out toward your performers, but keep some bend in the elbows, with the hands rather close to the body. Look at your musicians—not at the score—and most especially on the first beats of the piece. *Never* lean toward your performers. It looks terrible from the audience. Eliminate knee action and excess bodily motion. Show poise, dignity, and sincerity, and the audience will respond with appreciation and respect.

STARTING THE SOUND: THE PREPARATORY BEAT

Your first problem will be starting the sound. It takes courage! Plus what is called "impulse of will." When the impulse of will is anemic, everything is lost. There is no conducting. When the impulse of will is strong and the technique is weak, the conductor is eternally confronted with feelings of frustration. His muscles tend to tense up and he tries to substitute mental and emotional drive for physical technique. When the impulse of will is strong and the technique is secure, then the ensemble truly has a leader who can unify the musicianship of all into one secure interpretation. Such a conductor has the finely developed technical skill and the confident drive to convey by his gestures exactly what he wants without confusion or misunderstanding on the part of the players, and he appears at ease.

To start the sound, the conductor has to signal his forthcoming intentions regarding speed, dynamic, and style. This he does in a special motion, called the *preparatory beat*, which precedes the first playing beat.

The speed with which this beat is executed shows the coming tempo. It must, therefore, be absolutely accurate rhythmically. When the baton *starts to move* (in the preparatory gesture), the rhythm of the piece begins. This means, then, that *the preparatory beat must take the time of exactly one beat of the time-beating gestures to follow*. In very slow tempos the half-beat often suffices.

The size of the preparatory beat usually gears itself to the loudness of the coming dynamic. In general, the larger the preparatory beat, the bigger the sound to follow.

The style of the preparatory beat (legato, staccato, tenuto, light, heavy, sustained, ponderous) should set the mood of the music.

The slant of the preparatory beat should be slightly *upward*. *Too much downward curve in the preparatory beat can be mistaken by some of the players as a command to play—with unhappy results.*

The preparatory beat says, "Look out! Here it comes." The next beat says, in no uncertain terms, "Play!" or "Sing!" The beat that commands the sound to come forth should have a downward trajectory, plus impulse of will.

The preparatory beat moves upward and in a direction opposite to the "playing" beat. Samples are shown by the broken lines in Figures 13 and 14. For example, if the piece is to start on the fourth (last) beat of a measure in 4/4 meter, then direction of the preparatory beat would be from left to right (third beat of the measure) but in a slightly upward direction. When the piece starts on Two, make the preparatory beat (One) downward but very small and then enlarge the lead into Two. (Figure 14 (b).)

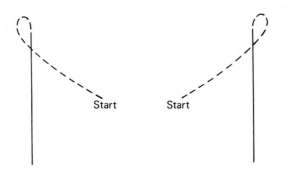

Figure 13.   The preparatory gesture for starting on the first beat of the measure.

There are two basic types of preparatory beat. The first type connects the line of preparation directly to the playing beat (most commonly used). The second type makes an infinitesimal stop between the preparation and the command-to-play beat. Type (a) is most often used. Conquer it first. Type (b) is specialized. It functions when the first played note is to be heavily accented, or when the entrance comes on an afterbeat. Type (b) is to be shunned like the plague if there are three or more notes to be played on the very first sounded beat. In this case, type (a) is imperative.

It is not good to hold the hands in the "Ready!" position for too long a period before beginning the preparatory beat.* It can become confusing to the winds and/or singers who have to prepare the breath. However, the hands should stand perfectly still during the ready position. The instant

---

*The novice conductor should form the habit of glancing around quickly at his musicians when he raises his hands to the "Ready" position to make sure that they, too, are prepared to start.

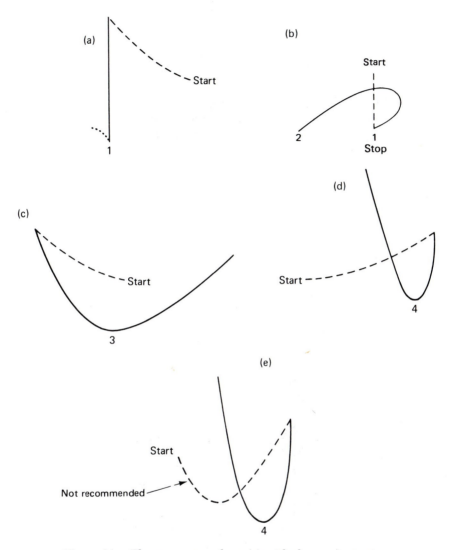

Figure 14. The preparatory beat (a) with the music starting on One; (b) with the music starting on Two; (c) with the music starting on Three; (d) with the music starting on Four; (e) common error, too much drop in the preparatory beat, causes accidents.

they start to move, the rhythm has begun. **Note:** Young conductors are often prone to making a long, slow preparatory beat followed by the real tempo of the music. This results in a ragged performance of the first measure. Reiterating, *the preparatory beat must be in the tempo of the piece.*

SETTING THE TEMPO

Before starting the preparatory beat, the tempo should be well in mind. During the preliminary score study, the process is this:

1. Check the composer's requested tempo indications: Presto, Lento, etc.
2. Study the melody line. Try several slight variations of tempo within the composer's designation. Choose what you deem best.
3. Glance through the composition, noting especially the faster notes and making sure that they are playable at your chosen tempo.

Beware of letting your natural heartbeat tempo influence your conducting tempo.

STOPPING THE SOUND

Figure 15 shows the looping gestures used to signify the stopping of the sound. Train each hand in the several directions shown and apply

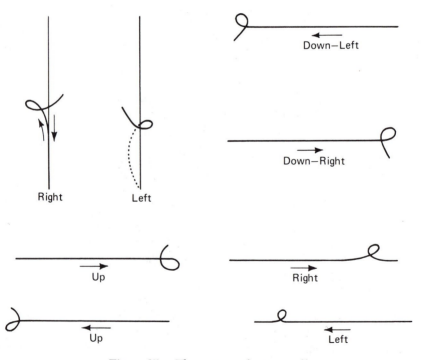

Figure 15.   The gesture of cutting-off.

them as needed—to end the piece, to cut off notes before long rests, and, in choral music, to control precisely the pronouncing of a final consonant. (Figure 15.) The hand stops still at the end of the cut-off gesture.

Timing the Cut-off

In fast tempos, when a cut-off occurs on a short note, the gesture is made exactly on the beat of that note. The cut-off becomes the beat. Exceptions: slower tempos, long ending notes, and fermatas. When the cut-off note is followed by one or more beats of rest, the cut-off is made on the first of the silent beats, thus ensuring the length of the closing note of the phrase. *The cut-off gesture should show definiteness, but not accent. Beware of too much "impulse of will."*

The Phrase Ending

It is not necessary to show cut-offs on phrase endings within the piece when the music continues without interruption. Phrasing itself may be shown simply by slowing the speed of the hand's motion (not the speed of the takt) leading to the last note of the phrase, and stopping momentarily on the ending note. The preparation for the next beat follows immediately.

Guard against letting the hand rebound suddenly and forcefully after a phrase ending. Control the stop. There is plenty of time to make the stop and continue without interrupting the steady, forward rhythm of the takt.

The cut-off itself may be transferred to the left hand—a valuable technique on certain fermatas and at places where some instruments (voices) drop out while others continue.

For further cut-off information, see Chapter 6, The Fermata.

THE TIME-BEATING GESTURES

There are several schools of thought regarding the time-beating patterns and several ways of diagramming the beats. One school emphasizes that every beat should touch a given horizontal base line. (Figure 16 (a).) Another school maintains that every beat-point should land in an identical spot in space. This one is almost impossible to diagram! (Figure 16 (b).) A third type of pattern raises all beats after the first one; thus in 4/4 the pattern resembles a cross. (Figure 16 (c).) Yet another pattern is preferred by some conductors. (Figure 16 (d).) **Danger:** Be careful that the beat-point shows at the lowest moment of the arc, not at the top of the rebound. The last pattern raises only the final beat of the measure or, in divided beats, the last group of subdivisions. This is the recommended pattern here.

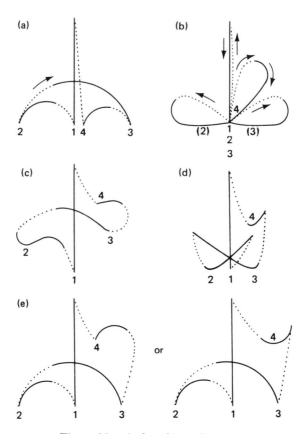

Figure 16.   Styles of time-beating.

Each beat-point is clearly defined and it requires no speeding up of the motion of the hand on the last beat of the measure. (Figure 16 (e).)

Regardless of which type of beating is preferred, three things are universally important: a good sense of rhythm, a lack of tension in the arm muscles, and a readable beat (especially for the first beat of the measure). Let us now make an analysis of a time-beating gesture and in so doing set up a useable terminology for what follows.

Every time-beating gesture has three parts: the **preparation** (the motion leading into the beat-point), the **beat-point** itself (the *ictus*), and the **rebound** or reflex after the tip of the stick has tapped the beat-point.

The Preparation

Just as the preparatory beat at the beginning of a composition should warn the musicians of what is to follow, so the preparatory part of any time-beating gesture should become a *declaration of intent* on the part of the conductor. This will not have great significance for the student at this time, but as his time-beating becomes habitual and the interpretative or expressive gestures are introduced, the declaration of intent will assume an important place in his work (see page 46).

The Ictus

In beating time it is of vital importance that the exact moment of the beat-point be clearly recognizable. This indication of the precise instant of the rhythmic pulse is termed the **ictus** of the beat. The steady reiteration of beatpoints we shall call the **takt**. The tip of the baton (or the fingers of the hand if no baton is used) should have the feel of tapping the beat and then of bouncing away (rebounding), the ictus being the instant of the tap. The rebound, immediately after the ictus, would correspond to the upward flick of the hand after its contact with the bouncing ball. This defining of the ictus is a function of the hand in a flexible wrist joint. After the recoil, the arm swings in an arclike motion toward the next ictus-point. The student can best clarify this by glancing ahead to the diagrams for three and four beats per measure, pages 25 and 26. Notice the well-curved arc joining one ictus to the next. Sir Adrian Boult (London Symphony) called the ictus the "click" in the beat.

The Reflex or Rebound: First-Beat Readability

The control of the reflex or rebound after the first beat of each measure is the foundation underlying clarity of time-beating. The important principle is this: *Except in time-beating in* ONE-to-the-bar, *the rebound after One should not be more than half the height of the initial beat of the measure. Center the rebound in the hand and wrist.* A rebound from the elbow usually climbs too high. Beat Two then looks like another One. Confusion follows. A professional player likes to be able to recognize the "down-beat" easily. If *he* needs it, how much more is it necessary for the amateur player! When one of the performers asks, "Are you beating this in TWO or in FOUR?" the conductor should be instantly alerted to the fact that perhaps his time-beating is not as readable as he presumes it to be.

THE TIME-BEATING PATTERNS (TRADITIONAL)

Note: For future ease in searching out needed information, the time-beating gestures are given here in logical sequence according to the number of beats per measure. However, it is strongly recommended that time-beating in THREE and FOUR be studied before going into ONE and TWO. When the time-beating in ONE is studied first, the student immediately forms the high rebound habit. It is then difficult to break or control this habit later on. Start with THREE and FOUR and train the proper rebound first. Work for a free, swinging motion in the arm without wrist rigidity. Avoid shrugging the shoulders, and avoid a wholly perpendicular type of conducting. Add the horizontal motions. In the following time-beating diagrams, the preparatory beat is shown by the broken line; the main gesture by the solid line; and the reflex or rebound by the dotted line. All measures start down and all measures end up.

Time-Beating In ONE (Down)

The motion of time-beating in 1-to-the-bar is straight down. The distinctive feature of this beat is that *its reflex springs back* immediately *to the starting point.* This is the *only* time-beating pattern where this should occur. See Figure 17 and Example 1.

In time-beating of One-to-the-bar, many young conductors have a tendency to pause momentarily with the stick at the ictus-point. This is not good. The single feature that distinguishes time-beating in ONE from other types of time-beating is the immediate full-length rebound to the starting point. For a more legato character, the rebound in ONE is sometimes curved as shown in Figure 17 (b). This curve may go right or left, outward or inward.

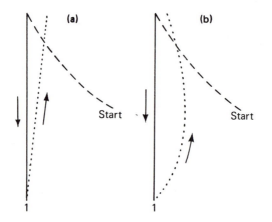

Figure 17.   Time-beating in ONE.

Time-Beating in TWO (Down-Up)

For time-beating in Two beats per measure, see Figure 18.

Very seldom does one see a conductor in school music festival competition use any other style of TWO. This is a most legitimate and accept-

Example 1.   Dvořák, *Slavonic Dance*, Op. 46, No. 1, in C Major. Measures 18–29. (Tacet instruments not shown.)

able shape for the 2-beats-per-measure, but it has one danger-point. The hazardous factor is that the rebound of One, which swings to the right of the ictus, often rises too high. Beat Two thereupon becomes indistinguishable from the downbeat, especially for the players sitting at the far right and far left of the conductor. In this type of TWO the upswing to the right should ascend only half as high as the peak of the initial One. (Example 2.) The forms of TWO shown in Figure 19 are also traditional.

Example 1. *(cont.)*

The two-beat patterns are pertinent to music in 2/4 meter, cut time
(¢), and the faster 4/8, 5/8, 6/8, and 7/8 rhythms.* One caution is necessary here, however. In music of the earliest classic periods the cut-time
signature often appears in Andante and Adagio movements. In such cases

---

*In 5/8 and 7/8, beaten in two beats per measure, one beat is of longer duration than
the other beat. See page 96, Figure 41.

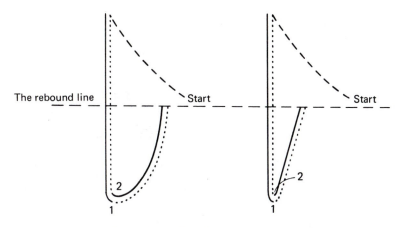

Figure 18. Time-beating in TWO.

Example 2. Haydn, *Symphony No. 94 ("Surprise") in G Major*. Finale, beginning.

23

Example 2.   *(cont.)*

Full score uses: 2 Flutes, 2 Oboes, 2 Horns, 2 Trumpets, Timpani, Strings (all tacet at the beginning.)

it means, very simply, two major pulses per measure. The four-beat pattern, or the divided TWO (Figure 48 (e)), would be used, in keeping with the slow character of the music. In modern scores, the cut-time marking usually means a faster tempo with only *two* beats per measure.

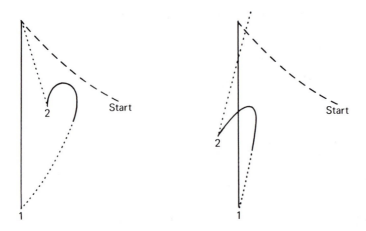

Figure 19.   Variations in the shape of TWO.

Time-Beating in THREE (Down-Right-Up)

This pattern is so standard that it needs no explanation other than to call attention to the fact that the *second beat* of the measure moves to the *right*. See Figure 20 and Example 3.

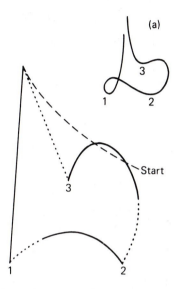

Figure 20.   Time-beating in THREE.

There exists in the French school of conducting a type of THREE pattern where the second beat moves to the left. When one sees it today, it is usually in the opera pit, and upon special occasions as given on page 128.

The THREE pattern is used in the slower 3/4 time signatures, often in the 9/8, and in the Adagio 3/8 meters when subdivision of the beat is not found to be necessary.

Time-Beating in FOUR (Down-Left-Right-Up)

Here again we have a very standard pattern that needs no explanation. Beginning with four beats per measure, the second beat moves to the *left*. See Figure 21 and Example 4.

Caution: Students sometimes perform the four-beat pattern as shown in Figure 22. This out-of-kilter design is caused by stiffness in the elbow, not allowing the arm to swing far enough to the right to include that half of the ensemble under the stick.

Example 3. Haydn, *Symphony No. 101 ("The Clock") in D Major.* Third movement, beginning.

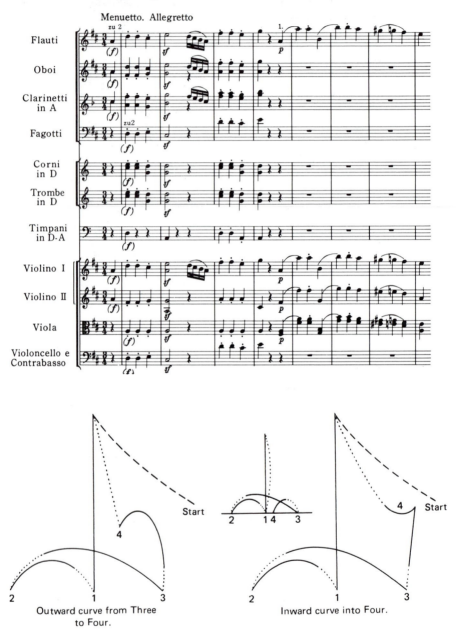

Outward curve from Three   Inward curve into Four.
to Four.

Figure 21. Time-beating in FOUR.

Example 4. Tchaikovsky, March from the *Nutcracker Suite*, beginning (condensed and transposed to C Score).

Figure 22. Unbalanced design pattern in FOUR.

MULTIPLE BEATS

The "Divided-Beat" in THREE and FOUR

In order to understand the structure of time-beating beyond four-beats-per-measure, it is practical, first, to become acquainted with the "divided-beat" patterns—those that show one or two small-sized supplementary beats attached to the main gesture. For example: In the slow-moving Adagio (it may well incorporate thirty-second notes into its scheme of notation), the "And" beats have to be delineated for the sake of good ensemble. To show the "Ands" (the half-beats), the conductor simply adds to each principal beat a second smaller beat, moving in the same direction as the main gesture. Notice, however, that *the "And" following One goes in a direction opposite to the next principal gesture.* (Figure 23.)

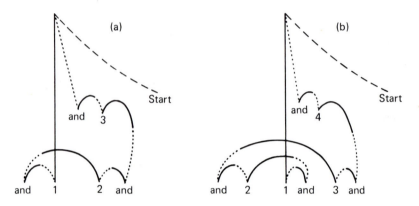

Figure 23.   Showing the "And" beat.

Patterns with Multiple Beats

A three-beat pattern, plus **two** added subdivisions per beat, becomes a nine-beat measure; a four-beat pattern with the added pulses handles the twelve-beat notation. (Figure 24.)

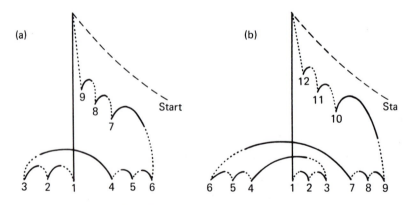

Figure 24.   Time-beating in NINE and TWELVE.

Time-Beating in FIVE—The Unbalanced Beat

Here we see the unbalanced or "mixed subdivisions" beats. One half of the measure may add one pulse to each beat; the other half, two subdivisions per beat. The takt is steady throughout.

Simple time-beating in FIVE takes one of the following forms: 3 + 2 (One-and-and/Two-and) or 2 + 3 (One-and/Two-and-and). The downbeat line, One, divides the pattern and *the long, horizontal line, crossing from left to right, shows where the second half of the measure begins.* Figure 25 and Music Examples 5 and 6. Fast FIVES in TWO, pp. 95-96.

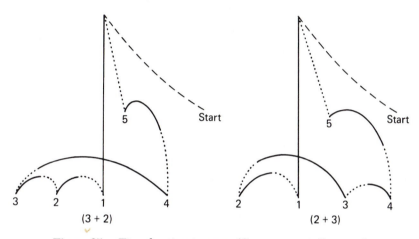

Figure 25. Time-beating in FIVE. (Contemporary Patterns.)

Example 5. Stravinsky, *The Rite of Spring.* (a) Sacrificial Dance: The Chosen One (measure 155). (b) Mysterious Circles of the Adolescents (measure 6). Copyright 1921 by Edition Russe de Musique. Renewed 1958. Copyright and Renewal assigned to Boosey & Hawkes, Inc. Revised Edition Copyright 1948 by Boosey & Hawkes, Inc. Reprinted by permission.

Example 6.   Barber, *Medea's Meditation and Dance of Vengeance*, Op. 23A (measure 104). Copyright © 1956 by G. Schirmer, Inc. "Used by Permission." Rhythm only here.

3 + 2

Caution: When the composer writes a 3 + 2 measure, followed by a 2 + 3 in the next measure (and vice versa), the conductor should show the change in the baton. See Example 49, page 96.

There is an older form of FIVE (traditional) that is gradually becoming obsolete. It is comprised of a large THREE pattern with a small TWO pattern attached, higher up in space. In TWO-plus-THREE, the TWO is large. Such designs are encumbered with two downbeats in the same measure. The change of size in the two patterns is confusing visually and dynamically. (Figure 26.)

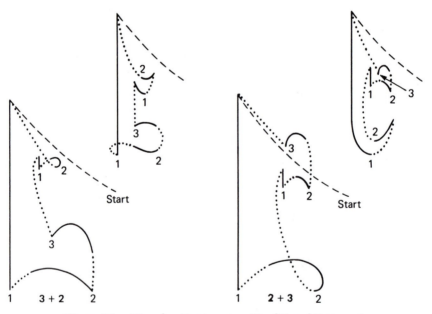

Figure 26.   Time-beating in FIVE. (Traditional Patterns.)

The traditional pattern was current at the time that Tchaikovsky wrote his famous "Five-Beat Waltz." (Example 7.)

Example 7. Tchaikovsky, *Symphony No. 6 in B minor*, Op. 74. Second movement, beginning.

When the composer places a bar-line between the two-beat and three-beat measures, and they alternate consecutively throughout, then the normal patterns are used as notated. (Example 8.)

Example 8. Stravinsky, *The Rite of Spring*. Evocation of the Ancestors (measures 28–31). Copyright 1921 by Edition Russe de Musique. Renewed 1958. Copyright and Renewal assigned to Boosey & Hawkes, Inc. Revised Edition Copyright 1948 by Boosey & Hawkes, Inc. Reprinted by permission.

Time-Beating in SIX

The true SIX may be thought of as springing from an enlarged FOUR: two pulses to the left of One and two to the right of One, with One and Four remaining unchanged. (Figure 27 (a).) The designs shown in (b) and (c) are also functional. They can be particularly useful when the musical interest moves from the conductor's left (b) to his right (c). (Figure 27.)

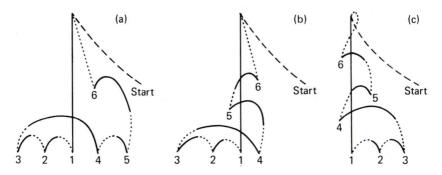

Figure 27. Time-beating in SIX.

Caution: Make a proper distinction between a Divided-Three accentuation, 2 + 2 + 2, Figure 23 (a), and a true SIX (3 + 3), Figure 27 (a). Apply the correct pattern as the music demands.

Example 9 depicts visibly the two types of accentuation. Rhythm only quoted here.

Example 9. Tchaikovsky, *Symphony No. 5 in E minor*, Op. 64. First movement (measures 97–100).

Time-Beating in SEVEN:

Its many complications are extensively treated in *Time-Beating II*, pp. 99–102.

Time-Beating in EIGHT:

Use the Divided-FOUR pattern, Figure 23 (b). It is most often used in Adagio movements.

Time-Beating in NINE:

Apply the Double-Divided-THREE, Figure 24 (a), to Example 10.

Example 10. Prokofiev, *Symphony No. 5*, Op. 100. Third movement (measure 128). © Copyright 1946 by MCA MUSIC, a division of MCA Inc., New York, New York. Reprinted by permission. All rights reserved.

Time-Beating in TWELVE:

Use the Double-Divided-Four, Figure 24 (b). See Example 11.

In all of the above, keep the added pulses small. Let the principal

Example 11.   Debussy, *Prélude à l' après-midi d'un faune* (measure 31). By permission of Jean Jobert, Editeur, Paris. Société des Editions Jobert, 76 rue Quincampoix 75003 Paris.

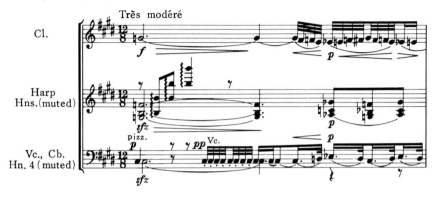

pattern emerge visually. Do not make more than three gestures consecutively in the same direction.

THE UP-ICTUS

Caution: One will, upon occasion, see a type of time-beating where the ictus, the playing point, comes at the top of the rebound. The hand, instead of "bouncing the ball" on each beat, acquires the feeling of tossing the ball. *The moment of impact shows at the top of the rebound instead of at the bottom of the beat.* This is something to be avoided as a basic habit. It makes life difficult for the performers since the beat-point is no longer at the lowest moment of the gesture. Rhythmic precision suffers and rehearsal time is lost. In choral music, the *rare* conductor who uses this beat feels that it gives "lightness" to the tone and helps to keep the pitch from sagging. (Figure 28.)

There is, nevertheless, one place where the up-ictus is useful and that is in the One-to-the-bar waltzes. Once the rhythm has been established, the conductor can subtly slip over to the up-ictus. It can add a charming lilt to the performance.

We have mentioned the up-ictus at this time because one should be able to recognize it when it is seen. But we caution against its use as a general facet of time-beating.

As a final word for this entire chapter: Teach your performers to see and recognize the first beat of each measure—and then be dead sure your own downbeat is clearly recognizable as such.

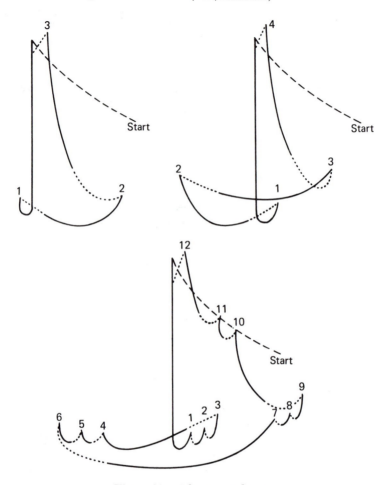

Figure 28.   The upward ictus.

EXERCISES FOR PRACTICE: TWO HANDS AND THE MIND

Note: The first nine of the following exercises are the preliminary studies. Numbers 10 through 13 are more difficult, requiring faster mental responses. Numbers 14 through 17 should wait until the preceding exercises have become easy. Unless otherwise specified, practice all exercises with both large and small gestures. The hand that is not actively engaged in functioning at the moment should hang in a completely relaxed manner, showing no tension.

1. Review the physical exercises of Chapter 2, Exercises 1 and 2, pp. 10–11.

2. **Right Hand (RH):** Time-beating in THREE: down-right-up. Drill.

3. **Left Hand (LH):** Time-beating in THREE: down-left-up. Drill.

4. **Both Hands Together (BH):** Time-beating in THREE. Drill.

5. **Time-Beating** in THREE: RH two measures (2M) / LH 2M / RH 1M / LH 2M / RH 2M / LH 3M / RH 2M / LH 1M / RH 1M / LH 1M / BH 3M / RH 2M / LH 1M / BH 3M / RH 1M. Take it slowly enough to think!

6. **Right hand:** Time-beating in FOUR: down-left-right-up. Drill.

7. **Left Hand:** Time-beating in FOUR: down-right-left-up. Drill.

8. **Both Hands Together:** Time-beating in FOUR. Drill.

9. **Time-Beating** in FOUR: RH 2M / LH 2M / RH 3M / LH 2M / BH 2M / LH 2M / RH 1M / LH 2M / BH 4M / LH 1M / RH 1M / LH 2M / BH 3M / LH 2M / BH 2M / RH 2M / BH 4M.

10. Alternating THREE and FOUR **Patterns:** Three measures on each change. RH in THREE / LH in THREE / RH in FOUR / LH in FOUR / BH in FOUR / LH in THREE / RH in THREE / BH in THREE / LH in FOUR / RH in THREE / LH in FOUR / RH in FOUR / LH in THREE / BH in FOUR / BH in THREE / RH in FOUR.

11. Repeat No. 5, making all right-hand gestures large (forte), all left-hand gestures small (piano). Then reverse hands on the size.

12. Repeat No. 9, making two units large, then two units small.

13. When all beats are conquered individually as such, then try the following exercises, repeating each many times consecutively with no break between and until the change from one pattern to the next becomes easy and habitual. See that the speed of the takt is a constant throughout. All beats, for the moment, are evenly spaced, regardless of their relationship later on in the repertoire. Practice each exercise with each hand.

   a. Two measures in TWO and one measure in THREE (Notice that each of the following notations will require *this same type of time-beating.*)

b. Two measures in FOUR and one measure in THREE.

c. Two measures in THREE and two measures in TWO.

d. Two measures in THREE and one measure in FOUR.

e. One measure in SIX and two measures in THREE. (Remember, the speed of the takt is the same throughout, as 6/8, 3/8, 3/8.)

f. Two measures in FOUR and one measure in ONE.

g. Two measures in THREE, one measure in TWO and one measure in ONE.

h. One measure in NINE and one measure in DIVIDED-FOUR.

i. Two measures in TWO and one measure in DIVIDED-FOUR.

j. One measure of very slow 4/4 and two measures of DIVIDED-FOUR, the speed of the *quarter notes* remaining the same throughout.

k. Two measures of DIVIDED-THREE and one measure of THREE without the division, *quarter notes remaining the same* throughout (3/4 signature).

l. Two measures of slow 3/4 and one measure of 9/8, the quarter note of the 3/4 having the same length as the three eighths of the NINE. In other words, each beat of the original THREE is subdivided into three parts in the NINE measure.

m. Three measures in ONE and one measure in THREE, the speed of the quarter notes remaining the same. (See the music.)

n. Two measures in FIVE (3 + 2) and one measure in FOUR, the speed of the beat remaining the same throughout.

o. Two measures in THREE and one measure in FIVE (2 + 3). Pay attention to making the +3 of the FIVE in smaller gestures than the two measures in THREE.

p. One measure in a very slow 4/4 and one measure in TWELVE, each beat of the 4/4 being divided into three parts in executing the TWELVE. Pay attention to the direction of the small beats following One.

q. One measure in NINE and two measures in TWELVE, the takt of the eighth note remaining constant throughout.

r. One measure in TWELVE and one measure in DIVIDED-FOUR, the eighth note remaining constant throughout (12/8, 4/4 Adagio).

14. Make up other studies for yourself similar to those above. Think your coming change and execute it right from the mind itself.

15. Now try the following exercises, the takt (speed of the beats) remaining a constant throughout:
    Time-beating in:

    (a) 4 2 3 1 4 1 2 5 3 2 1 4 2
    (b) 4 1 2 1 3 1 2 1 4 2 1 4 3 1 2
    (c) 4 1 3 2 5 1 2 4 3 2 4 1 5 1 3
    (d) 3 2 4 1 3 1 2 4 2 1 3 2 3 1 4
    (e) 3 4 5 2 4 3 1 2 6 1 2 4 2 5 1 3
    (f) 6 2 4 2 6 5 1 4 6 2 1 4 3 6 2
    (g) 2 1 3 6 4 3 1 6 2 5 4 1 3 6 1

16. Make up your own series similar to the foregoing. When the more difficult beats have been acquired, practice Exercise 17.

17. Try the divided beats as follows (the takt is the eighth note throughout): Divided 4/4, 9/8, divided 4/4, 12/8, divided 3/4, 9/8, divided 4/4, 6/8, 12/8, divided 3/4, 9/8. See that the small beats go in the correct direction and that the downbeat, One, is clearly recognizable.

RECOMMENDED REFERENCE READINGS (SEE APPENDIX G)

BLACKMAN, CHARLES. *Behind the Baton*. See especially the chapter on The Function of the Conductor.

EARHART, WILL. *The Eloquent Baton*. Chapters II-V, pp. 4–38. Time-beating patterns, and Chapters IX-X, pp. 68–84, "Nine, Twelve, Five, and Seven Beat" and "Divided Beats."

FARKAS, PHILIP. *The Art of Musicianship*. Section 4, "Tempo," pp. 17–20.

EIGHT EXCERPTS
FOR INITIAL
CLASSROOM PERFORMANCE

Note: The ability to imagine the sound of the printed notes is the foundation upon which score study rests. *The only way to make the vocal cords function is to think the sound to be produced.* Therefore conducting classes should do a certain amount of singing. The following excerpts are to be sung, played, and conducted; switch octaves as the voice range demands. Excerpts 1–5 have been adapted from the *Fifteen Sonatas, Op. 1, for Flute and Figured Bass*, by George Frederick Handel. They deal here with two important fundamentals, the melody line and the bass line. Three- and four-part scorings follow thereafter.

1. *Sonata No. V,* Fourth movement, beginning, Bourree.

*Use the 8ᵛᵃ for instrumental performance.

2. *Sonata No. XI,* First movement, beginning.

3. *Sonata No. VII*, Third movement.

4. *Sonata No. IX*, Fifth movement, beginning.

5. *Sonata No. V*, Third movement.

6.   *Trio in C major, Op. 87,* for two oboes and English horn, by Ludwig van Beethoven. Beginning.

**Use lower notes for singing and for non-transposing instruments.

7.   *String Quartet in D minor, Op. posthumous,* ("Death and the Maiden"), by Franz Schubert. Second movement, beginning and ending.

8. *String Quartet in A minor, Op. 29,* by Franz Schubert. Beginning.

4

Beyond Time-Beating:
The Expressive Gestures

We now come to a most important concept in all conducting—the concept of the conductor's "declaration of intent." To explain this term fully, let us diagram a four-beat measure thus:

$$1----2----3----4----$$

The performers will start to play when the baton shows the ictus of the first beat. Once they have begun to sound that beat, no power on earth can get them to change, within that single beat, what they have already started to do. This means, then, that as soon as the baton has shown an ictus (a beat-point), it is thereafter released of responsibility and is free, during the remainder of the beat, to show what is to happen on the next beat. This is what is called the **declaration of intent.** As the expressive gestures are studied and mastered, this declaration of intent will become the means for ensuring that changes in style, tempo, or dynamics will be grasped by the performers in time to occur exactly when and where the conductor may desire. **Note:** In very slow tempos, the latter half of the beat will provide enough time for showing the declaration of intent. See also *rubato* on page 64.

46

THE EXPRESSIVE GESTURES

The expressive gestures may be divided into two categories: the *active gestures*, requiring a response from the players (singers), and the *passive gestures*, which ask only for silence, no sound, from the members of the ensemble. The active gestures are accompanied by much impulse of will on the conductor's part; the passive gestures show an *apparent* lack of this factor, possessing instead a quality that clearly says, "Do not play yet."

In making the following classification of gestures, we now become entangled in two approaches—a question of basic philosophy. One approach considers the *conductor's contribution* to the gesture; the other pays more attention to the *result attained* by the gesture—the effect the gesture has on the musicians themselves. These are two different ideas. Affected most disturbingly is where to classify the preparatory beat. It is active for the conductor in that he must show tempo, dynamic, and style—but it is passive for the performers since no sound is to be made. This author leans toward favoring the *results* of the conductor's gestures, therefore the preparatory beat has been placed in the passive category.*

1. ACTIVE	2. PASSIVE
Demanding a response from the players:	Requesting only silence from the players:
Characterized by the presence of "impulse of will"	Characterized by the lack of "impulse of will"
1. Legato	1. "Dead" gestures
2. Staccato	2. Preparatory beats
3. Tenuto	
4. Gesture of Syncopation	

THE ACTIVE GESTURES

1. *Legato gestures.* The legato gestures are the most common of the expressive gestures. They are those which show the *smooth, flowing connection from ictus to ictus*. They seldom move in straight lines, but instead are curved motions, arclike in character. The diagrams of the basic time-

---

*This is the *classification* used by Dr. Malko. It appears to be the simplest and most direct route to understanding and proficiency. Nicolai Malko, *The Conductor and His Baton* (Copenhagen: Wilhelm Hansen, 1950), p. 65.

beating patterns as given in Chapters 3 and 7 show these curves between the beat-points.

The danger in the use of this gesture is that the ictus may become too smooth, lacking sufficient definition of the beat-point. Here the "click" mentioned by Sir Adrian Boult is important. The arm makes much of the motion in the legato gestures but the ictus is defined, in the long motions of the legato, by "give" in the wrist delivering a dip to the tip of the baton.

The legato gesture is, by far, the easiest of the gestures to acquire. It is used wherever the music flows along gracefully without undue stress or effort. This makes it the basic gesture for the time-beating. The legato gestures lend themselves easily to variation in size. The larger gestures are usually associated with the louder passages although it is possible to perform large gestures so gently that the texture of the resulting sound will be as fine as a delicate silk veil and correspondingly soft. Further, a sudden forte, following some measures of piano, can be made small but with such sudden, unexpected vigor and intensity that the dynamic change occurs instantly, startling the audience.

The customary small gestures for piano passages are centered in the hand and wrist, the tip of the baton preserving clearly the beat-pattern. (Example 12.) Smaller gestures for the triple piano with added intensity.

Example 12.   Schubert, *Symphony No. 8 ("Unfinished") in B minor*, Op. posth. Second movement (measures 92–95).

Legato gestures may be varied in size within the measure to show dynamic or phrasal contour, the larger gesture coinciding with the climax of the phrase. See Example 81, by Haydn where the fourth measure is often conducted as an echo of the third measure, the contouring remaining similar but the size being adjusted. Figure 29 diagrams this contour. The sweep of the "And" of Three, in the Haydn example done lightly, brings

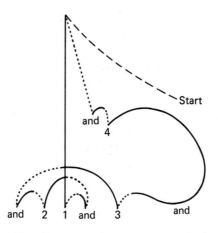

Figure 29.   Variation of gesture size in the legato.

with it a reaction of a longer, lighter bow in the first violins—a case again of texture. Dynamic control is aided by the left hand.

The size of the gesture is also affected by the tempo of the music. In very fast tempos, there is no time for extremely large gestures. Young conductors must be brought to realize this, for often in their emotional response to the excitement of the music they "let themselves go," the gestures become huge, and the tempo invariably slows down. The first reaction is to blame the musicians.

When great smoothness is desired and the rhythm is safe, the ictus-point may be smoothed out as shown in Figure 30.

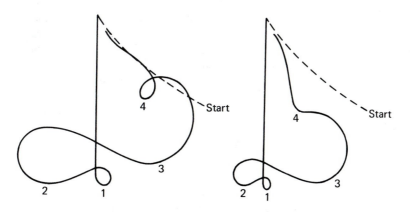

Figure 30.   The curved ictus in legato.

2. *Staccato gestures.* The staccato gestures are characterized by the *momentary stop* of all motion in the stick, hand, arm *immediately after the reflex.* The student can acquire the feel of this gesture in the wrist if he will practice flicking imaginary drops of water off the end of the baton. The flick is performed by the sudden motion of the hand in the wrist joint, ending in an abrupt stop at the end of the rebound.

In practicing, wait (no motion) after each staccato gesture, until the momentary rigidity of the arm muscles relaxes. Then make a preparatory arc into the next staccato. The important thing is the *control* of the stop. (Figure 31.)

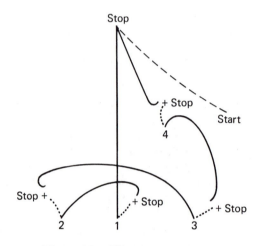

Figure 31.   The staccato gesture.

There is no true staccato if motion continues in any part of the hand or arm. The stop must be perfect—as clean as the staccato sound the conductor expects from his players. **Danger:** Particularly difficult is the stop at the top of the last beat of any measure.

The staccato gesture should be used whenever there is a possibility that the performers may fail to observe the composer's important staccato dots. (Beethoven was most conscientious in marking his staccatos. Observe them!)

In general, the more sudden the stop in the baton, the shorter the resultant sound from the performers. When the music shows continuous florid passages, unslurred and marked staccato, it is best to use the legato gestures, conducting the *line* of the music rather than its style. In slow tempos, with notes of longer duration, the baton can show the length of the staccato note and then stop after the reflex. Interpretatively, there are a thousand varieties of staccato and we choose the one that fits the passage.

Note: The staccato sound is inevitable when spiccato bowing is used. See page 243.

In Example 13 we see a typical passage requiring the staccato gesture in the baton.

Example 13.   Schubert, *Symphony No. 8* ("Unfinished") *in B minor*, Op. posth. First movement (measure 77).

A type of heavy staccato gesture is sometimes used to indicate accentuation of certain notes in the score. Such a gesture could, if desired, be used on the second page of the *Leonore No. 3 Overture* (page 167) to bring clean articulation and precise ensemble on the first note of each slur throughout the page.

Another excellent place for the heavy staccato is shown in Example 14.

Example 14.   Schubert, *Rosamunde,* Overture (Allegro vivace, measure 25).

3. *Tenuto gestures.* These gestures might also be called the *very heavy legato* gestures. They signify great cohesion in the musical line. The hand, in executing these gestures, feels as if the tip of the baton has become very heavy.

The chief characteristic of the tenuto gesture is that the tip of the stick drops below the hand and wrist. Instead of a relaxed, automatic rebound, the hand seems to *pull* upward or sidewise after each beat-point. One can acquire the feel for this gesture by pointing the stick straight down toward the floor and then pulling upward, the left hand pulling downward on the tip of the stick at the same time. (It is an application of the practice gesture in Chapter 2, Exercise 2, page 11.) To make a distinction: in the legato, the tip of the stick points upward; in the tenuto, it points downward, lagging behind the hand. The motion in tenuto is controlled and *condensed* and less distance is covered, thus adding to the appearance of heft and tenuousness. Care should be taken not to release the intensity as the baton changes direction between the beats, especially the last beat of one measure and the first beat of the next. Each beat is placed, carried through and sustained into the following beat.

The gesture tenuto is used whenever the composer writes "*ten.*" over any note, often where the wind player would use the "du" tonguing, where the legato-articulated slur occurs in string music (written with a line under each note plus a slur, *louré* bowing), and wherever the sustaining power of the tone is of vital importance. See Example 15, second and fourth measures, second full beat.

Example 15.   Haydn, *Symphony No. 94 ("Surprise") in G major.* Second movement (measures 1–4)

In Example 16, the pianissimo might start with legato gestures, move into a soft tenuto in the second and third measures and return to the legato as the third measure goes into the fourth. Such conducting would help the players to feel the legato line and to sustain adequately the last note of the first slur, so that this note would not be clipped in execution. In performing the given gestures, the conductor must guard his tempo.

Example 16.   Schubert, *Symphony No. 8 ("Unfinished") in B minor,* Op. posth. First movement (measures 352–355)

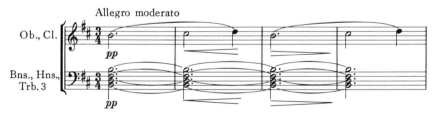

There is also a second way of performing the tenuto gesture. The hand bends upward from the wrist and pushes outward with the lower palm stating exactly the length of the note. This is invaluable as a replacement for the cut-off on soft endings. At the end of the gesture the hand retracts instantly. The conductor "stops conducting." The sudden retraction acts as a cut-off. See the last quarter-note, Example 17.

Example 17.   Schubert, *Symphony No. 8 ("Unfinished") in B minor*, Op. posth. First movement (last two measures).

4. *The gesture of syncopation.* The terminology for this gesture is not ideal. In practice, it is the gesture that the conductor uses when he wishes to control an entrance coming *after the beat.* Thus it should rightly be called the "gesture for controlling things that happen *after* the beat instead of *on* the beat." But this is a long and unwieldy terminology. So, for brevity, we call it "the gesture of syncopation" (G.o.S. for short), since syncopations start *after* a beat.

When the musicians have to enter after a beat rather than on the beat, the greatest help the conductor can give is to show, with utmost clarity, exactly where the beat is. (Example 18 at the ×'s.)

To control this gesture, the hand stops completely *one full beat before the beat that requires the after-beat response.* The hand stops on beat One in measures 2, 4, 6 of Example 18. The baton remains perfectly still until the exact instant of the takt of Two, then makes an *unprepared* sudden, short, sharp upward gesture, staccato in nature (the ×'s in the example). This pinpoints the precise instant of the beat. The musicians then respond after the beat. The stopping of the hand calls attention to the written rest and also highlights the instant of the gesture of syncopation itself. The size of the gesture of syncopation controls the dynamic. Varying the speed of the gesture can either delay or precipitate the after-beat response. In any case, there must be *no preparatory motion* in the baton before the gesture of syncopation. The gesture will not work if it is pre-

Example 18.   Mozart, *Symphony No. 12 in G Major*, Koch. verz. 124. Finale, beginning.

ceded by a loop or other motion in the stick. It must come instantly, without preparation, exactly on the takt. (Figure 32.)

Note: The difference between a gesture of syncopation and a staccato is that the stop comes *before* the gesture in the G.o.S. and *after the rebound* in the staccato. A staccato has a preparatory motion: the G.o.S. does not. The gesture of syncopation is *not* used when the music calls for continuous syncopations. The conductor must "nail" the beat instead.

Most difficult is a G.o.S. on One. The stop at the top of the last beat, at the end of the preceding measure, must be clean.

In Example 19, the baton stops on Two and makes the gesture of syncopation on the takt of Three. The stop, here, on Two also produces a cleaner rest on Three. Figure 32 (b) shows such a procedure.

Example 19.   Tchaikovsky, *Romeo and Juliet Overture-Fantasia* (Double bar, Allegro giusto, measure 111–113).

Gesture of Syncopation on Three

In Example 20, the suddenness of a G.o.S. on Two can startle the players into accenting before they can think!

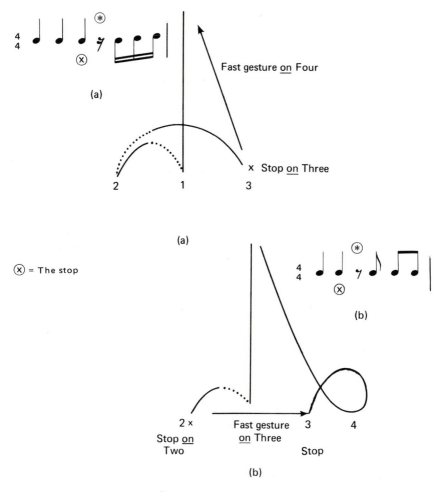

Figure 32.   The gesture of syncopation for entrances after the beat.

Equally effective is a G.o.S. on a tied-over note, producing good ensemble thereafter.

When the conductor wishes to control a sixteenth-note entrance after a dotted eighth note or rest, he can stop the baton on the immediate beat and make the gesture of syncopation on the "and." Control of the gesture itself should be perfected before this use of it is attempted.

In slower tempos, a leisurely push forward with the heel of the hand (the lower palm) starting after a stop and exactly on the takt, will produce the desired entrance on the second half of the slow beat.

Example 20.   Rimsky-Korsakov, *Russian Easter Overture*, Op. 36. (Allegro agitato, measures 7–10).

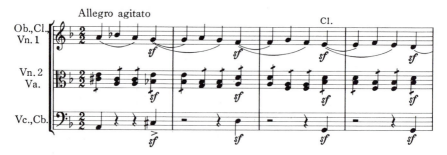

In Example 21 the use of the slower gesture of syncopation is illustrated. The *Andante non troppo* marking would preclude the use of the faster variety of this gesture. Regardless of whether the motion is to be fast or slow, one must remember that the success of the gesture of syncopation depends upon the momentary stopping of motion before the gesture itself is performed and that the motion must not start until the exact moment of the takt.

Example 21.   Tchaikovsky, *Romeo and Juliet Overture-Fantasia* (measure 40).

Let us now analyze a complete passage, as given in Example 22. The quoted rhythm is a series of forte chords performed by tutti winds, timpani and cymbals against a steady flow of unslurred sixteenths in the strings. The bass viols join the winds on the third measure.

When this passage is conducted, the violins are ignored, since there are no rhythmic problems in the string parts. The conductor concentrates his attention on helping the instruments who are playing the dangerous rhythm quoted. When a note comes after a beat, the gesture of synco-

Example 22.   Tchaikovsky, *Romeo and Juliet Overture-Fantasia* (measures 142–146) (rhythm only).

pation is performed *on that beat*. But when a note comes exactly *on* the beat, then the conductor must make a preparatory gesture before that beat, leading into the beat itself. A complete analysis is as follows: in the first measure, prepare Four and stop; measure 2, use a gesture of syncopation on One and prepare Four; measure 3, prepare Two and use the gesture of syncopation for Three; measure 4, gesture of syncopation on One followed instantly by Two, then prepare Four; last measure, gesture of syncopation on One and prepare Three. The tutti rests are the smallest of "dead" gestures. (See the discussion of these gestures given below.)

This example definitely belongs to the category of advanced conducting. The quoting of such an example at this time is not intended to be a challenge. It is inserted only for the purpose of aiding the understanding. When the skill has arrived to handle it well, the conductor will find that it is possible to produce a perfect rendition of the rhythm of the passage from unskilled players who have no music in front of them. But the conductorial technique must be perfect to do so.

THE PASSIVE GESTURES

1. *"Dead" gestures*. The "dead" gestures are those that are used when the conductor wishes to show the passing of rests (silent beats) or the presence of any single tutti rest. See the tutti rests at the beginning of the second measure of Example 23.

Example 23.   Mozart, *Così fan tutte*. Overture (measures 11–12).

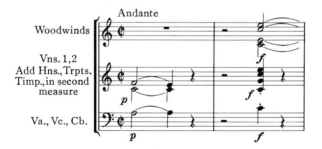

The connotation of this dead gesture is, "Do not play. Be patient and I shall show you when." It must be lacking in impulse of will in order that no one shall respond actively to it.

To perform the dead gesture, the conductor shows *only* the *direction* of the beats by absolutely expressionless straight-line motion in the baton. The gestures are *small* and no ictus is defined as such in the beat-pattern. Figure 33 (a) shows four beats of "dead" gesture; (b) One-Two as playing

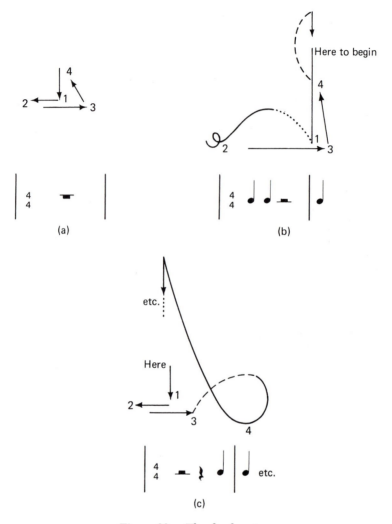

Figure 33. The dead gesture.

gestures, Three-Four "dead;" (c) shows One-Two-Three "dead," then a preparatory loop warns that Four will be "active," requiring an entrance into the music. Like the gesture of syncopation *a dead gesture has no preparatory beat.*

Any slight rebounding or curving of the line from ictus to ictus will show impulse of will, or "personality," and will make the gesture appear active instead of passive. In performing the dead gesture, the conductor's hand should become completely devoid of expression—as if he has disowned it. The straight-line motion shows the passing of beats in accordance with the takt, and does so in the quietest manner possible. The marvelous quality of silence is not to be disturbed. This gesture can become hypnotic in quality, holding the audience breathless.

When the dead gesture is used to show the passing of several measures of tutti rest (such as those that occur when accompanying a soloist), only the first beat of each measure is given. A dropping of the stick downward with an immediate return to the top is all that is needed. Such a single down-up gesture is also used to designate a measure marked G.P. (Grand Pause). This beat should be shown, to account for the measure which may come in the middle of a series of vacant measures (for certain performers) and has to be designated.

When tutti rests occur within a measure, they are generally beaten as dead gestures coincident with the takt. However, in recitatives, one may outline these missing beats unrhythmically, then pause in position for the next sounding gesture. (See pp. 195-97 for the Recitative.)

In closing chords interspersed with rests, the silent beats within the measure are generally not conducted. The baton simply stands still while the time goes by. However, if there is a whole measure of silence, it should be indicated by a small dead One. (Example 24.) A preparatory gesture precedes each on-the-beat chord.

Example 24.   Beethoven, *Symphony No. 5 in C minor*, Op. 67. Finale (last seven measures).

2. Refinement of the preparatory beat. Since the preparatory beat requires no sound from the performers, it can be classified as far as they are concerned under the heading of passive gestures. However, as has already been stated, the preparatory beat is active for the conductor. It is his "declaration of intent" leading to his command to "Play!"

The preparatory beat after a fermata, a completely silent measure, or a sustained whole note, is similar in character to that at the beginning of the piece. It should again set tempo, dynamic, and style.

In time-beating of One-to-the-bar, the preparatory beat states one full measure of the music. Make it an upward rhythmic motion that says "Ready," followed by a downward "One" that says "Play!" See also page 61.

The preparatory beat in Adagio need not necessarily take the time of one full beat. Often the half beat is sufficient and especially when the divided beat is being used.

A specialized type of preparatory beat may be used on a composition that starts with a double-forte. The baton is positioned high in space. It descends suddenly and returns immediately to the starting point, and the performers attack at the top of the beat. Charles Munch of Boston Symphony Orchestra fame was seen to use this type of brilliant forte beginning.

An unrhythmic preparatory beat with a "breathing gesture" preceding it, may be used when the first measure is comprised of a forte or double-forte tutti whole note or a fermata. (A sustained tone is rhythmically static, therefore a rhythmic preparatory beat is not essential.) To perform the breathing gesture, the hands assume a ready position slightly away from the body. The hands then move horizontally to center front. The conductor takes the breath simultaneously with the performers during this motion. The baton stops momentarily, center front, and then suddenly (unrhythmically) moves up-down with great vigor and the attack bursts forth with tremendous brilliance. The attack is followed by a sustained tenuto in the baton. Time-beating as such starts as a rhythmic preparatory beat leading into the following measure. (Figure 34.)

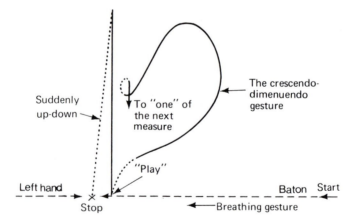

Figure 34.   The breathing gesture.

Example 25 shows this type of beginning. In the following Example 26, the breathing gesture would be omitted since only the strings play the

Example 25. Beethoven, *Egmont*, Op. 84. Overture (measures 1–2).

Example 26. Beethoven, *Coriolanus Overture*, Op. 62 (measures 1–3).

sustained C. The first beat of the second measure would be shown by a small dead gesture, for the sake of the winds who are "counting measures."

When the instruments have to execute a very short note (or a grace note) at the beginning of a piece, the conductor can arrange with the musicians beforehand that they are to play the small note exactly on the principal beat. This is applicable to the faster tempos, but not necessary in slow tempos.

Finally, two important "tricks of the trade:" 1. When the first played beat is divided into three or more notes of even value (♪♪♪ or ♪♪♪♪), the *preparatory beat will have to take the form of a legato line that moves into the playing beat without stopping. The length of the line states precisely the length of one beat of the coming tempo.* 2. For a piece that starts on an afterbeat: Make a small flick of the left-hand fingers indicating one preliminary beat that does not appear in the score. Follow rhythmically with a Gesture of Syncopation in the baton, on the beat immediately preceding the entrance. The beat's duration has then been precisely stated, from left hand to right hand. The baton must not move during the time between the flick and the sudden Gesture of Syncopation. See also page 63.

FROM SLOW TO FAST TEMPO

Important: When the music changes from a slow to a fast tempo at a double bar, without accelerating or ritarding, place the last ictus of the slow tempo *low* in space. Bring the baton to the center front near where the ictus of One took place. The baton will stop momentarily to permit the slow tempo to complete itself, then will make a sudden rhythmic preparatory beat upwards to set the new tempo. Figure 35 diagrams this technique.

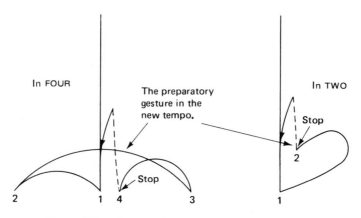

Figure 35.   Change of tempo—the return to center.

Example 27 presents a pertinent passage. Here the baton has to prepare the coming Presto by a fast legato gesture after the ictus of Four in the slow tempo. Note the reiterated notes on the first fast beat in the violins. Since these players enter after an eighth rest, the conductor will do well to look sharply to the ictus of his first Presto beat. When the music starts *after* a beat rather than on it, at the beginning of the piece or after a fermata, a special technique may be used. (Example 28.)

Example 27.   Mozart, *Così fan tutte.* Overture (measures 14–15).

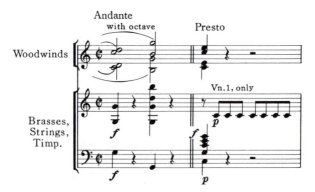

Example 28. Weber, *Oberon*. Overture (measures 22–23).

Here the musicians have to begin playing in a new tempo on the end of a beat which is preceded by sustained silence. Showing only the beat on which they enter is highly dangerous. It is impossible to divide anything into equal parts before one knows what the unit is in its totality. To insure excellent rendition of the opening notes of the Allegro, the conductor may resort to the following trick: a small flick of the *left hand* (without any preparatory beat before it) is made in order to show where the third beat of the measure would have occurred *in the allegro tempo*. This is followed, rhythmically, by a gesture of syncopation in the baton on the fourth beat, the entrance beat. The time-elapse between the left-hand flick and the gesture of syncopation in the baton states exactly the duration of one beat in the allegro tempo. This enables the musicians to proceed securely, with good ensemble.

Caution: The baton must stand perfectly still during the flick of the left hand. If the baton makes *any kind of a motion* before the exact instant for its beat, the result will probably be ragged.

The Beethoven example quoted in Example 29 is pertinent here. The flick of the left hand can show the cut-off of the fermata at the same time

Example 29. Beethoven, *Symphony No. 1 in C major*, Op. 21. Finale (measures 5–8).

that it states beat One in tempo allegro. The baton then performs the gesture of syncopation on the sixteenth rest and the music is off to a good start.

Note: Some editions do not show the caesura before the sixteenth rest, others do. If the conductor has made a long fermata, very soft, he may wish also to prolong the silence a bit. In this case, the fermata is cut off completely, and thereafter the left-hand, right-hand technique takes over as described above.

SUBTLE TEMPO VARIATIONS

If the student will set a metronome going while playing a fine recording of a major work by a major symphony orchestra, he will perhaps be surprised that the two will not continue to coincide in the takt. Music is a living thing and as such it cannot become entirely mechanistic. But, in the hands of a skilled conductor, it can give the illusion of perfectly timed beats without sacrificing the right to breathe freely.

Tempo variations, when they exist and are not indicated by written directives, must be very subtle. It is easier to fool the human ear than it is the metronome. When these variations occur they must be so skillfully performed that they do not call attention to their existence as such. The adding of a bit of tenuto to a certain note in a legato passage may lend color to the whole passage—but, inconspicuously, it has stretched the beat, which stretching is often compensated for by an equally inconspicuous deletion in the next following beat. When the composer himself requests such performance, and wishes it to be of a slightly more obvious nature, he does so through the use of the word *rubato*. It is a delightful word which permits emotion to reign with an authority superior to the inherent majesty of the takt. The French interpretation of the word is one that recognizes irregularities *within* the measure, but keeps the length of the measure itself intact.

When it is necessary for the conductor to hold back the tempo, the addition of more tenuto in the gesture can accomplish it. When he wishes to urge ahead, the use of staccato gestures will help. Also, a factor in urging ahead is the cheating, slightly, of the longer notes. Gestures become smaller, not larger.

In very slow movements (especially in Adagio tempos) the entrance of the second theme is usually the signal to relax the intensity and to urge the tempo ahead slightly—enough to negate any monotony that might otherwise prevail.

In Example 30 the tempo is sometimes subtly broadened after the

Example 30.   Weber, *Der Freischütz*. Overture (measures 287–292).

Vn. 1 quoted here
Passage fully
orchestrated

fermata with a *very gradual* accelerando all the way to the end of the piece. This makes for a thrillingly brilliant ending.*

Accelerandos and ritardandos marked by the composer are not quite so subtle. The important thing with these devices is that the change of motion in either case be gradual, not sudden, and that both may be brought under control again when the music demands the resumption of its original tempo. For immediate changes from slow to fast tempos, see page 61.

THE CLOSING MEASURES

A few words now about the almost imperceptible tempo deviations that lead to the final note of a composition.

Some pieces end with a tremendous rush of time-beating right to the last note which is performed as a brilliant cut-off. Accellerando is well nigh unavoidable. Other compositions lead to a gorgeous sustained sound, crowned with a fermata. When the fermata exists, pay attention to it. Usually it tells you that the composer intended some broadening of the sound (and tempo) with a consequent lengthening of the last note beyond its notated value. Try to achieve the nobility inherent in such an ending.

Note: A fermata over a bar-line signifies only the termination of a certain section of the piece and does not affect the performance.

For the diminuendo into silence, keep the hands moving downward in a tenuto gesture until the sound disappears. When silence reigns, the conductor stands perfectly still for a moment before releasing the audience from the spell of utter quiet.

Another type of ending must be mentioned. It is the hair's-breadth delay of the very last note where no ritard has occurred. It is pertinent to pieces of a light, airy, and often humorous character that bounce along right up to the end with no ritard. The performance of the last note, just

---

*There are two accepted interpretations for the passage given here. The second is as follows: The tempo is slightly slower following the fermata, tutti rest; it then resumes it original brilliance at (a).

later than the audience expects it, brings with it a bit of a chuckle and a storm of applause. It has a charm that is difficult to match in any other way. Example 31 shows a place where the delayed last note can be used.

Example 31.   Lalo, *Symphonie espagnole*, Op. 21, for Violin and Orchestra. Second movement (last four measures).

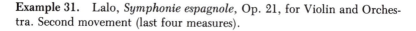

A second example of the delayed last note occurs in the Minuet forms. On occasion the bass instruments have an ending note on the second beat of the measure. This is usually in the form of an octave skip. In cases where there has been no ritard, this last note is generally played a fraction of an instant late. The effect is that of putting a definite period on the end of the sentence.

The necessity often arises, in theatrical performances, to stop the music in the midst of its onrush, as it were. When the "act" finishes, the applause must start, regardless. The old circus bands customarily resorted to their C-major chord, playing it instantly when the act terminated and holding it forte until the applause was well established. In the theater often the tonic chord of the selection being played is used for the ending chord and it is inserted whenever the applause is due. The theater orchestra understands that one of its biggest jobs is to crescendo the endings so that the audience reaction will be enthusiastic, spontaneous, and sustained.

Finally, let us mention the old "showmanship" ending. This is used when the theater orchestra is performing on the stage and is itself the main attraction. The conductor wishes to force the applause to start before the orchestra has finished playing its last note. (This presupposes a loud ending.) He can warn the musicians, during the rehearsal, to "keep pouring it on" until the applause starts. He then forces the applause by turning suddenly to the audience while still holding out the last note and, if necessary, jerking the baton upward a little, very quickly. It is almost foolproof in its results if the conductor has confidence in himself when he does it. The cut-off for the orchestra is performed after the applause has started and while the conductor is still facing the audience. Remember, this is pure showmanship—not formal concert etiquette.

EXERCISES FOR PRACTICE: DEVELOPING EXPRESSION IN THE GESTURES

1. Practice applying the gestures legato, staccato, tenuto, dead, and gesture of syncopation to the beat-patterns of Chapter 3 and 4. Watch the tip of the stick in the mirror as you practice, until each beat shows the distinctive style being worked on at the moment.

2. Practice Chapter 3, Exercise 13, applying each style to the examples given. Then change the style in the middle of each exercise, keeping the takt even throughout.

3. Practice the following exercises, repeating each several times without stopping. Be careful not to change the speed of the takt when the style changes to staccato. *Keep the takt steady.*

   a. Six measures in ONE staccato and six measures in ONE legato.

   b. Four measures in ONE staccato, forte, and four measures of dead gesture (silence). Use very small beats for the dead gesture here; center them in the wrist only.

   c. Three measures in ONE tenuto and one measure as a gesture of syncopation with the group playing *after* the beat. See below:

   d. Two measures in TWO staccato and one measure in TWO tenuto.

   e. Two measures in THREE tenuto and one measure in TWO silent (dead gesture).

f. Two measures in THREE with after-beats on the second and third beats (gesture of syncopation on Two and Three) followed by two measures in FOUR legato. Sing the after-beats as you make those gestures.

g. Two measures in FIVE (3 + 2) staccato and two measures in FOUR tenuto.

h. Two measures in TWO with the phrase ending on Two of each measure, followed by one measure in THREE staccato.

4. In the following exercises, three factors change in the middle of each exercise: the number of measures, the number of beats per measure, and the style. These are a challenge to the mind and they will help to activate the ability to think ahead. Do not be discouraged if they are difficult at first. As you practice, the mental aspect will improve and as it improves you will feel a real technique coming into your hands. Remember to watch your gestures in the mirror as you practice. Repeat each study without stopping, several times or until it becomes easy.

a. Two measures in TWO staccato and one measure in THREE tenuto.

b. Three measures in THREE legato and two measures in TWO staccato.

c. Two measures in FOUR tenuto and one measure in THREE silent.

d. Three measures in TWO tenuto and two measures in ONE staccato. See that your ONE pattern is distinctive from your TWO.

e. Two measures in FOUR legato and one measure in TWO, afterbeats (G.o.S.).

f. Four measures in ONE tenuto and one measure in TWO staccato.

5. Write out musical examples to go with Exercises 3 and 4 above, after the manner of the following:

Problem: Two measures in TWO staccato and one measure in THREE tenuto.

(Notice that the "problem" is applicable to each of the following notations, although the music for each is completely different.)

6. Now take a score such as Schubert's Symphony in B minor ("Unfinished"), first movement, and study it through, applying the various types of gestures to the music as written. Where would you use legato, staccato, tenuto? Where should the dead gesture be used? (**Note:** any score may be used here—chorus, band, or orchestra. The Schubert is suggested because it lends itself so well to the first application of the gestures.)

7. Take a score and look for after-beat entrances, or for accents after the beat where the gesture of syncopation would be applicable.

8. Practice the following exercises showing a *change to a faster tempo* when the meter changes. Make the change exactly on One of the new measure, and use a precise preparatory beat *in the new tempo*. Start with several measures in the first tempo. Remember to control the rebound of the last beat of the slow tempo, returning the baton to center-front and making a gesture of preparation thereafter in the new fast tempo.

   a. 4/4 to 3/4
   b. 2/4 to 3/4
   c. 3/4 to 6/8 in SIX
   d. 2/4 to 5/4 in FIVE
   e. 3/4 to 4/4
   f. Divided 3/4 to 4/4
   g. 4/4 to 2/4
   h. 5/4 in a 3 + 2 pattern to 6/8 in TWO
   j. 6/8 in SIX to 4/4
   k. 4/4 to 5/4 in TWO, 3 + 2 division
   l. 4/8 in TWO to 3/16 in ONE
   m. 6/8 in SIX to 3/4 in THREE

   From here on the student should be conscious of both *score* and *interpretive technical means.* This signifies that in studying a score he should carry in his mind the auditory image of the sound he wishes to extract from the musicians at any one place in the music and HOW he is going to conduct that passage to get his results.

As the drill exercises get easy, add to them dynamic variations as the styles change. Use smaller gestures for the *piano* and larger for the *forte*.

Learn the score thoroughly; practice the gestures until they say what they are intended to. Then proceed to *conduct*. Do not spend the time talking.

RECOMMENDED REFERENCE READINGS (SEE APPENDIX G)

BRAITHWAITE, WARWICK. *The Conductor's Art.* Chapter IV, pp. 22–35, "Sudden Changes of Time."

CHRISTIANI, ADOLF F. *Principles of Expression in Pianoforte Playing.* In applying Christiani's writings to massed performance groups, substitute the word *emphasis for accent.* This is one of the great works on expression in music.

EARHART, WILL. *The Eloquent Baton.* Chapters VI, VII, VIII, pp. 36–67, "Phrasing" and "Phrasing Beats"; "Other Properties of the Beat."

KAHN, EMIL. *Conducting.* Chapter 20, pp. 146–154, "Phrasing."

MALKO, NICOLAI. *The Conductor and His Baton.* Chapter V, pp. 123–220, "The Conductor's Gestures." (This is probably the greatest single chapter in print on this subject.)

MCELHERAN, BROCK. *Conducting Technique.* Chapter 9, pp. 37–46, "Dynamics, Accents, Phrasing, Tempo, Character."

PRAUSNITZ, FREDERIK. *Score and Podium.* Newest book in the field. Well written, much good advice for all conductors.

5

The Development
of the Left Hand

The technically developed left hand plays an important part in the overall musical result. While this hand should be able to beat time efficiently, it should not constantly mimic the rhythmic motions of the right hand. The left hand has its own eloquent language to speak and it should eventually be trained for *independent* action.

To introduce this facet of the technique, it is helpful if the reader has some understanding of the structure of the brain. The human brain is comprised of two "mirrored" halves, each complete in itself. Medical science has shown that the left half of the brain controls the right side of the body; the right half links up with the left side of the body. The two halves can set up independent controls, aided by habit formation, so that each hand can do a different kind of work, simultaneously with and independently of the other.* Witness the violinist!

By use of the Positron Emission Tomography (PET) scan, the intuitive, spatial recognition, and music centers have been located in the right half of the brain; the emotions occupy the frontal portion. When trained musicians judge musical pitches, both halves of the brain show activity. This should tell us something about how important it is to have both halves

---

*Each hemisphere contains the control centers for several activities that can occur simultaneously." Excerpts from *The Brain: The Last Frontier* by Richard M. Restak, M.D., p. 186. Copyright © 1979 by Richard M. Restak. Reprinted by permission of Doubleday & Company, Inc.

of the brain developed, especially in our field of physical-mental-emotional-creative conducting.

The two hemispheres are interconnected by an intricate network of fibers called the *corpus callosum* that acts to correlate the functions of both halves when, for example, simultaneous or similar actions of the two hands are desired.* If you have read the footnote you will realize that as a young conductor you can have confidence that you are "built to function!"—but it takes practice.

BUILDING INDEPENDENT ACTION IN THE HANDS

During the activating of the right side of the brain (to train the left hand to perform), the right hand will be functioning largely by habit—the habits you have established in your conducting thus far. Two goals now emerge: first, to be able to activate and deactivate the left hand without upsetting the time-beating in the right hand; and second, to be able to perform long, smooth, slow motions with the left hand without showing either pulses or momentary stops in its motion while the right hand continues its time-beating.

The First Step: Activating and Deactivating the Left Hand

Let the left arm hang loosely downward from the shoulder, completely relaxed. Begin time-beating in FOUR with the right hand. Bring the left hand up in a fist gesture on a third beat and then drop it back immediately to its full-length relaxation. Do this every second measure while the right hand continues to beat time. See that the rhythm of the right hand is not upset by the left-hand motion. Remember that you are using two different halves of the brain to perform these motions. When this exercise is easy, bring the left hand up on the first beat of each measure. This is more difficult because the right hand will be coming down while the left hand is coming up. Continue with 4, 3, 2, 1 (in consecutive measures), then 1, 2, 3, 4. The left hand returns to *complete relaxation* each time.

---

*Restak, p. 172. "Events in one hemisphere can be immediately telegraphed over this 200-million-fiber network [corpus callosum] to the opposite hemisphere. If we suppose that each fiber has an average firing frequency of twenty impulses a second, the *corpus callosum* is carrying something like four billion impulses a second right now as you are reading this sentence."

Repeat this same study starting with the left hand resting on your belt buckle. Return the hand to this position after every gesture.

The Second Step: Cuing Gestures

Choose a time-beating pattern for the right hand. Bring the left hand into play and actually direct a cue toward this or that group of musicians. Visualize your performers as you cue. Cue sopranos, basses, trumpets, first violins, and so on. Cue *on* the beat for now.

Next, bring the left hand into play in time to make a preparatory gesture (rhythmic) before the cue. This begins to make you conscious of the timing factor.

Each of these exercises should be practiced from the full-length relaxation position and also from the "belt" position of the left hand.

The Third Step: Smooth Motion vs. Time-beating

Beat eight measures in TWO with the right hand. The left hand is going to make a four-measure crescendo motion upwards followed by four measures of diminuendo as it returns downward to its starting position. Let the palm of the hand face upward on the crescendo gesture, as if actually carrying the sound up. At the peak of the upward motion (forehead level) the hand is turned to face the performers and comes back down to the starting point at the side, indicating diminuendo. You will find that at first the left hand will not perform smoothly. Watch it with your eyes. Its motion will tend to pause here and there and to be somewhat jerky, influenced by the rhythmic motion of the right hand. Smoothness comes rather quickly, however. Later, the right hand can vary the size of its time-beating gestures to match the crescendo-diminuendo dynamic of the left hand. When this exercise becomes smooth and easy, you can be assured that the two hands have established their fundamental independence. The Brain has gone through its period of initial development.

The Fourth Step: Contouring the Phrase

Let the right hand beat a two-measure group in 4/4. Let the left hand carry the phrase upward in about a twelve-inch arc, its peak coinciding with the beginning of the second measure; then turn the palm toward the floor and bring the phrase back down again. Example 32 (a) and (b) presents two passages where phrasal contour gestures may be used effectively. In (a), two four-measure phrases are shown with the peak at the beginning of the second measure; in (b), a series of two-measure phrases of increasing intensity is given.

Example 32.   Dvořák, *Slavonic Dance*, Op. 72, No. 2, in E minor. (a) Measures 1–8; (b) Measures 17–24. First violin only quoted.

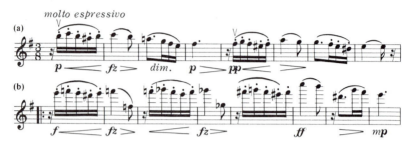

CUING

In order to give effective cues you must know where the various singers or instrumentalists are positioned in the organization you are about to conduct. If you are in doubt, it is permissible to ask at the beginning of the rehearsal. It is best if you can be provided with a seating chart beforehand. Several types of seatings are to be found in Appendix A.

When Are Cues Given?

Cues are customarily given under the following circumstances:

1. When an instrument or group of instruments enters the music for the first time after the piece has already begun.
2. When an instrument or group of instruments enters after a long rest.
3. When a single instrument begins an important solo or melodic line.
4. When an entire section takes over the main theme.
5. When melodic interest or rhythmic figures (motifs) are tossed from one instrument to another.
6. Whenever entrances are tricky and difficult.
7. When the conductor wishes to control exactly the moment of the sound.
8. When instruments enter on *double forte* attacks.
9. When there is a cymbal crash or an entrance of the cymbals for a prolonged passage.
10. When there are isolated pizzicato notes or chords.

How Are Cues Given?

Cues are given in the following ways:

1. By the baton, in the manner of a time-beating gesture directed specifically toward a player or group of players customarily seated on the conductor's right or in the center of the orchestra.
2. By the left hand in a special motion (not a time-beating gesture), sometimes with a preparation gesture preceding the cue and sometimes with just an indication on the beat-point. The left-hand cues are used for players sitting left of center.
3. By the eyes, a lift of the eyebrows, or a nod of the head. This last is used in very quiet passages where anything other than the most subtle of motions would disrupt the mood. These gestures are also used when both hands are already fully occupied with other necessary conductorial gestures.

Caution: The two hands should not cross over each other in giving cues. *Do not lean over toward the performers when giving a cue.*

OTHER FACETS OF LEFT-HAND TECHNIQUE

In addition to its duties in cuing, the left hand gives valuable assistance in controlling dynamics and adding to the emotional drive. When the palm faces the players it is usually read as a caution to soften; when it faces the conductor, the musicians read it as a command for more power. *Keep the three middle fingers together in using the left hand.* For the piano subito bring the left hand up suddenly, palm toward the performers and fingers pointing *straight up*. The more sudden the motion, the softer the response.

A left hand, working without panic, can often prevent mistakes from happening. It can say "Not Yet" so beautifully.

Note: The more difficult problems for further development of the left hand are outlined in Appendix F, pages 257-58. The use of the left hand in conducting fermatas is dealt with in the next chapter.

EXERCISES FOR PRACTICE: CUING AND LEFT-HAND INDEPENDENCE

Repeat each of the following exercises many times without stopping. Repeat until easy.

1. Beating time in FOUR, cue with the left hand on One of the first measure and on Three of the second measure; on One of the third measure and Three of the fourth measure, and so on.

2. Beating time in THREE, cue on One of the first measure and on three of the second measure and repeat. Direct the cues toward two different players in an imaginary ensemble.

3. Beating time in ONE, cue on the first beat of the third, fifth, and ninth measures.

4. Beating time in FIVE, cue on the fourth beat in the first measure and the second beat in the second measure and continue in the same manner. Use the various types of FIVE patterns, both traditional and modern, and drill each type thoroughly on the given exercise.

5. Beating time in FOUR, cue on the first beat of the first measure, the second beat of the second measure, the third beat of the third measure, and the fourth beat of the fourth measure, repeating instantly from the beginning.

6. Taking the patterns given in Exercises 13 and 14 of Chapter 3, cue on the last beat of the first measure and the second beat of the third measure throughout.

7. Take also Exercises 15 and 17 of Chapter 3 and cue on predetermined beats as you pass through the measures.

8. Beating time in TWO, let the left hand show four measures of steady crescendo (upward rise) and four measures of steady diminuendo (downward gesture, palm toward players).

9. Beating time in SIX, let the left hand show a two-measure crescendo, a three-measure diminuendo, a three-measure crescendo, and a four-measure diminuendo and repeat.

10. Beating time in FOUR for four measures, the left hand is to show a phrase contour, rising and falling in a curved arc from left to center front, ending the phrase on the second beat of every second measure.

11. Practice cuing on all of the full-score excerpts in Chapters 10, 11, and 12. Direct the cues to the proper place in the imaginary band, chorus or orchestra. (Seating Charts may be found in Appendix A.)

RECOMMENDED REFERENCE READINGS
(SEE APPENDIX G)

BRAITHWAITE, WARWICK. *The Conductor's Art.* Chapter VII, pp. 46–50, "Use of Left Hand and Arm."

CLYNES, MANFRED. *Music, Mind and Brain.* Specialized research.

EARHART, WILL. *The Eloquent Baton.* Chapter XI, pp. 88–93, "The Left Hand and Signaling."

GROSBAYNE, BENJAMIN. *Techniques of Modern Orchestral Conducting.* Chapter XII, pp. 75–80, "Left Hand."

KAHN, EMIL. *Conducting,* pp. 74–75, "Cuing."

MALKO, NICOLAI. *The Conductor and His Baton.* Chapter VI, pp. 251–266, "The Left Hand."

RESTAK, RICHARD M. *The Brain: The Last Frontier.* Chapter 10, pp. 164–206, "The Jekyll and Hyde Solution."

6

The Fermata

Every fermata ($\frown$) is a law unto itself. Only one thing do they all have in common and that is a nonrhythmic execution. The fermata is held out as a sustained tone with no rhythmic pulsation and, except in chorales, is lengthened beyond the written value of the note.*

The fermata is used in two ways:

1. In early church music (chorales), the fermata indicates the ending of the phrase. Sometimes this ending is elongated, but this is not an invariable custom.

2. In other types of vocal composition and in instrumental music, the fermata is written to lengthen a particular note when the drama of the situation demands it or the expressive qualities of the music require such highlighting.

When the young conductor begins working with the fermata, he must clarify his ideas on three points:

*It is of serious concern today that the length of the fermata is being so greatly disregarded. One hears performance after performance of the less-than-professional choruses, bands, and orchestras where the fermata is being given exactly the length the note would have had if the composer had failed to write the fermata above. The ability to *stop* the rhythmic feeling inside of oneself seems to be a lost art. In asking many teachers of conducting, both here and in Europe, "What is the most difficult thing for the students to acquire?" the answer has been, invariably, "The handling of the fermata."

1. What the emotional quality of the particular fermata is, and therefore, *how long it should be held;*

2. *Whether it cuts off completely at its termination or leads directly into the next note* with no moment of silence between;

3. In the event the fermata is to cut off completely, *what direction this cut-off should take in order that the baton may be in position to move easily into the next following gesture,* whatever it may be. (Check back on the cut-off diagrams on page 16.) Every fermata should be "solved" in the light of the three points mentioned above before an attempt is made to execute it with the musicians.

DEFINITION OF THE FERMATA

The fermata is a cessation of rhythm. In Italian, the word fermata means "stop." One does not beat time during a fermata. The hands simply perform a sustained tenuto gesture during the length of the sound.

In general, it is preferred to keep the baton moving slowly while sustaining, but there are sometimes occasions which warrant the striking of a dramatic pose with the stick and "freezing." When this is done, intensity must show in the baton grip. The tension in the hand keeps the players sounding their tone until a cut-off occurs or the music continues. Upon occasion this intensity is shown by a small but purposeful shaking of the stick. When the baton stands still, there is always the danger that a diminuendo may occur. The sustaining motion may be transferred to the left hand if preferred, the stick remaining static.

FERMATAS CLASSIFIED BY LENGTH

There are two basic types of fermata by length.

1. The fermata which is determinate in length: The duration is a certain definite span in relation to the speed of the takt, such as twice as long as the composer's written notation of the fermata note. This type of fermata appears in certain places in Haydn and Mozart, especially in fast movements of solo accompaniments. It is, however, the exception to the rule.

2. The fermata which is indeterminate in length: The duration of such a fermata is left entirely up to the conductor, but it should be *longer* than the written value of the note or rest over which it is placed. This is the more common type of fermata. In handling either type, *no time is beaten.* One's inner feeling of continuous rhythm must halt. The fermata must not be curtailed. One is reminded of Wagner's "as if Beethoven cried, 'HOLD my fermatas!'"

The cutting off of the fermata should leave the baton (hand) in position to move easily into the next gesture. In many cases the left hand can be most serviceable in showing the termination of the fermata. This hand is also valuable in helping to control the general fermata dynamic, in reinforcing the sustained tone, and in adding a hypnotic quality to a very long diminuendo-fermata.

Important: After any fermata there must be a rhythmic preparatory gesture if the following note comes directly ON a beat. But if the entrance comes after a beat (on part of a beat), the use of the gesture of syncopation ON the beat will be sufficient to ensure accuracy of execution. (Examples of after-beat entrances: No. 33; 34, last measure; 36.)

THE FERMATA THAT CONTINUES
THE MUSIC WITHOUT A STOP (Caesura)

Note: The caesura lines (//) indicate a complete cut-off, a complete stop but of momentary duration.

Certain fermatas lead directly into a continuation of the music without a complete cut-off. The musical thought carries on through the rhythmic interruption contributed by the fermata. The next six examples deal with fermatas of this type.

Example 33 shows the fermata slurred to what follows. Here the baton sustains the fermata while moving slowly (tenuto) to the right and slightly upward. To terminate the fermata, the baton shows Two (after

Example 33. Beethoven, *Symphony No. 3 ("Eroica") in E♭ major,* Op. 55. Finale (measures 95–96).

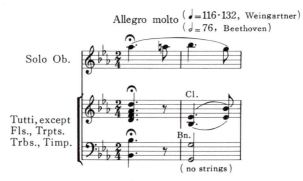

the manner of a gesture of syncopation). This gesture actually states the dot on the fermata note and the music continues in the given rhythmic tempo. No preparation is necessary. The showing of Two terminates the fermata at the same time that it resumes the tempo of the music.

Example 34 shows a tutti fermata with no caesura indicated. At the termination of the first hold, the baton loops directly into One of the next measure. The cut-off of the second fermata is Two of that measure, again stated suddenly as a gesture of syncopation (no preparatory loop), thus resuming the rhythm. The downbeat of each fermata measure should be shown by a very small down-up in the stick as it sustains the tie from the preceding measure. The left hand becomes valuable here also in preserving the sustained sound. The reason for not cutting off the first fermata completely is given by Felix Weingartner (an authority on Beethoven): the passage is "a closed harmonic and melodic complex," thus not allowing a break in its sequence.

Example 34. Beethoven, *Symphony No. 1 in C major*, Op. 21. Finale (measures 234–236).

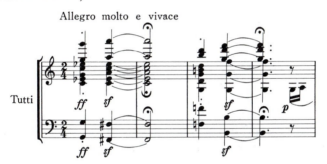

Example 35 presents another type of direct continuation of the music. The fermata is held on One, the baton moving to the right and slightly

Example 35. Beethoven, *Symphony No. 7 in A major*, Op. 92. First movement (measure 88).

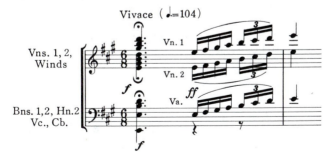

upward. This motion changes to an outward, rhythmic preparatory loop and Two is stated with good impulse of will. This cuts off the fermata at the same time that it commands the strings to continue the music *on* Two.

In Example 36 we see Beethoven's very careful notation of just exactly what he means. The pizzicato A-flat in the strings is to continue immediately on the heels of the fermata. Notice Beethoven's notation of the fermata *between the rests* in the string parts. This signifies that the gesture of cutting off the fermata becomes a rhythmic Two.

Example 36. Beethoven, *Symphony No. 3 ("Eroica") in E♭ major*, Op. 55. Finale (measure 31).

Not infrequently a fermata appears just before a double bar. This is seen in medleys and overtures. If the pause is on a dominant seventh chord, a complete cut-off is out of place. It leaves the resolution chord, to the right of the double bar, stranded. Sometimes an arranger marks the cut-off. Be wary in such places.

When the fermata before the double bar precedes a change of tempo, the fermata is held, after which the baton makes a *rhythmic preparatory gesture in the new tempo* leading into One. (Check p. 61, Slow to Fast Tempo.)

In Example 37 the first beat of the new tempo entails the playing of

Example 37. Beethoven, *Nameday Overture*, Op. 115 (last measure of the slow introduction and first measure of the Allegro).

six notes on that first beat, violins and violas. The allegro preparatory gesture should be legato and connected directly to the downbeat. (Refer to p. 14.)

Finally, in Example 38 we find a leading-through on the fermatas with an interesting articulation in the timpani (stems down in the bass clef line). In measure one, the timpanist is shown his ending note by a gesture of the left hand as the right hand begins its rhythmic preparatory loop into the first beat of the second measure. In measure Two, after the timpanist has performed his roll, the conductor gives him the left-hand cut-off gesture. But now Beethoven has written a fermata on a rest, *after* the timpani cut-off, showing that the fermata is still in effect and is to be sustained after the timpani stops.

Example 38.   Beethoven, *Consecration of the House Overture*, Op. 124 (measures 200–202).

THE FERMATA FOLLOWED BY A COMPLETE
CUT-OFF (A rest or caesura)

In dealing with fermatas on rests, the duration of the silence is influenced by the dynamic preceding it. Extreme pianos or massive double fortes usually lead to a longer silence. In Example 39 the note preceding the rest is a phrase ending. The cut-off can be handled effectively by the

Example 39.   Beethoven, *The Ruins of Athens Overture*, Op. 113 (measures 23–24).

left hand. The baton stops on Two and stands still during the fermata-rest; then makes a rhythmic preparatory beat into One.

When the fermata cut-off is followed by a single full beat of rest, the silent beat is used only to make a rhythmic preparation for the next entrance. If there are several beats of tutti rest, the left hand can control the silence while the baton makes very small dead gestures showing the passing of the beats; or the baton can move directly into position for the next beat and wait until it is time to make the preparation. If time is beaten, the small gestures should be in the direction normally taken by the pertinent time-beating pattern.

When the composer has not specified rhythmically how long a silence should last, then it depends upon the conductor's own innate musical taste. In general, the longer the fermata, the more the silence can be stretched in that magic moment following the cut-off.

THE FERMATA WITH CAESURA LINES, //, CONTINUING IMMEDIATELY

The caesura lines indicate a complete break between the fermata and what follows—just enough of a break to show that the fermata is not connected to what *immediately* follows.

The Fermata on One

In 4/4, the line of sustaining for a fermata on One would move to the right; the cut-off gesture would circle upward, counterclockwise, and cut to the right, leaving the hand in position to move leftward into Two. (Figure 36.) In 3/4 meter, the line of sustaining would move left, the loop would be clockwise cutting left, and the hand would be in position to make the customary Two to the right. In every case, a slight lift of the stick after the stop would act as a preparatory motion into the next beat—as if you were saying "And Two," "And Three," as the case may be.

Figure 36.

From the foregoing, it will be seen that (except in time-beating in One) when the fermata occurs on One, the line of sustaining will move in a direction *opposite* to that of beat Two when that second beat follows immediately. **Note:** When conducting a fermata, if the cut-off and reentrance feel clumsy, check on the direction of the circle used for the cut-off. Reversing the direction will often solve the problem.

The Fermata on Two

Figure 37 shows the fermata on Two in 4/4. In (a) the line of sustaining continues leftward and slightly upward after the ictus of Two. A clockwise loop cutting left is made and the baton arches into Three. In 3/4 the fermata sustains to the right, uses an upward counterclockwise gesture, cuts to the right and proceeds into Three. **Important:** Look now at figure 37 (b). After showing the ictus of Two, the hand would now sustain to the *right* so that the cut-off could be made on the customary ictus-point of Three (the tie of the farmata note), and would then be in position to loop directly into Four. This is an example of what is meant by "baton in position for the next beat after the cut-off." Be sure the baton stops cleanly after a cut-off.

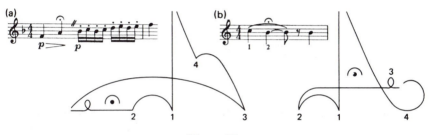

Figure 37.

The Fermata on Three

When the fermata is on Three (in 4/4), the line of sustaining moves to the right, the cut-off loops counterclockwise and cuts to the right. Figure 38.

Figure 38.

The Fermata on the Last Beat of Any Measure

With the fermata occurring on the last beat of any measure, it is necessary to keep the *rebound of the preceding beat* low. The ictus of the last beat will then be also in a low position. The line of sustaining has two choices. It can move normally upward, very slowly so as not to go too high; the cut-off can circle right or left, leaving the hand ready for a short preparatory motion into One. (Figure 39.) Or, if the fermata is to be extremely long, the baton can take a horizontal sustaining line, to the right and back or to the left and back, before starting its climb upward. If there is a rest on One, the baton can simply cut the fermata on One, beaten rhythmically, and then prepare Two. **Note:** The slow-moving horizontal line is the preferred line, in general, for sustaining. The wrist can lead the hand (Exercise No. 1, p. 10) with the thumb facing the ceiling; the hand is then always in position to take the next beat. *Perpendicular* lines are usually time-beating in character.

Figure 39.

SOME MORE DIFFICULT TYPES OF FERMATA

As you have seen, every fermata requires intelligent study. Of all composers, Beethoven stands out in precision of notation and in a variety that is all-encompassing. Every rest, every dot, every caesura says exactly what he means. We shall close this chapter by dealing with some specialized types of fermata.

The Rebeaten Fermata

In Figure 40 we have a series of fermatas that playfully interrupt the melody's rhythm but *not its sequence.* Imagine that this same melody has occurred earlier in the piece without the fermatas. In order to perform this music, breaking the rhythm but not the melodic sequence, the conductor has to show *two* second beats in each measure, one to start the hold

Figure 40.

and another to signify the ending of the fermata and the resumption of the rhythm. The first of the two second beats will show its ictus and move into a slow, tenuto gesture of sustaining. This sustaining gesture will go to the right. This will be followed by a sudden gesture of syncopation also to the right stating "Two" again and proceeding rhythmically into Three.

Example 40 shows a different type of rebeaten fermata. Here we have a triple meter, beaten in One-to-the-bar. The measure preceding the fermata is often taken in THREE in order to gain precision in the ensemble for the slight ritard marked by the composer. If THREE is used, the first two beats of the measure are in tempo, the ritard being reserved for the third beat. The fermata rises upward from the ictus of One. The cut-off is made upward and becomes, rhythmically, the first beat of the fermata measure, rebeaten in tempo, the musicians playing on the last one-third of the beat. The gesture of syncopation is practical for this rebeaten One.

Example 40.   Beethoven, *Symphony No. 5 in C minor*, Op. 67. Third movement (measures 7–9).

Specialized Problems

In Example 41 we have a gentle rhythmic interruption in a continuous melodic line. Compare Example 41 with Figure 40. In Example 41, there is no break: The fermata is held out on a sustained Two, the hand then looping without a stop into One. Beat One cuts the fermata as the new instrument enters. On the last measure of the example, a small One is shown in the baton, the sustaining motion moves to the right and up-

Example 41.   Beethoven, *Symphony No. 4 in B♭ major*, Op. 60. Finale (nine to six measures from the end).

ward, preparing the stick for the sudden down-up, double-forte ictus of Two.

In Example 42 the caesura lines are missing. The usual solution for handling this famous place is to consider the downbeat One of the third measure as the cut-off of the fermata. However, the author has seen at least one of the great conductors use a very quick cut-off gesture upward with an instantaneous One. In this instance the auditorium was a large one and he may have resorted to this device in order to clarify the written eighth rest for the audience.

Example 42.   Beethoven, *Symphony No. 5 in C minor*, Op. 67. First movement (measures 1–6).

One other comment on Example 42: Your attention is called to the fact that the fermata in the fifth measure comes on the *second* downbeat of that note. Both downbeats must be shown, the second One very small so as not to interrupt the tenuto motion of the tie.

In Example 43 the cut-off is performed whenever the conductor wishes to end the sound. The following rest is used only for the purpose of making a preparatory gesture into One of the next bar. The rest is a tutti rest.

Example 43.   Berlioz, *The Damnation of Faust*, Op. 24 (last measure of Scene XVI and first measure of Scene XVII, recitative).*

Example 44 presents a fermata written against a moving voice. This type of fermata is rather common. Although the fermata appears to begin on the first beat of the measure for those instruments playing the whole

*This type of fermata is very rare. There are hundreds of examples to be found with notes followed by fermata-rests, but very few with fermatas followed by *rhythmic* rests for the balance of the measure. (See also Example 86.)

Example 44.   Beethoven, *Fidelio overture*, Op. 72b (measures 247–248).

note, actually it does not start as a *fermata* until the last beat of the measure. The position of the fermata in the *moving voice* (in this case the first violins and the cellos) states the inset of the hold as such. In conducting this type of fermata, *the time-beating continues until the last beat of the moving voice.* When that beat begins to sustain, the real fermata starts.

The Adagio marking with the cut-time signifies two major accents in the measure, but a time-beating pattern in Four. Beethoven, in writing six notes in this fermata measure, has stretched his phrase with a subtle type of written ritard. Beats One and Three would be emphasized in the preceding measure. They would become rhythmically One-Four of this last Adagio measure, beaten in a SIX pattern.

In Example 45, the fermata is placed over the rest, indicating two things: (1) the last note before the rest must be given exactly its written value, and not lengthened unless qualified by the word ritard: (2) There is a long moment of silence following the note before the next entrance is made.

In the quoted example, the first beat (One) would be cut on Two. In measure 2, after the cut-off, the baton stands still as long as the conductor wants the silence to last. Then he makes a tiny flick with the fingers of his left hand, which hand is not seen by the audience. This flick tells

Example 45.   Rossini, *L'Italiana in Algeria.* Overture (measures 31–32).

the players, "Here is Two *in the Allegro tempo*." The baton then beats Three as a sharp gesture of syncopation and everything follows in due course. The flick of the left hand shows the ending of the fermata-rest and simultaneously states Two in the Allegro tempo. Three is the gesture of syncopation, after which they play. Careful timing is necessary here to see that Two-Three are exactly in tempo.

When there is no change of tempo after the fermata, and the silence is of rather short duration, the left-hand flick is not needed. The tempo of the piece has already been well established in the minds of the players during the rendition of the measures preceding the fermata. The baton beat alone is sufficient to reestablish the tempo.

Some pieces start with a fermata on the very first note. This is a dramatic call to attention and is usually a double forte. It means *no rhythm* on the first note. See page 60, "breathing gesture."

In Example 46 we have a fermata followed by two beats of tutti rest. When this type of notation is used, it signifies the immediate resumption of the rhythm when the fermata is cut off. The baton shows One and sustains to the right. The gesture of cutting off becomes Three (to the right) while Four (moving upward) prepares for One, the pizzicato chord.

Note: When a single pizzicato note, surrounded by rests, is to be played ON a beat, use a legato preparation that leads directly into the pizzicato without stopping. If a stop occurs between the preparation and the command to play, the result will probably be ragged. The stop "reads" as a gesture of syncopation with the note coming after the beat.

Example 46.   Rossini, *Semiramide*. Overture (measures 173–174).

Finally, let us mention a specialized type of fermata. It is that which occurs on a sustained tone or a rest for certain members of the ensemble while one or more instruments perform cadenza-like passages. Here a bimanual handling is usually best; one hand devotes itself to controlling the non-solo instruments (the fermata) while the other hand beats as necessary, if necessary, to give the needed direction for the cadenza performance. The beat following the cadenza must be made in the correct direction of the time-beating. A good reference score is *Scheherezade*.

While the foregoing examples provide some methods for studying fermatas, and some solutions for handling them technically, it is important to caution again that every fermata is a law unto itself. Its proper handling is determined by the context in which it occurs. Intelligent thought should be brought to bear upon the problem each presents, and the gestures ought to be practiced in order to insure effective performance of the fermata and efficient resumption of the rhythm thereafter. The fermata is inserted for the chief purpose of making the note *longer* than its written value. HOLD the fermatas!

EXERCISES FOR PRACTICE: HANDLING THE FERMATA

1. Practice diligently on all of the examples given in this chapter.

2. Practice making cut-offs on all beats of the various types of time-beating patterns, picking up the rhythm again on the next following beat. Practice with and without lengthy caesuras. When the caesura is long, use a preparatory gesture before the next time-beating gesture. Make all gestures in the proper direction (preparations and beats.)

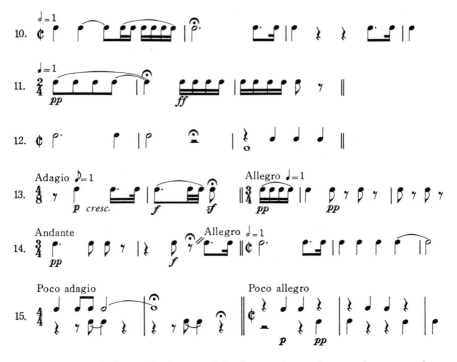

3. Compose melodies to fit the stated rhythms and sing them as these examples are practiced.

RECOMMENDED REFERENCE READINGS
(SEE APPENDIX G)

GROSBAYNE, BENJAMIN. *The Technique of Modern Orchestral Conducting.* Chapter XIII, pp. 81–96, "The Hold."

MALKO, NICOLAI. *The Conductor and His Baton.* Excellent examples from the repertoire are given and analyzed in the section dealing with the Fermata, pp. 220–239.

RUDOLF, MAX. *The Grammar of Conducting.* Chapters XVIII, XIX, pp. 166–201, "Holds."

7

Time-Beating II: Fast Fives, Sevens: Twentieth-Century Innovations

Rhythm is universally defined as heavier emphasis followed by lighter emphasis, repeated—a succession of heavy–light recurrent accentuations.

In basic time-beating, you encountered the "divided" beat where all beats were of the same length (duration) and the number of pulses between beats was constant throughout.

Now, in the twentieth century, composers have chosen to upset the duration of primary beats, so that some beats may be extended by an extra half-beat, others curtailed by an equal amount. (Example 47, second measure.)

If the second measure is beaten in ONE, it must account for an extra "And" beat; beaten in TWO, the second beat would have to be shortened

Example 47. Stravinsky, *L'Histoire du soldat.* Introduction: Marche du soldat, measures 78–80. © 1924 by J. & W. Chester, Ltd. By permission of the copyright owners, J & W Chester/Edition Wilhelm Hansen London, Ltd.

by a half-beat. All of this has resulted in what we have termed *lopsided* time-beating. All beats will not be rhythmically even.

LOPSIDED TIME-BEATING

In addition, the composers have chosen to *regroup* the smaller pulses within the measure. What was formerly a nicely balanced nine-beat measure (3 + 3 + 3) may now become an uneven grouping of 4 + 5, or 5 + 4. Such groupings occur most often in faster tempos where the smaller pulses are not shown as such, but their existence is accounted for by lengthening (or shortening) the duration of the primary beat. (Example 48.)

Example 48. Stravinsky, *The Rite of Spring*. (a) Sacrificial Dance: The Chosen One (measures 15–19; rhythm only); (b) The Play of Abduction (measures 19–21; rhythm only). Copyright 1921 by Edition Russe de Musique. Renewed 1958. Copyright and Renewal assigned to Boosey & Hawkes, Inc. Revised Edition Copyright 1948 by Boosey & Hawkes, Inc. Reprinted by permission.

When conducting these complicated rhythmic variations, the conductor must think in the value of the shorter notes (in (a), the sixteenths; in (b), the eighths), and then adjust the duration of his primary beats to accommodate the added (or deleted) pulse where it occurs. In (b) the composer himself has indicated his groupings by the addition of parenthetical signatures and dotted lines of demarcation.

FAST FIVES

There is a helpful adjustment in the time-beating pattern, to accommodate measures beaten in TWO where lopsided beats are called for. (Figure 41.)

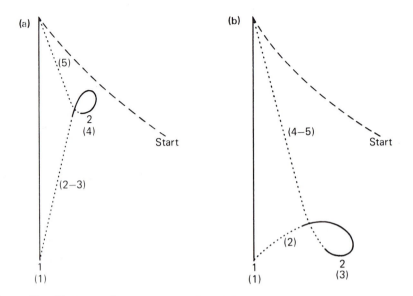

Figure 41. Fast FIVES beaten in TWO (lopsided pattern). In fast SEVENS (a) = 4 + 3; (b) = 3 + 4.

In Figure 41 (a), the high rebound of One accounts for the added duration (the 3), leaving only a shorter line for the curtailed half of the measure (the 2). In (b), the rebound of One is kept low, leaving the long upward line for the lengthier second beat (2 + 3). The speed of motion of the gestures will vary appreciably, faster on the short gestures, slower on the longer.

Example 49 shows a 3 + 2 followed by a 2 + 3 in the second measure: (Figure 41(a) followed by 41(b) is an excellent example for reiterated practice.)

The patterns of Figure 41 can also be adapted to the fast SEVENS, 4 + 3 and 3 + 4, beaten in TWO. Reemphasizing, the conductor must keep

Example 49. Stravinsky, *L'Histoire du soldat*. Music from the first scene: Little Tunes Beside the Brook, measures 64–65. © 1924 by J. & W. Chester, Ltd. By permission of the copyright owners, J & W Chester/Edition Wilhelm Hansen London, Ltd.

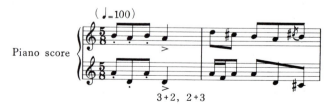

the pulse-notes clicking through his mind *in even succession* as he shows their groupings with his unbalanced gestures.

STRANGE COMBINATIONS OF PULSES IN SLOW TEMPOS

Figure 42 presents diagrams for showing odd combinations of phrasings within the measure.

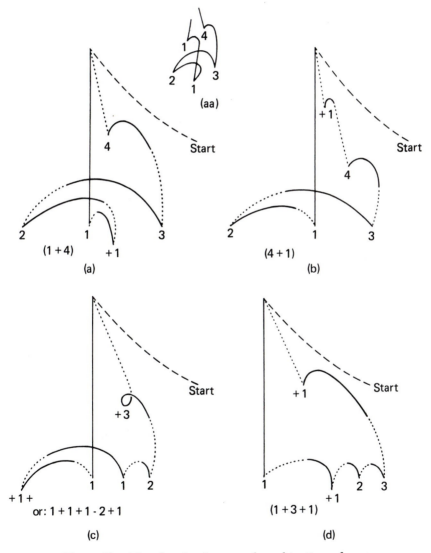

Figure 42. Time-beating in unusual combinations of FIVE.

Diagram (a), (1 + 4), a heavy downbeat followed by an attached FOUR pattern, tells us that the composer has written a forte One and a subsequent four-beat phrase. Diagram (aa), with a small first One, would be applicable to the excerpts given in Example 50 (a) and (b).

Figure 42 (b) shows the 4 + 1 pattern—a normal FOUR plus an extra small beat at the top for the fifth beat.

FIVES may also be found in combinations of 1 + 1 + 3 (diagram

Example 50. Stravinsky, *The Rite of Spring:* (a) The Sacrifice (measure 55) (b) Games of the Rival Tribes (measure 27). Copyright 1921 by Edition Russe de Musique. Renewed 1958. Copyright and Renewal assigned to Boosey & Hawkes, Inc. Revised Edition Copyright 1948 by Boosey and Hawkes, Inc. Reprinted by permission.

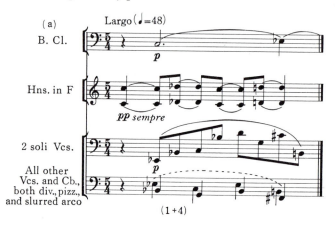

Example 51. Stravinsky, *The Rite of Spring.* Games of the Rival Tribes, (measure 22). Copyright 1921 by Edition Russe de Musique. Renewed 1958. Copyright and Renewal assigned to Boosey & Hawkes, Inc. Revised Edition Copyright 1948 by Boosey & Hawkes, Inc. Reprinted by permission.

(c))*, 1 + 3 + 1 (d), and 3 + 1 + 1. In (d) there are three groupings within the measure and a basic THREE pattern is feasible adding the small pulses as demanded by the music. Example 51 shows 1 + 3 + 1.

The Principle for Creating Gestures

To create gestures for things not yet written: Choose the primary beat-pattern by the number of groupings within the measure and add the subdivisions as notated. The long lines of the primary beats lead to the beginning of the following pulse-grouping. Such patterns define precisely the structure within the measure and are visually clear for the musicians performing the notes.

SEVENS

Seven beats to the bar may be broken up into the following groupings: 3 + 4, 4 + 3, 2 + 3 + 2, 3 + 2 + 2, 2 + 2 + 3, and combinations of a 1 and several 2's. If there are two or four groupings in the measure, start with a four-beat pattern. (Figure 43 (a).) If there are three groupings, use three primary beats—a three-beat pattern. (Figure 43 (b).)

Figure 43 (a) shows the deleted divided-FOUR; (b) the augmented divided-THREE. Diagram (b) could serve either a 3 + 4 phrasing beaten

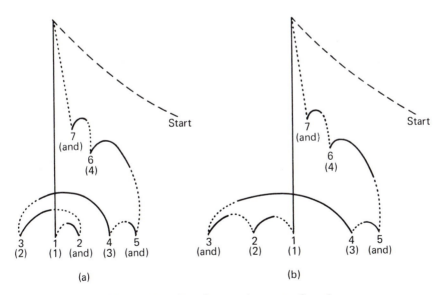

Figure 43. Time-beating in SEVEN: 3 + 4.

*Notice (c) would also handle a 4-grouping of 1 + 1 + 1 - 2 + 1.

in THREE or a 3 + 2 + 2 grouping. The choice would depend upon subtleties found in the score.

In Example 52, the composer's dotted lines state a 3 + 2 + 2 pattern. (Fig. 43 (b).) The left hand would be useful in cuing the horns (top score) and the violins at the end of the last measure if necessary. (Example 52.)

Example 52.   Copland, *Concerto for Piano and Orchestra*. First movement (measure 4). Copyright 1929 by Cos Cob Press, Inc.; Renewed 1958 by Aaron Copland. Reprinted by permission of Aaron Copland, Copyright Owner and Boosey & Hawkes, Inc., Sole Publishers and Licencees.

Example 53 might be conducted using either (a) or (b) of Figure 43.

Example 53.   Barber, *Medea's Meditation and Dance of Vengeance*, Op. 23 A (measure 110). Copyright © 1956 by G. Schirmer, Inc. "Used by Permission."

Figure 44 deletes the divided-FOUR pattern: In (a), 2 + 2 + 1 + 2 and in (b) 2 + 2 + 2 + 1.

Thus it shows the 4 + 3 patterns springing from a DIVIDED-FOUR. In (a) the "And" of Three has been deleted and in (b) the "And" of Four has been eliminated.

Figure 45 enlarges the THREE-beat pattern.

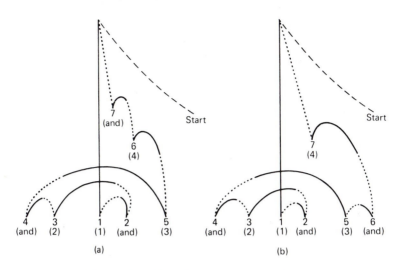

Figure 44. Time-beating in SEVEN: 4 + 3.

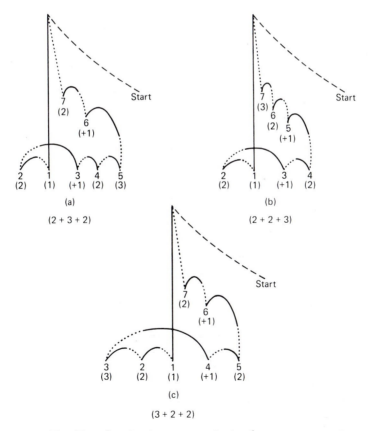

Figure 45. Time-beating in SEVEN springing from a THREE pattern.

Example 54 combines SEVENS and FIVES: 2 + 2 + 3 and 3 + 2.

Example 54. Stravinsky, *L'Histoire du soldat.* Music from the second scene (measures 35–37). © 1924 by J. & W. Chester, Ltd. By permission of the copyright owners, J & W Chester/Edition Wilhelm Hansen London Ltd.

Example 55 moves from 3 + 2 + 2 (Fig. 45 (c)), to 2 + 2 + 3 (Fig. 45 (b)), a "mirrored" image rhythmically.

Example 55. Stravinsky, *The Fire-Bird Suite.* (measures 41–42, melody line only). © 1920 by J. & W. Chester, Ltd. By permission of the copyright owners, J & W Chester/Edition Wilhelm Hansen London Ltd.

*The dotted lines are in the score

THE MISUNDERSTOOD EXAMPLE

Attention is now called to Examples 56 and 57: the first, written in FIVE and beaten in TWO; the second, written in SEVEN but beaten in THREE.

The tremendous ff and sff (strings) on the last notes of measure 1 immediately attract attention. The tendency is to accept a 3 + 2 and to apply it again as a 3 + 2 + 2 analysis of the 7/8 measure (Ex. 57), the conductor preparing and showing the last beat with great vigor. But this does not work in performance. What must be conducted here is the ff timpani line, using a sudden vigorous gesture (similar to a Gesture of Syncopation) on the final beat of each excerpt. The pattern is a 2 + 3 and a 2 + 2 + 3. The sudden percussion "whack" precipitates the grace notes which are the real problem in producing good ensemble. Trust the other

Example 56.   Stravinsky, *The Rite of Spring*. Glorification of the Chosen One (measures 1 and 18). Copyright 1921 by Edition Russe de Musique. Renewed 1958. Copyright and Renewal assigned to Boosey & Hawkes, Inc. Revised Edition Copyright 1948 by Boosey & Hawkes, Inc. Reprinted by permission.

Example 57.   Ibid measure 19.

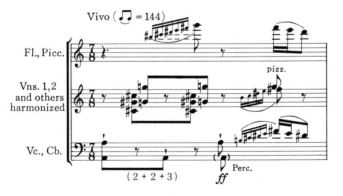

players who enter on those last three notes; they will be fine if they hear that percussion beat emphasized.

A simpler example is shown in No. 58. Again the bass line is the clue to solving the conducting.

Caution: In twentieth-century music, a distinction is to be made between the length of measure and the length of note. If the note length is a constant, then the measure length will vary; if the measure is to be uniform throughout, then the extra notes squeezed in will have to adjust. Try the following exercise:

Example 58.   Stravinsky, *L'Histoire du soldat*. Music from the first scene: Little Tunes Beside the Brook (measure 67). © by J & W. Chester, Ltd. By permission of the copyright owners, J & W Chester/Edition Wilhelm Hansen London Ltd.

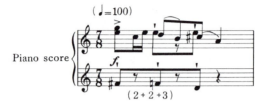

Steady Time-beating in THREE; the duration of each measure is identical.

Counting as follows, completing the count within the duration of the measure:

```
1 2 3
1 2 3 4
1 2 3 4 5
1 2 3 4 5 6
1 2 3 4 5 6 7
1 2 3 4 5 6 7 8
1 2 3 4 5 6 7 8 9
```

Note: An interesting example is to be found in Respighi's *Sonata in B minor for Piano and Violin*, second movement. The piano has a 10/8 signature against a 4/4 in the violin, further complicated, here and there, by measures containing two triplet figures in quarter-note values in the violin part.

STRANGE COMBINATIONS OF NINES AND TWELVES

Refer again to the basic principle as stated on page 98. See also Example 48 (b) on p. 95. With the discussion already completed in this chapter, the reader should be able to adjust the time-beating patterns to accommodate the demands of any combinations of NINES or TWELVES.

ELEVEN BEATS TO THE BAR

In cases where ELEVENS and other odd and rare meters are called for, the basic principle still is to use the long gestures when leading into the rhythmic accents (groupings) and to intersperse them with the short "And" gestures as needed. When the ELEVEN is comprised of eleven equally accented beats, a simple counting of eleven identical downbeats can be used. (Example 59.) When the conductor uses this solution, he should warn the players of his intentions verbally, then make the rebound of the eleventh beat move to a totally new position in space. This tells the performers that the next beat will be One of the next measure.

Example 59. Stravinsky, *The Rite of Spring.* Mysterious Circles of the Adolescents (last measure). Copyright 1921 by Edition Russe de Musique. Renewed 1958. Copyright and Renewal assigned to Boosey & Hawkes, Inc. Revised Edition Copyright 1948 by Boosey & Hawkes, Inc. Reprinted by permission.

Vn. 1 quoted here.
Same rhythm in
Timp., B. Dr.,
and all strings

CONDUCTING ACCENTS AND CROSS ACCENTS

In conducting accents, the conductor's gesture must show that the accent is to occur on the coming beat. The rebound of the preceding beat usually rises somewhat higher and sometimes the baton stops for an instant just before it swings into the accented beat. Stopping the motion momentarily after the ictus of the accent or suddenly retracting the hands helps to prevent a crescendo following the accent.

In nonprofessional ensembles there is always the tendency to make the accent loud and then to retain that dynamic. This is especially true in sforzatos on sustained tones. Such a rendition denies the accent completely. An accent is an accent only if the dynamic falls away instantly, following the accented sound. As to the amount of tone on the sforzato itself, the professional rule is "one degree louder than the passage in which it occurs." Lack of understanding of this dictum explains why so many amateur groups "crush" the sforzato in piano passages.

For accents occurring just *after* the beat, use the gesture of syncopation *on* the beat.

Cross accents are regularly recurring accents sounding in one meter but written in another. Example 60 is an excellent illustration. The clarinet is accenting in 5/4, the singer in 2/4 and the violas in 3/4, but all parts are notated in the 2/2 measure.

Example 60. Dallapiccola, *Divertimento* for Soprano voice, Flute (Piccolo), Oboe, Clarinet, Viola, and Cello. III: Bourée (measures 134–136). Reprinted with authorization of CARISCH S. p. A. Milan (Italy), owner of the author rights all over the world. © 1956 by Carisch S. p. A.

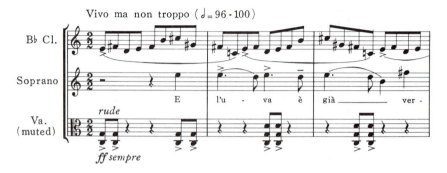

The most common form of cross accentuation is found in three-beat measures with the accent coming every two beats. Example 61 is a well-known case in point. To preserve the three-beat pattern and still show the accents, proceed as follows: Say to yourself One-Two, One-Two, One-Two, instead of One-Two-Three, One-Two-Three, while continuing the time-beating pattern in THREE. Then make a large, vigorous gesture each time you say One and a very small gesture when you say Two. The pattern that will emerge will look like Figure 46. The dangerous beats are the

Example 61. Schubert, *Symphony No. 8 (Unfinished) in B Minor, Op. Posthumus.* First movement (measures 134–142). Score condensed.

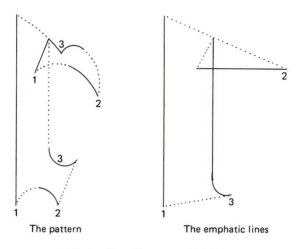

The pattern   The emphatic lines

Figure 46.   Cross accentuation.

small Two of the first measure and the small One of the second measure. Control will be needed to keep them small.

Note: The Aleatoric ("allowing for chance") score is discussed on p. 188.

ACCOMPANYING

Almost every instrumental organization will have to do a job of accompanying sometime in its career. It may be that a chorus has been added to the production, or a special soloist is to perform with the group. Or the accompanying activity may be just a simple background for a solo-melody-line within the composition itself. In any case, accompanying is an art in its own right and merits a few words here.

First and foremost: *the soloist must be heard.* This may mean cutting down on the size of the accompanying group, or just an underplaying of the marked dynamics. Second, the conductor, in general, follows the soloist and does his best to give the soloist confidence and a feeling of musical ease in the performance of the number. (After all, the success of his program at the moment depends upon that soloist.) The conductor should know the soloist's part about as well as the soloist himself knows it. He must also know how every note of the accompanying part fits against that solo line. He must be alert to quick adaptation to the soloist, and the musicians must watch with all attention to catch instantly any new subtlety which may be added to their previous rehearsing of the score. The timing of the conductor's preparatory gestures is of vital importance in order that the beat itself coincide with the soloist's rendition.

When the accompanying group has an interlude, this interlude should enhance the general character of the drama of the music itself. It should also act as a momentary release—a breath for the audience—from the concentrated intensity of the solo. The interlude should take over in its own right, furnishing the contrast of the full beauty of the instrumental ensemble to the continuing line of the music. In light opera, the orchestral interlude often heightens the characterization on the stage, sometimes humorously, as happens in many Gilbert and Sullivan operettas. A bit of overplaying, even in a single measure of interlude, can add a humorous touch to the comedy going on beyond the footlights. In all interludes, the accompanying instruments carry the burden of the performance. When accompanying the soloist, total control of the softer dynamics is imperative.

In instrumental works that have a lengthy passage, unaccompanied, for the soloist, the conductor can show the first beat of each measure by a dead gesture One, and nothing more. Go straight down and *immediately* up. Wait at the top of the beat for the next One. When the solo passage happens to be a long cadenza, the conductor does not beat time. He simply tells the musicians, "I shall begin to beat again____measures before our entrance."

Note: The accompanying of the Recitative is discussed on pp. 195-97.

THE METRONOME

This little beast must not be entirely ignored in a book on conducting. Many are the sins which may be laid at its feet, but it is nevertheless a good thing for the young conductor to test himself every so often against the metronome. When he does so, he subjects himself to a severe, but conscientious, taskmaster, and a little disciplining now and then is good for almost anybody.

The metronome came into existence during Beethoven's lifetime. He himself placed metronome markings in his scores, but because of his deafness, conductors do not always accept them as accurate. When the conductor sees metronome markings on scores predating Beethoven, he knows that they are suggestions of the editor of the music, not of the composer himself. When the metronome marking is authentic, it should be given intelligent attention.

A metronome marking at the beginning of the piece and at double bars with change of tempo signifies that the given note, or its equivalent, occurs the stated number of times per minute, for example, *metronome: quarter note at 126* means that the quarter note value comes 126 times per minute.

It is important to work out the mathematical relationships at double bars where tempo changes occur. **Problem:** Andante, 4/4, quarter note equals 80; followed by Allegro vivace, alla breve, half note at 120. (Tchaikowski, *Fifth Symphony*, Finale.) Dividing 80 and 120 by 4, we have 20 vs 30 or 2 vs 3. The lowest common denominator for 2 and 3 is 6. On the last beats of the Andante, think triplets:

Andante, 4/4 at 80:	Beat One			Beat Two			Beat Three			Beat Four			
Think:	1	2	3	4	5	6	1	2	3	4	5	6
Allegro vivace, in TWO:	1	2	1	2	1	2	1	2	1	2	1	2
half note at 120:	One		Two		One		Two		One		Two		

The speed of reiteration of the numerals is a constant *throughout*, unvaried. The Allegro will be one-third faster than the Andante in this case. **Problem:** Metronome is quarter note at 60. How to get five even quarter notes at 60? Thus: 60 divided by 4 equals 15; 60 divided by 5 equals 12. Dividing 15 and 12 by 3 (the lowest common denominator) we have a 5 to 4 relationship. For the four quarter notes, think: 1 2 3 4 5 on each quarter; for the five quarter notes, think 1 2 3 4 on each note. Again the speed of reiteration of the numerals is a constant.

```
X               X               X               X
1  2  3  4  5  1  2  3  4  5  1  2  3  4  5  1  2  3  4  5
1  2  3  4  1  2  3  4  1  2  3  4  1  2  3  4  1  2  3  4
X            X            X            X            X
```

To conquer this rhythm conclusively, try this: Draw a circle around the first vertical column, X 1 1 X. Do the same with the following upper X's, encircling, vertically, X 1 2; X 1 3; X 1 4. This will show visually where the multiple beats correlate. Now count aloud, 1 2 3 4, steadily and continuously. Tap the lower X's with the left hand and the upper X's with the right hand. Notice that the two second X's and the two last X's come a beat apart and that the third X of the upper line comes exactly halfway, rhythmically, between X3 and X4 of the lower line—a momentary One-and, One-and effect. When all of this is functioning satisfactorily, then replace the time-counting with a steady Ta, Ta, Ta . . . etc., throughout. Eventually the correlated rhythm materializes—ping, ping-ping, ping - ping - ping, ping-ping.

At the time the author was studying with Dr. Malko, the following advice was given:

"Sing a common tune—one that is so common it almost ceases to be music. Take the tempo which is your own most natural way of rendering it, and then find this tempo on the metronome. Remember that such-and-such a tune correlates with such-and-such a marking on the metronome. When you have built up a good collection of these tunes together with their metronome markings, you will be able to arrive quite accurately at the marking requested by the composer even when the metronome is not present."

It is, as all of his advice notably was, very good advice.

EXERCISES FOR PRACTICE: SKILL IN MODERNIZATIONS

1. Practice the exercises given in Exercise 13 (a) through (o), of Chapter 3, varying the pattern designs according to the diagrams given in this present chapter.

2. Practice Exercise 15 of Chapter 3, varying the shapes of all two-beat measures.

3. Try the upward ictus on time-beating in ONE.

4. Study the following and decide how you might vary the contours of TWO in this music:

5. Now try this: use the basic swing to the right throughout the exercise given in No. 4, above, changing to the clockwise loop in measures 2, 5, 6, 10, 12, and 15. Use the counterclockwise loop in measures 13, 14, and 16.

6. Choose the FIVE pattern you believe would be best for each of the following and give your reasons for your choice.

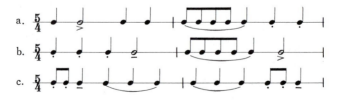

7. What would you do with the following?

8. Choose a SEVEN pattern for each of the following:

Irregular Time-Beating and Cross Accents

9. Practice Examples 48 through 58, using fast tempos throughout.

10. Practice the following irregular time-beating sequences as described under (a), (b), and (c). In (a): All beats as quarter notes, the FIVES being 3 + 2 beaten in TWO, the SIXES as 3 + 3 beaten in TWO. In (b): The same, with the

FIVES being 2 + 3. In (c): Time-beating in TWO for the FIVES and SIXES which are eighth notes. All other notes are quarter notes. Keep the eighths running through the mind throughout. Use both 3 + 2 and 2 + 3.

Sequence: 2 3 2 5 6 4 3 1 1 2 5 3 4 6 5 1 1 5 4 2 1.

11. Same as (a), (b), and (c) above: In the sevens, use 3 eighths plus 4 eighths beaten in TWO, for (c).

Sequence: 4 2 5 3 2 7 4 3 5 7 2 2 6 3 5 2 7 1 1.

12. Time-beating in THREE, accenting every second beat. Continue the THREE pattern but say One-Two to yourself throughout.

13. Time-beating in TWO, accenting every third beat. Beat in TWO but say to yourself, One-Two-Three throughout and give the large beat on One each time you speak it.

14. Time-beating in FOUR, accenting every third beat. Beat FOUR, say to yourself One-Two-Three and accent on the Ones.

15. Choose five common melodies and gear them to the metronome at your own tempo. Check several days in succession to see that your own tempo is consistent.

16. "Yankee Doodle" at a moderate tempo will give 60 (a quarter note each second), beaten in ONE. This can be tested against the speed when one speaks the following: One thousand one, One thousand two, One thousand three. Make a beat on the last word of each group. Check this with 60 on the metronome. If it does not work for you, then try to find your own recipe for 60. It is a valuable tempo to have instantly available.

17. Practice all of the musical exercises given above, melding the half notes or notes of longer duration.

RECOMMENDED REFERENCE READINGS
(SEE APPENDIX G)

BOULT, ADRIAN C. *A Handbook on the Technique of Conducting*. Section 10, p. 26, "Accompanying."

BRAITHWAITE, WARWICK. *The Conductor's Art*. Chapters II-III, pp. 13–21. Exercises in Fives and Sevens at the ends of these chapters. Chapter VI, pp. 40–45, "Indefinite Problems"; Chapter XII, pp. 80–82. "On the Conducting of Concertos."

CHRISTIANI, ADOLF F. *Principles of Expression in Pianoforte Playing*. Chapter XVII, pp. 296–303, "Sudden Changes of Tempo."

COOPER, G. W. and L. B. MEYER. *The Rhythmic Structure of Music*. Very erudite. Everything that deals with rhythm.

GROSBAYNE, BENJAMIN. *The Techniques of Modern Orchestral Conducting.* Chapters V-XI, pp. 20–74. Variety in gestures may be found here. Chapter XIX, pp. 166–179, "Orchestral Cadenzas and Accompaniment."

MALKO, NICOLAI. *The Conductor and His Baton.* Chapter III, pp. 63–108, "Time-beating." Certain phases of time-beating that are not in print elsewhere, such as how to perform transitions from one meter to another (pp. 95–103).

READ, GARDNER. *Modern Rhythmic Notation.* Fine discussions of modern metrical concepts. Also *Thesaurus of Orchestral Devices.*

8

Psychological Conducting and The Virtuoso Technique

As the student's baton technique clarifies, he will find it possible to produce from an ensemble, *on a static pitch, musical excerpts for which the performers have no music and which they have never seen nor heard before*. This is termed **Psychological Conducting.** The baton technique alone is sufficient if a *real technique has been built*. Examples follow.

Example 62. Robert Jager, Class example (seventeen measures). Used by permission.

Example 63.   David Bates, Class example (thirteen measures). Used by permission.

When true independence of the hands is gained, it is not impossible to perform a dual rhythm such as that given in Example 64. In this case, the ensemble is divided into two groups, one of which follows the directions given by the conductor's right hand while the other responds to the signals of the left hand.

Example 64.   Don Wilcox, Class example (nine measures). Used by permission.

(It might be a good idea to mention that the examples used here were taken from student-performances on final examinations. The examples were written by the students themselves and successfully performed as one phase of the final test. Only two copies existed—one for conductor, one for instructor. Singers had no music to read.)

In the quoted examples the staccato dot signified the use of the staccato gesture, the long line over a note showed the tenuto gesture in action, unmarked notes were simply performed legato, notes of more than one beat's duration were "melded" (see pp. 131–34), and notes coming after the beat were handled by use of the gesture of syncopation. Rests were indicated by dead gestures. Notes followed by rests were conducted as cut-off gestures *on the beat on which the note was written.* The cut-off replaced the time-beating gesture. This is necessary when the performers do not know that a rest is about to occur. It would be overconducting if the participants were reading from music or singing music already memorized. After a rest (dead gesture), a preparatory motion is made if the next note comes *on* the beat. If it is after the beat, the gesture of syncopation follows the rest. A gesture of syncopation followed immediately by a note on the next beat must show an instantaneous preparation for that note, precipitating the beat. We shall now deal in detail with psychological conducting.

PSYCHOLOGICAL CONDUCTING: TECHNICAL PROFICIENCY

"Psychological Conducting" is the technical phase of the virtuoso technique. It tests the readability of the conductor's gestures, his impulse of will, and his mental alertness.

Psychological conducting we now define as the process of getting a group of singers or players to respond, *on a single pitch throughout*, to the messages it receives from the conductor's hands and baton **alone.** The group has no music to read and the conductor announces nothing. The terminology implies *a transfer of ideas from the conductor's mind to the performer's mind through the medium of correct and precise conductorial technique without the use of verbal directions or written notation.*

All time-beating and expressive gestures must be perfected before such psychological conducting can be successfully performed. In addition, the conductor's impulse of will must be sturdy, and his mental control from mind to hands instantaneous. The melding of beats (pp. 131–34) has to be workable and fast "thinking-ahead" functionable.

The practical application of the diagram, on p. 46, now becomes of basic importance. We are entering that stage of "advanced conducting" where the declaration of intent is all-powerful. If the performers are to react successfully to the gestures of the conductor, they must be informed (during the time-space between beat-points) of what they are to do on the following beat. **Caution:** Psychological conducting cannot handle everything that can be written in music. For example, it cannot show more than one note per beat unless the time-beating is so very slow that a divided beat can be inserted here and there. The things that are possible are listed on page 118.

Let us now become specific. Figure 47 deals with the performance of the cut-off gesture, mentioned a moment ago, synchronized with the beat itself.

In the second measure of Figure 47, the second beat is a quarter note. This is followed by a rest on the third beat. The tempo is allegro moderato.

The second beat of this second measure will, therefore, be conducted with a *cut-off gesture instead of a time-beating gesture*. This cut-off occurs on the ictus of the time-beating gesture. If the regular time-beating gesture is made, followed by a cut-off, the latter comes too late and the group sings a note on the rest. This again emphasizes that every conductorial gesture has to be made in sufficient time for the group to respond properly to it. Continuing with the example, beat Three may be conducted either as a dead gesture or simply as a preparatory motion leading into the fourth beat. Beat Four must show good impulse of will.

Allegro moderato

Figure 47.

Beat One of the next measure will again have to be an active gesture of cutting-off. In all of this, the underlying rhythmic pulse should be steady and exact. **Note:** The cut-off, performed simultaneously with the beat, is *not* necessary when the group is reading music, but it becomes a valuable piece of technique, repertoirewise, in very fast tempos. In slower performance tempos it is perfectly safe to show the beat with the cut-off following on the rest—but not in psychological conducting.

For psychological control of all entrances *after* the beat (the eighth rest followed by the eighth note in all of the foregoing examples), the gesture of syncopation is used. Remember, the stick must stand perfectly still momentarily before this gesture, and the sudden, sharp motion of the gesture must coincide exactly with the moment of the takt of the beat after which the note is to be sounded. This gesture gives no warning that it is about to happen. It is seen too late for the group to respond ON the beat and they therefore respond *after* the beat.

WRITING EXAMPLES FOR PSYCHOLOGICAL CONDUCTING

In all musical examples used for psychological conducting, the notation must be limited to notes requiring *one or more* beats for their performance, or to *single-note entrances after the beat*. This is true throughout unless the beat is so slow that it can be adequately subdivided to show the "And" and, therefore, the presence of two eighths for that beat. (Example 62 shows this.)

The student should now write his own exercises for psychological conducting. Two copies should be made. One is used on the conductor's stand and the other is given to the instructor in order that the latter may see whether the young conductor is producing from the group what he intended. There is no better way to develop the "impulse of will" than practice in "psychological conducting."

The following list of possibilities will serve as a guide in the writing and conducting of the original examples.

1. Write one note per beat, or notes requiring more than one beat per note.
2. Notes requiring more than one beat per note may be performed by use of the melded gestures.
3. Any number of beats of rest may be written and conducted by use of the dead gestures. All tutti rests are to be so shown during these drill studies.
4. The last note before a rest must be beaten as a cut-off gesture in moderato and faster tempi. The cut-off replaces the time-beating ictus.
5. The eighth note followed by the eighth rest is usable if a *very short* staccato gesture is made to indicate it, or if each beat so written is performed as a very demanding and very short cut-off gesture.
6. The eighth rest followed by the eighth note is usable and may be produced by the gesture of syncopation on the rest.
7. The dotted quarter with eighth is usable since the conductor can control the eighth by making a gesture of syncopation on the second beat of the quarter note. When he does this, however, he will have to "drive" for the next beat following the eighth note. Unless this following beat has great impulse of will, and is made precipitously, the singers will not sing a new note on it.
8. Fermatas are always usable and good.
9. All dynamics may be used and should be carefully marked in the written example.
10. All of the expressive gestures may be used and should be indicated in the manuscript as follows: a dot over or under a note indicates the staccato gesture; a long line signifies tenuto; no marking for notes of the simple legato character.
11. Accelerandos and ritards are usable and good.
12. Crescendos and diminuendos are usable and good.
13. Changes of meter are excellent.
14. The left hand may bring in or cut out some of the singers independently of the right hand.
15. Accents of individual notes may be shown by enlarging the preparatory gesture leading into the accent.

The young conductor who can produce what he wants in the fore-going categories from the musicians, who have no music and to whom he gives no verbal instructions, need have no worries about his control of the situation when he is working with his future orchestra, band, or chorus. His technique is a true technique of the stick. He is no longer cheer-leading but he is turning into a Conductor.

Since this is the last chapter of a technical nature, the reader will now find added here a section requested by my fine student-critics who have read this manuscript in its pre-publication form. Their feeling that the following unit would be of value to them when they themselves were out in the field has persuaded the author to add it here. It amounts to a quick checklist to avoid backsliding.

First may we say, however, that it is the undying conviction of the writer that *positive* thinking is of far greater value than negative thinking. Correct results come when the mind concentrates on *what to do* rather than what *not* to do. The following list, then, may be of value in stating the problems, but the student is urged to think "Do this" and *not* "Don't do that."

COMMON TECHNICAL ERRORS AND THEIR
NEGATIVE EFFECT ON THE PERFORMING GROUP

1. The unrhythmic preparatory beat causing ragged performance of the first measure.

2. Letting the heel of the stick slide to a position under the little finger so that the tip points leftward and becomes invisible to the players on the right.

3. Indecision on the part of the conductor. This results in uncertain and timid response from the group.

4. Stiffness or undue tension in the shoulder (shrugging) or arm, resulting in unrhythmic time-beating and harshness of tone quality in the group.

5. A crookedly curved wrist, wrist toward the left and hand toward the right, in the effort to get the stick straight in front of the conductor. The line should be straight from elbow to knuckles of fingers. Adjustment for straightness in the baton can be made by sliding the point of contact of the heel of the stick more under the base of the thumb. When the right wrist (not hand) curves to the left, it interferes with good flexibility in the wrist and produces whole-arm conducting. This makes for a lack of def-initeness in the beat-points as shown by the tip of the stick.

6. Too much impulse of will in cut-off gestures. Results in an unpleasant accent at the end of the note.

7. Reaching toward the group with the baton in general or with the left hand in making cues. Tends to push the music away from the conductor and audience. The purpose of the performance is to get the music out into the auditorium. Pull it from the players. Do not cram it back into their throats. Also, reaching toward the musicians often brings with it a bending of the torso which is anything but graceful in the view presented to the audience. It is entirely unnecessary.

8. A general tendency to make soft (*p* and *pp*) gestures much too large. This results in a lack of dynamic control and dynamic variety in the performance and produces a monotonous rendition.

9. Too high a rebound (reflex) in the stick after the downbeat. This results in an unreadable time-beating. It springs, usually, from too much emphasis on the rhythmic pulse and not enough attention to the forward-flowing line of the music. There is too much vertical motion and not enough horizontal distance between the beat-points.

10. Carelessness in the straight-line motion of the stick, especially in the vertical plane. When too much of the curved motion is permitted, the ictus of the beat is often out of sight. The tip of the stick may even flick back over the conductor's right shoulder at the top of the rebound, or drop below the music stand. In the horizontal line the second beat in FOUR is dangerous, curving too far leftward and thereby becoming invisible for the players on the conductor's far right.

11. Too much accenting of the rhythmic pulse. This produces a strident tone from the group. It is cheerleading, not conducting.

12. Thinking ahead too late to show a good declaration of intent, thus handicapping the group's response.

13. Fear of subtle tempo changes and variations when the music itself is fairly crying for relief from monotony. This results in static performances and mechanistic renditions.

14. Poor indications of coming tempo changes in crossing double bars. This results in ragged setting of the new tempo and poor ensemble for a measure or two. (After the last beat in the old tempo, the baton must make its preparatory beat in the new tempo.)

15. A jitter in the stick (not nervousness, but lack of real control) when it should be standing still before the gesture of syncopation. Instead of a confident entrance after the beat, the group responds with indecision and raggedness.

16. Lack of a good preparatory gesture after rests or fermatas. This results in indecisive attack.

17. Too large time-beating gestures when the group is silent or static on a sustained tone. This is annoying to the audience.

18. Lastly and most important of all, lack of flexibility in the baton wrist (it should "give" on each ictus). This results in a lack of definition in the *tip* of the stick itself. The motion is poured over the whole stick instead of being centered neatly and clearly in the tip of the stick. It eliminates any chance for the tip to describe the music—which is its function. The horizontal line between ictus-points should be well arched. Rigidity in the arm tends to produce a strident tone.

A little psychological conducting in front of your band, orchestra, or chorus once a week or so will soon tell you whether you are slipping. It is a good drill for the players, too. They watch, understand, and become flexible when these drills are used often. Conductor and conducted benefit mutually. Don't be afraid to use them!

EXERCISES FOR PRACTICE: DEVELOPING
THE PSYCHOLOGICAL CONDUCTING

Produce the following studies by conducting someone who has no music to read from. (The conducted person can be a singing or playing musician, or a non-musician who hums a monotone in response to the gestures.)

Staccato = •
Tenuto = −
Legato, no marking

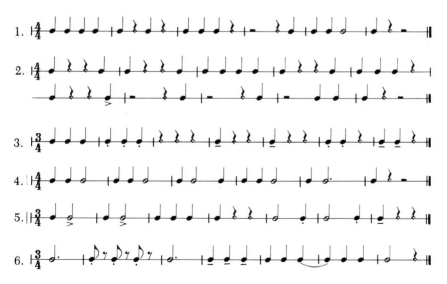

Used by permission

THE VIRTUOSO TECHNIQUE

Thus far the future conductor has been building his manual skills, setting up good, readable habits that will come into play automatically as the notation demands. The test of technical competency will be passed when the material of Psychological Conducting has been conquered.

When the gestures alone can produce musical effects from a group of players (singers) who have no music to read, then the conductor's command is adequate to control most situations that may arise in the rehearsal and performance.

The Shift from Technique to Music Making

Music is not a static art. It plows through time, measure by measure, in an ever-changing panorama. As the student's skills mature, he finds that his active concentration on technique is gradually being replaced by his personal emotional response to the music itself, influencing his gestures and lending an individual quality to his work, which quality differs from one conductor to another. No two mature conductors conduct exactly alike.

Musical consciousness eventually achieves supremacy, and with it comes the paramount need for flexibility and variety in the technique. Changeless repetitions in musical performance, as in other phases of our existence, are the soul of monotony. As we strive for interpretative variety in our gestures, we approach the virtuoso technique—the creative aspect of our work.

Creative Conducting

Freedom of expression is not a stereotyped thing. But it has, in conducting, one controlling factor; namely, that we do not become so "original" that our gestures are meaningless to the performers. It is not necessary to sacrifice clarity in order to be flexible.

Flexibility and the avoidance of monotony may be attained in several ways:

1. by variety in shape of beats.
2. by variety in size of gestures.
3. by variety in style of gestures (legato, staccato, etc.)
4. by variety in speed of gesture-motion.
5. by variety of position in space.
6. by variety of melding (combining time-beating gestures).
7. by variety in texture and emphasis.

All of these have their "imaginative" qualities, linked to the sound of music. When the ear takes over our existence, musically, for a space of

124   *Psychological Conducting and The Virtuoso Technique*

time, the imagination quickens and unpredictable things can happen. An unimaginative performance is a dead performance—a thing of skin, bones, cold notes, and ossified rhythms.

In the following exploration of possible variations from the norm, let us still retain, subconsciously, our commitment to clarity of communication with our players.

1a. *Variation in time-beating patterns: in* TWO. The greatest possible variety in adjusting the time-beating rests with the TWO patterns. Enumerating, we have (a) the straight down-up One-Two, termed the rigid takt, (b) the clockwise turn into Two, (c) the counterclockwise circle so helpful in phrase endings, and (d) the "common garden variety" which was introduced on pp. 21–23, shown here with its divided pattern(e). (Figure 48.)

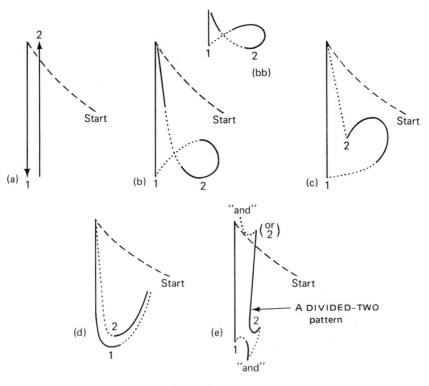

Figure 48. The modern TWO'S.

(a) *The rigid takt.* One is straight down, Two is straight up. Nothing more is shown. The ictus of One is at the bottom while that of Two is at the top. This type of time-beating is used when there are many rhythms going on simultaneously in the music, and all that the musicians desire from the conductor is to be shown the most exact definition possible of the takt—and then to be left alone. A passage such as that quoted in Example 65 might very well lend itself to this kind of treatment.

Example 65.   Barber: *Medea's Meditation and Dance of Vengeance*, Op. 21 A, measure 221, rhythm only, quoted. Copyright © 1956 by G. Schirmer, Inc. "Used by Permission."

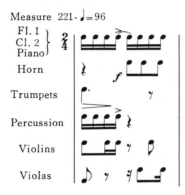

The rigid takt, in TWO, is also much used in the conducting of marches for the band where the musical content is somewhat subordinated to the rhythmic drive. In such cases it assumes a rather staccato character, changing to the traditional TWO for the more melodic trios of the march form.

(b) *The clockwise loop.* The baton rises sharply upward after One and makes a loop outward to the right, coming downward into the ictus of Two. Attention must be paid to the rebound after One so that it does not rise too high for good clarity.

This clockwise turn into Two is most valuable when the conductor wishes to carry a phrase into and through the second beat. It is endowed with tremendous sustaining power because of its possible extension of the horizontal line as shown in (bb) of Figure 48. Example 66 is a case in point.

(c) *The counterclockwise loop.* Here the baton spreads its rebound after One outward to the right rather than moving instantly upward. Contrast (c) with the much sharper reflex of (b) in Figure 48. After the outward swing to the right, the baton then curves back toward the downbeat line as it comes into the ictus of Two. When this counterclockwise gesture is used, the ictus for the second beat is somewhat higher up in space than was the ictus of One. This counterclockwise loop serves very well when the phrase ends on Two. To close off the phrase, the hand slows its speed

Example 66. Schoenberg, *Gurrelieder*. Part II (measure 420 of the Berg piano reduction, page 152 of the piano score). © 1912, renewed 1940 by Universal Edition A. G., Vienna. Used by permission of Belmont Music Publishers, Los Angeles, California, 90049.

of motion (not the speed of the rhythm) as it approaches Two, and stops still for an instant on Two.

The counterclockwise loop may also be adapted to the closing of a phrase on the last beat of any measure regardless of the meter. For a complete phrase ending, the beat is brought to a gentle stop on the ictus-point. Great delicacy and charm are possible.

Example 67 shows an excellent contrast of clockwise and counterclockwise loops. In the third and fourth measures quoted the clockwise loop is practical because the composer so obviously leads the phrase through One into Two. In the last two measures the counterclockwise gesture matches the reverse phrasing, the emphasis on One with the close on Two.

Example 67. Schubert, *Rosamunde*. Overture (measures 340–347).

(d) *The traditional* TWO. The traditional TWO depicts well a flowing motion, swinging along with great ease, showing two accents in each measure.

Erik Tuxen, before his death the conductor of the Copenhagen (Denmark) State Radio Orchestra, used all four of the TWO patterns very closely juxtaposed in the conducting of a certain Scherzo movement. The music was a 6/8 meter. A staccato section in the rigid takt was followed by the counterclockwise looping for several measures. This gave way to the clockwise gesture which, in turn, was followed by the traditional TWO. Then came a passage similar to that quoted in Figure 49, in which the conductor dealt most imaginatively with the rebound after One, gradually changing its height to match the contour of the melody.

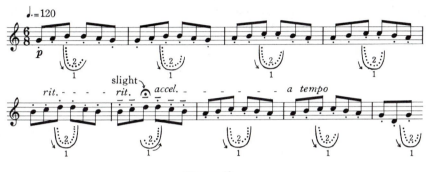

Figure 49.

(e) *The divided-*TWO *pattern.* This little-known pattern (down-down, up-up) is effective when, instead of resorting to a four-beat solution, it is preferred to retain the more visually obvious down-up of the principal TWO-beat design. An ideal excerpt for this type of divided-TWO is given in Example 68.

Example 68.　Rimsky-Korsakov, *The Great Russian Easter*, Op. 36 (measures 9–11 from the beginning).

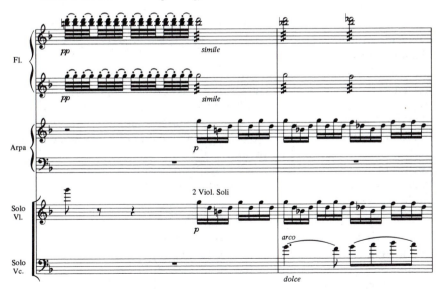

1b. Variation in Time-Beating Patterns: THREE and FOUR Varied. The patterns for THREE and FOUR are, in general, static. Their variations come largely under the heading of Melding, No. 6 below, pp. 131–34. One thing, however can be said here: The second beat of the THREE pattern is sometimes reversed in direction, moving left instead of right. Used upon occasion in the opera pit for ease of visibility by the stage performers, it can also show an antiphonal character between the violins (left on Two) and the cellos (right on Two). (Figure 50.)

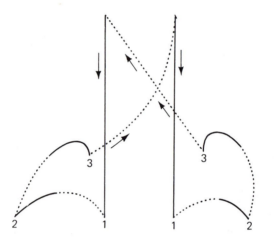

Figure 50.   Reversal of direction in time-beating in THREE.

In FOUR, the size of any single beat may be varied to show subtle changes in the phrasal dynamic within the measure. See Example 81 and details on pp. 48–49.

2. *Variation in Size of Gesture.* This has been previously mentioned, linked to the dynamic—large gestures for the fortes, small for the pianos. However, Nicolai Malko trained his students also to reverse the size of the dynamic gestures, showing a large, very gentle, floating motion that still reads piano; and, contrariwise, to be able to command a brilliant double-forte by a sudden, small preparatory beat of tremendous vigor with momentarily added muscular tension. This latter gesture was valuable when a large preparatory beat was undesirable, the intention being to take the audience by surprise.

3. *Variation in Style.* See all of Chapter 4.

4. *Variation in Speed of Gesture-Motion.* Here we have a facet of conducting technique too often ignored. While the rhythmic reiteration of the takt remains a constant, the speed of motion of the conductor's gestures will vary. This topic covers all of the unmarked subtleties: the illusion of stretching the beats, of dwelling momentarily on a particular note, of making barely noticeable accelerandos and ritards, and of closing off a phrase among other phrases. All of these musical attributes of the great performance rely upon skill in the variation of speed of motion, the takt remaining a constant.

The speed of the gesture is closely linked to the distance moved. Obviously, a slow gesture at a given tempo will not go as far, spatially, as a faster-moving gesture. (A foundation for this variation of the speed-distance factor has been laid in the divided-beat technique, the constancy of rhythm being preserved in the small pulses as well as in the longer lines leading to the principal beats.)

Expanding now upon this facet of the technique: Inserted among faster gestures, a suddenly slower motion gives the impression of dwelling upon a single note or of stretching the beat. The slower gesture conserves space and assumes a tenuto quality. In order to preserve the tempo itself, the slow gesture will give way to a speeded-up preparatory motion to bring the players, on time, to the next beat. Also, a faster gesture showing expended space among slower gestures will produce a dynamic swell.

The excellent drill-study (also a Malko technique) for acquiring flexibility and ease in gesture-speed variations is the following (a simple exercise but producing superb results in those already-established conductors who have taken it seriously):

Set the metronome at a chosen speed—92 is an effective tempo for the first attempts. Time-beating in FOUR using a well-balanced pattern. (Figure 21 (a), p. 26. Beware of an unbalanced design as in Figure 22.) Baton in hand, begin with a *quarter-inch square*. The four beats of the measure are confined within that square. Repeat several times. Then, without stopping, move to a half-inch square. Repeat. Go on to 1 inch, 2 inches, 3, 4, etc., up to 10 inches. Now 12 inches, 15, 18, 21, and 24. Gradually reverse the sequence, square by square, until you arrive again at the quarter-inch. Guard the balanced pattern throughout. Interpretatively, some measures will require several changes in speed of motion within the measure.

Note: The last rebound of the measure prepares for the next size when you are ready to move on. The smallest beats will require only finger control of the baton, or an infinitely small motion of the hand in the wrist-joint. Somewhere between 5 and 7 inches, the lower arm comes into play. When beats at 92 are easily functionable, change the metronome designation. Later, move from a small to a large beat in consecutive measures, and also try varying the size within one measure. Ten minutes a day is all it takes, practiced regularly until the technical freedom is acquired.

Timing: There is another facet of speed-change that should be mentioned here. *Not every gesture the conductor makes will be rhythmic!*

There are times when an unrhythmic gesture is necessary in order to produce an exact rhythmic response from the players. This now introduces the topic of "timing" the gestures—the most advanced skill of all and one that grows with experience in front of the ensemble.

We have what we call "precipitating the beat," usually addressed to players who are seated far from the conductor (particularly trombones, string basses, etc.), to ensure that their entrance is synchronized exactly with the players up front (violins, flutes, etc.). Very often such players cannot hear clearly these up-front instruments, or will hear the sound too late. To control the situation, the baton, raised above the line of vision of the front rows of players, will indicate the beat infinitesimally ahead of its rhythmic takt. **NOTE:** The sound waves of the lowest-pitched bass instruments are of such length that the pitches are not instantly heard.

Cautionary gestures, to prevent accidents, also require sudden, unexpected, and nonrhythmic motions.

5. *Variation of Position in Space.* One facet of this was mentioned in time-beating in ELEVEN, p. 105. A second aspect is found in time-beating in ONE at fast tempos, where a heavier stressed measure is followed by a second measure of lighter accentuation in a sequential series. Beating in ONE throughout, the ictus-point for the lighter measure is placed higher up in space and slightly to the right, thus accounting for the two-measure phrasal grouping. (Example 69 and Figure 51.)

Example 69.   Beethoven, *Symphony No. 6* ("*Pastorale*") *in F major,* Op. 68. Third movement (measures 1–2).

6. *Variation by Melding the Gestures.* The melding (combining) of gestures may be used whenever the length of a sound is stressed rather than its rhythmic content. To perform the meld, the ictus of the first of the combined beats is shown. This starts the sound. The baton then follows the general path that the melded gestures would normally have taken in the given time-beating pattern, but *no other ictus is shown during the meld.* The next ictus to appear is the one for the beat *following* the melded beats. The melding gesture is a sustained tenuto and takes up exactly the same amount of time the normal time-beating gestures would have taken.

Figures 52 through 55 show the melding of various beats in time-beating in FOUR. Starting with Figure 52: The time of beats One and Two is consumed while the baton moves from the ictus of One to the ictus of Three. Regular time-beating in FOUR resumes in the next measure.

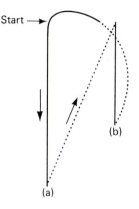

Figure 51. Change in the position of the ictus in time-beating in ONE. No preparatory beat shown here.

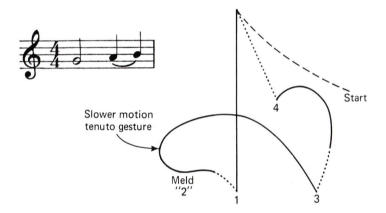

Figure 52. Melding the first two beats.

Melded gestures must not delete anything from the time values of the beats melded. Let us take another example. Suppose the class is told to sing "La" whenever the baton says to do so. The baton shows the ictus of One with a good strong impulse of will. The group sings La. The baton shows the ictus of Two. The group again responds with La. Now the baton moves through Three without showing any ictus, but showing only a tenuto, continuous sound. The group sustains its second-beat tone through Three. An ictus is now shown on Four. The group sings "La" again. Such a pattern would look like that shown in Figure 53.

Again let us emphasize that the melding must be very tenuous and very smooth in outline in order to leave no doubt in the minds of the

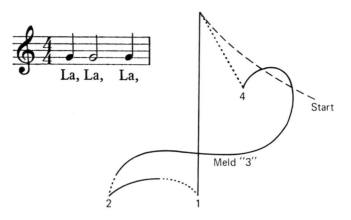

La, La,   La,

Figure 53.   Melding "Two-Three" in 4/4.

performers that they are to sustain the sound. The conductor must likewise have the feeling of continuous tone, not interrupting it with rhythmic pulsations in the baton. Figure 54 shows the melding of Three-Four.

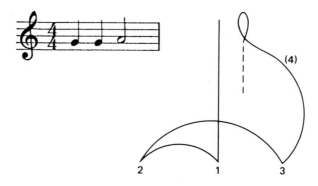

Figure 54.   Melding "Three-Four" in 4/4.

To show the presence of a tutti whole note, the ictus of One is shown and then all of the remaining beats of the measure are melded into one long gesture. The pattern might look like any of those given in Figure 55. Note the preparatory loop into the next measure, following Four.

As shown in (c) of Figure 55, the meld of the full measure is sometimes performed as a circular motion. The ictus of One is the lowest point of the circle. The second measure of Example 70 might be conducted as shown in Figure 55 (a).

The melded gesture is the very soul of **phrasal conducting.** Once the reader has become accustomed to recognizing it, he will begin to under-

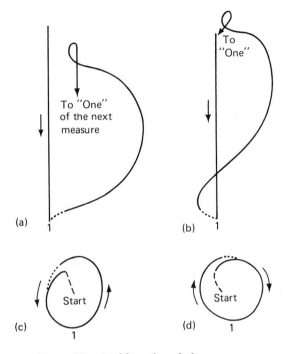

Figure 55.   Melding the whole measure.

Example 70.   Mozart, *Don Giovanni*. Overture (measures 17–19).

stand motions made in performance by many of the world's great conductors—motions which previously made but little sense to him. When
changing to phrasal conducting, the conductor must be sure that the
rhythmic drive of the music is such that the musicians can carry on perfectly without his time-beating gestures at that point. Melds are much used
in choral conducting.

Let us examine two more examples from the orchestral repertoire where phrasal or melded gestures may be successfully used.

In Example 71 the first two beats of measures 2 and 4 may be melded, the baton showing One, then moving toward the right where the third beat is performed as a cut-off gesture. The baton would stand still during this tutti fermata-rest. A sudden, sharp, upward gesture of syncopation would then state Four, precipitating the triplet entrance at the end of the measure.

Example 71.   Mozart, *La Clemenza di Tito*. Overture (measures 3–6).

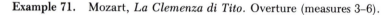

The familiar passage in Example 72 lends itself well to the use of phrasal conducting and the melded gestures. The first measure is beaten out fully, thus setting the tempo securely. Measure 2 melds the first and second beats, but shows the ictus for Three. Measure 3 shows One and then melds the remainder of the measure. The fourth measure is beaten out in full, indicating each of the quarter notes. Measure 5 is like measure 2. In measure 6 the first beat is shown. This is followed by a gesture of great sustaining power, double piano-tenuto. This last gesture sustains for three measures showing only the slightest dip for the first beat of measures 7 and 8. The entrance of the sixteenth notes in the ninth measure is prepared by a rhythmic, legato gesture on Three of the eighth measure. This gesture would be similar to the preparatory beat at the very beginning of a piece. Once the violins enter in measure 9, normal time-beating takes over.

Example 72.   Schubert, *Symphony No. 8* (*"Unfinished"*) *in B minor*, Op. posth. First movement (measures 1–8).

7. *Variation in Texture and Emphasis.* The quality of the line between beats bespeaks the texture of the sound. Gentle sound, gentle curves;

in fast tempo, vigorous beat-points with more angular connections for the big fortes, and so on. There is the Toscanini story where he tossed his open handkerchief into the air, letting it float down, to show the texture he was trying to produce in the sound.

In Conclusion: Summing up the virtuoso technique, let us refer to Beethoven's *Third Symphony* (the "Eroica"), first movement. This movement is a veritable symposium on time-beating in THREE. Much of the movement is done in ONE—the first two measures, for example. In THREE, measures 83–90. In THREE staccato: measures 65, 70, 186–193. Baton shows the slower-moving Two—the dwelling on Two starting in measure 44. One, Two-accented, with Three unbeaten, being used only to prepare the next One, starting in measure 236. Showing One, using Two, dead gesture, then preparing Three, measures 152–165 (second ending). Many passages show accents every two beats (cross accentuation): measures 25–26; 28–34; Figure 46, p. 107.

When the technique has become habitual, such interpretative conducting takes place without conscious effort, even in sightreading. Make a distinction in your mind between monotonous time-beating and interpretative conducting. Let your imagination take over. Coupled to intense listening, you have a source of infinite intelligent inspiration. The intelligent freedom you allow yourself becomes your individuality as a conductor.

RECOMMENDED REFERENCE READINGS
(SEE APPENDIX G)

BARRA, DONALD. *The Dynamic Performance*. Ideas on musical expression and interpretation. Worth reading.

BOWLES, MICHAEL. *The Art of Conducting*. Good chapters on interpretation.

FUCHS, PETER PAUL. *The Psychology of Conducting*. The title speaks for itself.

HANSEN, PETER. *An Introduction to Twentieth-Century Music.*

LEINSDORF, ERICH. *The Composer's Advocate*. Read this one by all means. A great conductor supports what the composer writes.

MARTIN, WILLIAM A. and JULIUS DROSSIN. *Music of the Twentieth Century.*

SALZMAN, ERIC. *Twentieth Century Music; an Introduction*. A well-written introduction to contemporary thought.

VAN ESS, DONALD H. *The Heritage of Musical Styles*. A great book, profusely illustrated with beautiful reproductions of art.

Introduction to Score Study

Score study deals with the mental approach to the music and with the musicianship of the conductor himself. The following step-by-step outline presents a logical approach to the score. Where markings are suggested, keep them neat. Do not blot out notes. Remember that *markings are for the purpose of learning the score,* not intended to be used as a crutch while you are conducting.

1. Check the instrumentation (or voices) needed for performance. Mark it in on pages where it is missing.
2. Check the tempo indications, signatures, and clefs used for the several parts.
3. Check on the transpositions (see page 146).
4. Glance through the entire work, page by page. Note form, solo passages, and thickly orchestrated climaxes.
5. Follow the melody line throughout, noting its progress from instrument to instrument.
6. Make a phrasal analysis—this is imperative. In choral works, the words can be helpful. In instrumental music, phrases are distinguished by melodic contour, changes in instrumentation, repetition of motif, dynamic groupings, harmonic sequences, and so on. The analysis should be marked in pencil below the bottom line of the score. To do this, the barline is extended downward to show the beginning of the *first full measure* of each phrase, disregarding an up-beat if it exists. The number of measures in the *coming* phrase are then indicated thus: 4 or 4–7–3–6–5 when a complicated series is about to follow. Upon occasion a new phrase will be found to start on the identical beat that closes off the

preceding phrase. This "interlocking" phrase may be marked $\frac{4}{4}$. The conductor's attention is given to the start of the new phrase, not to the closing off of the ending phrase. This type of analysis of the score reveals many things immediately that might be overlooked otherwise, and it is a tremendous time-saver in grasping the total picture.

7. Check the doublings and relate them to the strength of the melody line. Adjust dynamics so that the melody will be heard.

8. Read through each part separately, noting changes in clefs, transpositions, tunings (Timpani) where they occur *within the part.*

9. In pencil, mark necessary cues in the top margin where they can be instantly seen. Place abbreviation for instrument directly above cue-beat. For multiple soloists, place in score order. Circle in red the first cymbal crash of a series and isolated crashes where they exist.

10. Circle in red the forte mark under the top line of the score (applied to all winds) and under the first violin part (indicating all strings). Use blue for indicating pianos. If the dynamic is not uniform, mark the exceptions in the proper color. Important crescendos and diminuendos may be underlined in the corresponding color.

11. Half-circle each side of the sforzatos. Use the color for the surrounding passage (forte or piano). For a *fp* use a red half-circle on the forte side and a blue on the piano side.

12. Bracket thus [any place where a particular instrument should project.

13. To correlate the score, read it upwards, measure by measure, from lowest stave to highest.

RECOMMENDED REFERENCE READINGS
(SEE APPENDIX G)

For more detail on Score Study, you may wish to peruse Green and Malko, *The Conductor's Score,* Chapter 3 (Malko) "Studying the Score," pp. 12–27, and Chapter 4 (Malko) "Marking the Score," pp. 30–76. Also, Benjamin Grosbayne, *Techniques of Modern Orchestral Conducting,* Chapters 21–24, pp. 192–226. Fine material on Score Analysis, Editing the Score, and Preparing the Rehearsal. See Bibliography.

GAL, HANS. *Directions for Score Reading.*

GREEN, ELIZABETH A. H. and NICOLAI MALKO, *The Conductor and His Score.* Chapter 3 (Malko) "Studying the Score," pp. 12–27, and Chapter 4 (Malko) "Marking the Score," pp. 30–75.

GROSBAYNE, BENJAMIN, *Techniques of Modern Orchestral Conducting,* Chapters 21–26, pp. 192–236. Fine material on Score Analysis, Editing the Score, and Preparing the Rehearsal.

JACOB, GORDON. *How to Read a Score.*

ROOD, LOUISE. *How to Read a Score.*

9

Clefs and Transpositions

Before the student begins his perusal of the various types of conductor's scores, his attention should be called to two facts: (1) he will have to deal with the C clefs in addition to the G (treble) and F (bass) clefs, and (2), in the instrumental scores, he will come into vital contact with the problem of the *transposing instruments*. We shall take these up in order.

THE C CLEFS

The C clefs are not difficult to understand. The small pointer of the printed clef sign points to the line or space of the staff that is to be read as *middle C*, as shown in Figure 56.

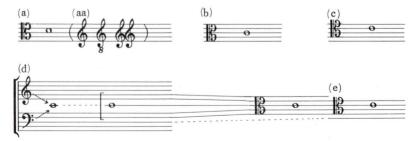

Figure 56.

There is a possible C clef for every line and every space of the staff. Those given in Figure 56 are the most used in present-day printing, although the reader will come across others as his experience with music scores enlarges. Figure 56 (a) is the C clef that is called the *vocal tenor clef*. It designates the third space of the staff as middle C. Since this third space, in treble clef, is also C, the lines and spaces of these two clefs have the same letter names. When this C clef is used for the tenor parts in choral music, it recognizes the fact that the male voice is *an octave below the corresponding female voice*. Nevertheless, it is not used consistently. The other designations for the tenor voice are given in parentheses in Figure 56 (aa).

Figure 56 (b) shows the pointer of the clef sign designating the middle line of the staff as middle C. This clef is called the *alto clef*. The viola parts in the orchestra are written in this clef, with occasional lapses into the treble clef to eliminate leger lines for the higher notes. For this reason the clef is sometimes referred to as the "viola" clef. But the violas do not exercise exclusive ownership since the first trombone parts, in the European editions of orchestral works, are often found in this clef. When it is used, the part is often called "Alto Trombone."

The third C clef, Figure 56 (c), is the fourth-line C clef called the instrumental tenor clef. This clef is used for the higher notes of the cello and bassoon parts and, in certain European editions, for the second trombone parts which are therefore designated "Tenor Trombone." Upon rare occasions the string basses may encounter this clef in their parts. Today the bass clef is customarily used for all trombone parts (especially in American publications), occasionally resorting to the use of the tenor clef for the higher notes of the first and second trombones. The third trombone part is invariably in the bass clef.

The instrumental C clefs are formed as shown in (d) and (e) of Figure 56. Starting with the grand staff, we know that between the treble and bass clefs there is one line missing, the middle C line. If this line is extended, it becomes the C line in the C clefs. Thus, for the alto clef, we borrow two lines from the treble clef above it and two from the bass clef below it and our new five-line clef is formed. When the lowest line of the treble clef is used above the C line and the three top lines of the bass clef are marked below it, we have the tenor C clef, instrumental. Bearing this in mind helps with the initial steps in reading these two clefs, but they should, certainly, be subsequently learned as individual clefs by practicing them at the piano.

An interesting use of the C clefs, vocally, is found in Schoenberg's *Drei Satiren*. The first song, entitled "Am Scheideweg" ("Concerning the Departure"), opens with the words, "Tonal or Atonal." (Example 73.) Such writing is seldom seen in our day, but, as the example shows, it does exist.

Example 73. Schoenberg, *Drei Satiren für Gemischten Chor*, Op. 28. No.
1: Am Scheidweg (Concerning the Departure) (measure 7). © 1926, renewed 1953 by Universal Edition A. G., Vienna. Used by permission of
Belmont Music Publishers, Los Angeles, California 90049.

THE TRANSPOSING INSTRUMENTS

The wind instruments are classified either as "transposing" instruments or as "nontransposing." Simply defined, the **transposing instruments**
are those that *sound pitches different from the notes actually written in
the score.*

The **nontransposing** instruments sound as notated. They match the
corresponding notes on the piano and are designated as C instruments. A
written C sounds C.

The transposing instruments are identified by title: clarinet in B-flat,
clarinet in A, French horn in F, and so on. What this means is that when
a transposing instrument plays a written C, it actually sounds the pitch
for which the instrument is named. A clarinet in B-flat playing C will
sound the B-flat.

The relationship between C and the name-pitch of the instrument is
called the **Interval of Transposition.** Each written note will sound below
(or, in a few cases, above) its printed pitch as determined by this Interval
of Transposition. **Caution:** A note that drops a whole tone in performance
must be written, by the composer, one whole tone higher than the desired
sounding pitch.

The resonanace of a wind instrument depends upon the length of its
air column. What this length is must be determined, for the particular

type of instrument, by three things: (1) the range of the notes it is to play, (2) the resulting efficiency and tone quality produced by the chosen length, and (3) its adaptability to the size of the human hand. The shape of the instrument, the manner in which the air is set into vibration and, according to some authorities, the material of which it is made, all add their bit to the resulting tone.

Through years of experimentation and improvement, certain standard instruments (as to length of air column) have emerged as functioning most efficiently for the player. This means that such instruments cover their entire usable range with good quality and fairly easy execution, and this accounts for the existence of the transposing instruments. See the Table of Transpositions on page 146.

The C instruments, sounding as notated are: flute, oboe, bassoon, trumpets in C, trombones, baritones and euphoniums in bass clef, and the Tubas. (For exceptions, see below.) The strings are all "C" instruments, matching the piano in pitch, with the exception of the string basses, which sound a octave lower than notated. Customarily, the string bass part duplicates, in the lower octave, that of the cellos.

Now a word about the brasses in particular. When Haydn, Mozart, Beethoven, and their contemporaries were writing, the horns and trumpets were not provided with valves as they are today. (By use of the valve mechanism, our present-day instruments have control over the complete chromatic range.) Instead, "crooks" were used. These were of varying lengths, and each crook placed the instrument in a certain key. The crooks were removable, and when the music modulated, the player had to have time to make the exchange. The use of the crook permitted the following notes to be played in the given key: root (not playable on some instruments), octave (not used on the trumpets and cornets), fifth above, double octave, third, fifth, out-of-tune seventh above the double octave, plus scale-wise progression thereafter, including the raised fourth; in other words, the succession of notes playable on the trumpet as open tones today. If the D crook was in the horn, the D major series would sound, and so on.

On the French horn, the player could also make other pitches by inserting his hand into the bell of the horn, but the tone quality changed on these notes and composers tended to avoid them.

Since these early horns and trumpets would necessarily play in the key of the crook, it is easy to see that accidentals had little or no place in the writing of such parts in those days. The composer stated the crook to be used and that took care of the situation. The accidentals of that key functioned automatically.

With our modern valve horns, any and all accidentals are playable.

The contemporary notation of the horn parts is generally without signature and with all accidentals marked in as they occur. In classifying a score as to the period in which it was composed, much can be inferred from the presence or absence of accidentals in the horn and trumpet parts.

The conductor will feel insecure with the early horn parts unless he is acquainted with the transpositions of various crooks in use during the eighteenth century. These will be explained under Rules for Transposition.

SOME ADDITIONS AND EXCEPTIONS

The following comments will give the reader some idea of the variations found in notational customs. This is not an exhaustive listing.

Certain C instruments sound at an interval of an octave above the notated pitches: piccolo in C, xylophone, chimes, and the celesta. The glockenspiel sounds two octaves higher than written. Richard Wagner preferred to write for it in its sounding octave!

When the bass clef is used for the bass clarinet, the written notes sound one whole tone lower. But this instrument may also find bass clef parts written in concert pitch and even designated "Clarinet in A." Notated in treble clef the sound drops a major ninth.

The contrabassoon sounds an octave below its notation. However, parts are to be found written at sounding pitch: Iberia by Debussy; Parsifal by Wagner.

The bass clef is used for the trombones and baritone (euphonium). They sound as written. When treble clef parts exist, they are B-flat transpositions. Customarily only one part is scored for these instruments; however, some English editions, as well as early American scores, include a specialized part for the baritone, written in treble clef.

The tubas sound as notated in the bass clef. A famous exception, however, is the sustained tone starting in measure 485 of Tchaikovsky's *Romeo and Juliet*. Traditionally it is played an octave lower than written. In certain French scores for band, tuba parts are found in BB-flat, E-flat, and C scorings. Professional orchestra players will change to the smaller E-flat and, F tubas for performing lengthy parts written in the upper registers. They sound as written.

In certain earlier English scores for military band, parts designated "E-flat piccolo and flute" are to be found. There does exist an E-flat soprano flute (in addition to the E-flat alto flute, rarely seen today), so that the conductor must, in such cases, determine whether piccolo or flute is intended. See the works by H. E. Adkins (military band) and Abe Tor-chinsky (tuba) in the Bibliography.

THE TWO BASIC RULES FOR TRANSPOSITION

There are two basic rules for transposition which can be mastered quickly by the young conductor. The first rule tells the conductor exactly what pitch should *sound* for each note written in the score—the *concert pitch*. The second rule tells the player what to do about it when the composer calls for an instrument other than the one the player has in his hands.

The First Rule for Transposition

Most prevalent are the transpositions that *sound* a pitch somewhat *lower* than the written note. To determine the downward interval of transposition, proceed as follows:

Write on the staff the note C. (In treble clef the third space is best: in bass clef use middle C.) *Below this note write the pitch of the instrument designated by the composer* (clarinet in Bb, trumpet in A, French horn in F or D or whatever is called for). The *drop* in pitch from the C to the name of the instrument will tell you the interval of transposition. Each written note will sound as much lower as the interval of transposition states. Refer now to Figure 57. This will state the most common of the transposition intervals.

With the exception of the four trumpets mentioned in Fig. 57 below, the early instruments with crooks all transposed downward. These were: trumpets in B (natural), Bb and A; French horns in Bb alto (one whole tone lower), A, Ab, G, F, E, Eb, D, C basso (an octave lower) and Bb basso (a major ninth lower). The designation "horn in C" generally refers to the "C basso." For further specific information, see the Table of Transposition Intervals at the end of the chapter, page 146.

When horn parts are notated in the bass clef, the transposition interval is the inversion of the interval in the treble clef. This is due to the fact that the direction of the notation is reversed in bass clef writing for the horns, each written note rising to the concert pitch *above* instead of dropping to the concert pitch below. This form of writing is not strictly adhered to in modern works. When the composer chooses to lay aside this custom he will call attention to the fact by a brief sentence in the score and parts.

A very few instruments transpose upward. These are: piccolo in Db

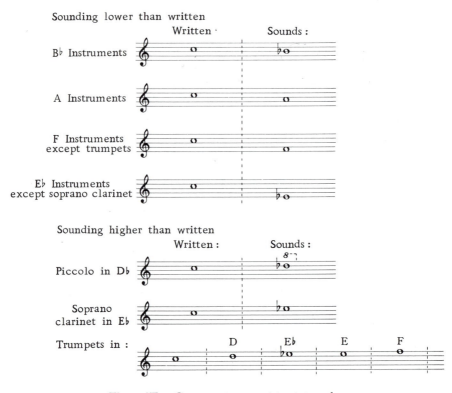

Figure 57.   Common transposition intervals.

(a minor ninth higher); soprano clarinet and trumpet in E♭ (a minor third higher); trumpet in D (a major second higher), in E natural (a major third higher), and in F (a perfect fourth higher). The student will have to memorize this short list of upward transpositions. Applying the first rule of transposition in these cases, the C will be written on the staff and the keynotes of these instruments will be written *above* the C. Each written note in the part will then sound at the resultant interval above. (The composer will have had to write it that much under pitch.)

The Second Rule for Transposition

This rule tells the player what to do when his instrument is not built in the key specified by the composer. Here again the rule is simple: the player writes on the staff *the key of the instrument he has in his hands* (as "horn in F," for example). The relationship between the instrument he has in his hands and the instrument called for will state his interval of transposition. He will have to read each note of the written part, transposed by that interval. In the case of a horn in F going to a written horn in D, each written note will be read downward a minor third. If horn in A were called for, the A would be written *above* the F since in the table of horn transpositions that is the A designated by "horn in A." Figure 58 will help to clarify this point.

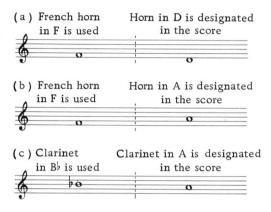

Figure 58.

Some students may need to think "the long way around." Write C for horn in F = [musical notation] . Write C for horn in D = [musical notation] . For horn in F to sound the required pitch of horn in D, the F-horn would have to transpose a minor third downward = [musical notation] . It is difficult to think in minor thirds downward. There is a short-cut. Notice that the horn in D part shows no written signature. The performer is therefore playing in *his* key of C (no sharps, no flats to read). Take *his* key and throw it through the interval of transposition (a minor third downward) and we arrive at the key of A which has a signature of three sharps. To play the D part on the F horn, the player proceeds as follows: Any note on a line is dropped to the next line below. Any note on a space is dropped to the next space below. And the player uses a three-sharp (key of A) signature. **Note:** The written part for horns with crooks will show a C signature. Throw the C signature through the interval of transposition to obtain the key for the transposed part. Again: *When going from instrument to instrument, start with the instrument in the players' hands and go from there to the instrument called for in the score.*

When the conductor names notes, he specifies "written pitch" or "concert pitch."

TABLE OF TRANSPOSITION INTERVALS

Timpani sound as written in all modern notations.

EXERCISES FOR PRACTICE: SKILL IN
CLEFS AND TRANSPOSITIONS

1. Play the following examples on the piano, or on your major instrument.

2. Refer to the orchestra scores given in Chapter 11 and play through all of the
C clef parts.

3. Refer now to the scores for both orchestra and band (the latter are in Chapter
12) and play through on the piano the correct *sounds* for clarinets, trumpets,
cornets, French horns, saxophones. (The piano is a "C" instrument.) Apply the
first rule for transpositions. Write the C, then the key of the instrument itself,
and proceed to play each note of the written part, sending it through the correct interval of transposition. Be alert in the reading of the trumpet parts. You
may find one or two which will transpose upward.

4. Reading from the bottom upwards, play each *sound* called for on the first beat
of each measure. Make the correct transposition for each instrument as you
come to its part. Remember, the string basses sound an octave lower than the
cellos when they are playing the identical written notes.

5. Sing Exercise 4 above, without help from the piano. Sing the *sound* for the
transposing instruments, not the written note. Place the pitches within your
own voice range.

6. Work the following problems:

    a. The composer writes for Horn in C and the instrument in hand is a horn
in F. What is the interval of transposition for the player?

    b. The composer specifies Trumpet in D with no Signature (the key of C for
that horn), and that instrument used is a trumpet in B♭. (The D trumpet
transposes up from B♭.) What will the interval of transposition be for the
player? What will be the key of the transposed part?

    c. Horn in E♭ is called for. Horn in F is being used. What is the interval of
transposition? What is the key for the new part if the original had a C
signature?

d. A band conductor has no bassoon in his organization. He hands the part to his Eb alto saxophone player and tells him to play the part as if the clef sign were printed treble instead of bass, the notes remaining just as printed. He also tells him to play in the key of three sharps, the original part being in the key of C. Marked accidentals are to be handled as follows: marked sharp, raise the corresponding note a half tone (written A sharp in bass clef, bottom space, would read F× in treble clef notation, the F being already sharped by the three-sharp signature): flatted notes lower the corresponding treble clef note by half a tone (Eb in bass clef would read C natural in treble clef, the C being sharped by the three-sharp signature and then lowered the half tone, since the E is flatted). Will the notes sounded on the saxophone be identical with those sounded in the original part, or will they be off by an octave?

7. Write out the first four bars of *America* in unison (or sounding in octaves) for the following instruments: violin, clarinet in Bb, French horn in F, trumpet in A, trombone in bass clef, viola in alto clef (C clef), bassoon in tenor C clef (instrumental), and alto saxophone in Eb. Remember that the written note must be *higher* then the sounding note for the transposing instruments. The tone drops as it goes through the instrument. Use the concert key of G-major.

RECOMMENDED REFERENCE READINGS (SEE APPENDIX G)

ADKINS, H. E. *Treatise on the Military Band.*

BOWLES, MICHAEL. *The Art of Conducting.* pp. 99–140. Specific information on each of the standard orchestral instruments, winds and strings.

FARKAS, PHILIP. *The Art of French Horn Playing.* Section 18, Transposition, pp. 70–75. It is all there, comprehensive and specific, for the French horn.

GOLDMAN, RICHARD FRANKO. *The Concert Band.* Chapters II-V, pp. 18–146. Very complete information on band instrumentation and the functions of the instruments.

KENNAN, KENT. *The Technique of Orchestration.* Complete information on the instruments of the symphony orchestra.

LANG, PHILIP. *Scoring for the Band.*

PIETZSCHE, HERMANN. *Die Trompete* (The Trumpet). The new American edition is filled with excellent information of a detailed nature on this instrument, its history, transpositions, and uses in the literature.

PISTON, WALTER. *Orchestration.* This is another fine book in this field.

RIMSKY-KORSAKOV, NICOLAI. *Principles of Orchestration.* Vol. I. Chapter I, pp. 6–35. The manner of presenting the instruments in this book is unique. It is highly recommended since certain information is available here which is not obtainable in other places. The resonance and power of the various instruments is compared on pp. 33–35.

WAGNER, JOSEPH. *Orchestration, A Practical Handbook.*

———. *Band Scoring.*

WEERTS, RICHARD K. *Developing Individual Skills for the High School Band.* Takes up each instrument individually.

10

Mechanics of the Choral Score

The first experiences with reading score present many new problems. These may be enumerated as follows: (1) the problem of the position of the several parts on the page; (2) the problem of spanning with the eyes a wide range of page *vertically;* (3) closely related to number two, the problem of reading the notation of the rhythm in a vertical direction so that cues may be properly made; (4) the problem of the instant recognition of the proper octave of the particular voice or instrument in the score; (5) the problem of the frequent encountering of the C clefs; (6) in vocal music, the parallel reading of words and music; and (7), in instrumental music, the problems presented by the transposing instruments and the shifting of the melodic line.

The present-day four-voice choral score, written on four staves, furnishes an excellent introduction to the problems of score reading. In the first place, all parts are singable. In the second place, the line-space letter names are those of the treble and bass clefs, even when the vocal-tenor C clef is used (The C clefs are explained in Chapter 9 on page 139).

It is suggested that the college student begin conducting with a choral score wherein the tenor part is written with the C clef sign. This will give him some experience in seeing the clef in its easiest form and in becoming cognizant of the octave in which this clef sounds.

CONSTRUCTION OF THE CHORAL SCORE

Choral scores range from two to a dozen or more parts for the singers. Example 74 presents a two-part work.

Example 74.   J. S. Bach, *Cantata No. 212 ("Peasant")*, for soprano and bass voices. First duet (measures 1–5).

In some scores, the piano merely doubles the voice parts, lending support thereby, but not adding to the musical thought. Example 75 shows such a use of the piano.

In other scores, the piano plays an entirely independent part and in many cases must be conducted as such. Example 76 presents an excerpt from a recent score where the accompaniment is given to two pianos requiring some definite attention from the conductor.

In still other scores the piano part is entirely lacking and these are called scores for *A Cappella* performance, that is, for unaccompanied voices. Example 77 shows an *A Cappella* work with a piano part marked "for rehearsal only."

The study of three-part scores (as for three women's voices), Example 78 makes an excellent background for the later study of the orchestral scores of Haydn, Mozart, and even Beethoven where three-part writing is often employed. The young conductor can gain valuable experience in working with the three-part voicing. The auditory recognition of such a structure, harmonically, will come in aptly in many places in scores of larger form. See Example 78.

It is interesting to compare this writing with the three-part structure shown in Example 83, pages 167–68.

Scores for large choral ensembles may divide one or another part, as first and second soprano, first and second tenor, and so on. Or a work may be written for a double choir comprised of two choral groups which are relatively independent of each other. Such writing is often encountered in opera scores, and a case in point is shown in Example 79, page 156.

In examining this excerpt the student will see that it is comprised of two solo voices; a five-part choir which, in the staging, is a group of towns-

Example 75.   Dvořák, *Stabat Mater*. Blessed Jesu, Fount of Mercy: anthem for mixed voices (words adapted by the Rev. Benjamin Webb) (measures 1–12). Taken from MASTER CHORUSES. Copyright © 1933 by G. Schirmer, Inc. "Used by Permission."

Example 76.   Copland, *The Tender Land*. Choral Square Dance: Stomp Your Foot, for male voices with piano duet accompaniment (words by Horace Everett) (measures 1–20). Copyright 1954 by Aaron Copland. Reprinted by permission of Aaron Copland, Copyright Owner and Boosey & Hawkes, Inc., Sole Publishers and Licencees.

Example 77.   Orlando Di Lasso, *Good-Day Sweetheart*. Chanson for mixed voices, a cappella, from the A Cappella Chorus Book, edited by Christiansen-Cain (words by Pierre Ronsard, trans. A. C. Curtis) (measures 1–11). 1933 by the Oliver Ditson Co. Reprinted by permission of Theodore Presser Company, Bryn Mawr, Pennsylvania.

Example 78.   Giovanni da Palestrina, *Tell Me, What Master Hand.* Canzonet for female voices (edited and trans. Henry Coates) (measures 1–7). Novello and Co., Ltd., used by permission.

people standing outside of the church; and a second choir which depicts the singing of the people inside the church. Attention should be paid to the brackets in the form of heavy vertical lines outlining these two choirs on the score. These heavy lines are placed at the beginning of the staff, before the clef signs. They will later on become a helpful part of the orchestral score-study.

Now let us look at the music itself. Notice that in the second measure, only five tones are actually being sung. The solo voices double the notes written on the two top lines of the "External Chorus" parts. (Santuzza is

Example 79.   Pietro Mascagni, *Cavalleria Rusticana*. Scene and Prayer (Schirmer's Standard Secular Choruses, No. 2415, page 30). Reprinted by permission of G. Schirmer, Inc.

* Piano reduction of the orchestral score.

the soprano and Lucia the contralto.) When the second choir enters in the second measure it, too, is singing the same pitches as the first choir. The independence of parts is established by the rhythm and the words. In the third measure, the four tones are expanded into seven tones through the splitting up of the soprano and bass parts in both choruses. The piano part as given here is a reduced orchestral part and shows a typical independence from the voices.

The study of these many types of choral scores carries over into instrumental score-study by laying the foundation for the quick recognition, in the instrumental score, of the number of parts actually occurring at any given moment. (A distinction should be made here in the reader's mind between the number of instruments playing and the number of rhythmically independent parts appearing on the page.)

Many times an instrumental score of from ten to twelve lines, fully orchestrated, will, upon analysis, boil down to a simple three-part structure such as a melody, a counter-melody and a chordal accompaniment. The detailed discussion of Example 83 (pp. 167–68) in the next chapter will bring further light to bear upon this point.

Finally, Example 80 shows eleven measures from Gian Carlo Menotti's *Help! Help! The Globolinks are Coming.* It is scored for eight soloists, twelve children (a few of them with minor solos), orchestra, and tapes. Here one can see how the tape cues are incorporated into the score and how the stage directions function. This section occurs before the first soloist begins to sing. A companion one-act opera by Menotti is *The Unicorn, The Gorgon, and The Manticore, or The Three Sundays of a Poet.* In this opus a new form emerges. The stage characters perform entirely in pantomime while a chorus replaces the orchestra in the pit, singing the story with charming tongue-in-cheek running comment.

When working with any fully orchestrated score, grouping the notes into units of the given beat, vertically, helps with the synchronization of the whole page. Reading upward from the bottom to the top highlights the string parts (at the bottom of the score) which carry much of the burden in choral music with orchestral accompaniment.

The foregoing discussions have served to introduce the reader to the mechanics of the score itself. The next two chapters will build upon the foundation laid here. For the handling of the chorus as such, we refer you to Chapter 13, *Interpreting the Vocal Score.*

Note: Opera scores will show the full instrumentation throughout. Scores for musical comedy are usually of the Piano-Conductor type—words, music, and piano—with the instruments indicated by abbreviations over their entrances.

Example 80.   Menotti, *Help! Help! The Globolinks are Coming.* Text and music by Gian Carlo Menotti. Piano Score, p. 5, from rehearsal numbers 6 to 7, eleven measures. Copyright © 1969 by G. Schirmer, Inc. "Used by Permission."

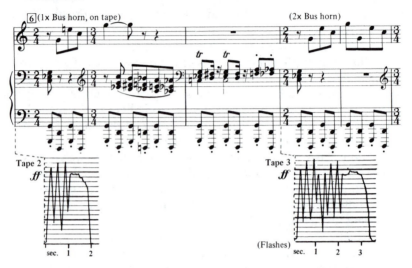

(The lights disappear where the almost invisible road curves behind a hill.)
(Die Lichter verschwinden, wo die fast unsichtbare Strasse um einen Hügel biegt.)

The hidden Globolinks signal to each other with strong phosphorescent rays.
Die verborgenen Globolinks geben einander Zeichen mit starhen, phosphoreszierenden Strahlen.

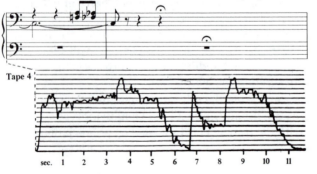

EXERCISES FOR PRACTICE: BEGINNING
THE SCORE READING

1. Take any easy four-part choral composition, preferably with the C clef tenor printing, and play the voice parts on the piano, reading from the bass note upward on each beat. As soon as one beat is played, sustain it with the pedal and immediately begin to prepare the hands on the notes of the next beat, again *starting with the bass and proceeding upward*. It will be slow work for those who are not expert pianists. If you yourself are one who belongs in this category, do not worry about the rhythm at first. Just get the mechanic established of the upward reading and the recognition of the notes in the various clefs. Place the fingers silently, one at a time, on the proper note as you look at each part and when all notes are correctly under the fingers, play the chord. Sustain it with the pedal while you place, silently, the next chord.

2. Sing each part throughout (same composition as in Exercise 1). Jump an octave in the part as necessary to make it fit your voice. Pay attention to the half-step and whole-step intervals as they occur. Concentrate on the pitches this time through, and let the words go. In singing long skips, the unskilled singer will do well to imagine mentally the sound of the missing scale-tones between the terminal notes of the skip. In this exercise, start with the soprano line.

3. Sing the notes on each beat vertically upward from the bass note. Place the pitches in your own voice range. Such an exercise is also fine if played on your major instrument, whatever it may be.

4. Conduct the number throughout, handling an imaginary chorus.

5. Now give the words a run-through, beating their articulations instead of the time, just as a practice routine. Sustain with the hand the syllables falling on the long notes of the music.

6. Practice conducting all of the longer examples given in this chapter. Imagine the sound of the voices and piano as you do so. Pay attention to the mood as set by the accompanying words of the poem. Try to depict it with your gestures.

RECOMMENDED REFERENCE READINGS
(SEE APPENDIX G)

CRIST, BAINBRIDGE. *The Art of Setting Words to Music.* This book contains analyses of the works of many composers. Many things of interest and help to the young conductor in the vocal field may be gleaned therefrom.

CROCKER, RICHARD L. *A History of Musical Style.* This book is filled with vocal examples. Traces the development of vocal music in all of its aspects.

DAVISON, ARCHIBALD T. *The Technique of Choral Composition.* The ranges of the various voices may be found on p. 17.

KJELSON, LEE and JAMES MCCRAY. *The Conductor's Manual of Choral Music Literature.* Music of various periods and styles.

ROOD, LOUISE. *How to Read a Score.*

11

Mechanics of
the Orchestral Score

The orchestral score is introduced immediately upon the heels of the vocal score for two reasons: first, because the orchestral score, during the two hundred years of its existence and development, has become quite standard as to form, and second, because it may be presented *in toto* in a somewhat simpler form than the score for full symphonic band.

In the following discussion, the subject matter will be interspersed with many references to the several illustrations of full-score pages. By studying these the reader will be able to achieve a modest understanding of the gradual development which has led up to our modern school of orchestral composition. In the process of doing so, he will also expand his ability to encompass more parts on the page and he will encounter the more difficult rhythmic problems in the conducting. This, in turn, lays a foundation for the study of the expanded score form necessary to the fully instrumented symphonic band, together with its problems of twentieth century repertoire.

FIRST ACQUAINTANCE WITH THE INSTRUMENTAL SCORE

Let us now examine the first page of Symphony No. 104 in D major ("London") by Haydn, often called the Second Symphony. (Example 81 next page).

The following items should be noticed:

Example 81.   Haydn, *Symphony No. 104 ("London") in D major.* First movement (measures 1–5).

1. The woodwind family occupies the top lines of the score, the brass family comes next, then the percussion, and last, the strings.

2. At the beginning of the staves, to the left of the clef signs, appears a heavy black line which groups the instruments of each family by bracketing them together. The reader will recall the similar bracket-lines for the choruses in Example 79.

3. Within each family, the instruments are placed on the page from highest to lowest, the highest occupying the top line for that family. The one exception to this is the position of the French horn parts. The horns occupy the top line of the brass family because they so often correlate with the woodwinds when the rest of the brasses are not playing. They are

therefore placed in the most favorable position for the conductor to see them easily in this relationship.

4. The bar-lines between measures break at the end of each family of instruments in a great many editions, thus giving the conductor further help in seeing the instruments in their proper relationship.

5. There is also an added bracket in the left margin joining the first and second violins. This extra bracket is used in the majority of editions whenever *identical* instruments occupy more than one line of the staff. For example, if there were four French horns instead of two, they would, of necessity, be written on two staves and those two staves would be bracketed. (On occasion the conductor will find curved lines for the bracket rather than the straight-line printing.)

6. The student will notice next that in orchestral scores the names of the instruments are often printed in foreign languages: Italian, German, French. Italy was the cradle of the stringed instruments, and the symphony orchestra as such began its development with the compositions of Haydn who was Austrian. The English-speaking countries did not produce their greatest orchestral writers until long after the "professional" vocabulary had been established. The few terms the musician has to learn should not bother him greatly; and being annoyed by them is rather childish when one compares our musical vocabulary with that needed by the medical student for his work.

Most troublesome will be the following terms:

		SINGULAR	PLURAL
French horn:	(Italian)	corno	corni
Trumpet:	"	tromba	trombe
Bassoon:	"	fagotto	fagotti
Cymbals:	"	piatto	piatti
Trombone:	(German)	Posaune	Posaunen
Viola:	"	Bratsche	Bratschen

With this introduction to the obvious difficulties, the reader is referred, for further information, to Appendix B, p. 238.

7. Next we see that certain instruments are marked "in A" or "in D," and so on. These are the transposing instruments, discussed in Chapter 9. The young conductor must continue to advance himself in the handling of the transpositions.

8. If there is a solo instrument (as in a concerto for solo violin and orchestra), the solo line usually appears in the score just above the string parts. Chorus parts, when they exist, are given a similar place on the page.

9. When the harp is used, it, too, may be placed after the percussion and before the strings.

10. In music written for younger orchestras, a condensation of the score often appears as a piano part, printed on the two lowest lines of the page.

11. The very first page of the score lists all of the instruments needed for the performance of the work, together with their transposition. In symphonies of several movements, the instrumentation for the single movement only is listed on the first page. Therefore, to know what instruments are needed for the performance of the entire work, the conductor must look at the first page of each movement.

12. After the first page, many scores list only the instruments playing during the measures occurring on each particular page. If, at a certain place in the music, only cellos and two woodwinds are playing, the score will be narrowed down to just three lines, omitting the staves on which the other instruments would be written. With a three-stave score, there is room on the page for several lines of the music instead of just the one line possible when the scoring for full orchestra is needed. The printer calls attention to this fact by placing a pair of heavy lines in the margin, signifying the break in the score and telling the conductor that the page has not been completed when one line of music has been played. See the left margin of Example 85.

13. If the reader will now look at Example 82, he will see that the instrumentation calls for "Timpani in H—E." In foreign language printings the H is used to designate B natural, as distinct from B♭ which is normally printed as B. The composer here is calling for the timpani to be tuned to B natural and E.

14. Occasionally, in early scores, the notes for the tuning of the timpani were stated by letters and then only C and G were written in the score. The drum which was tuned to the tonic of the key would play all notes written as C, and the other drum, tuned to the dominant of the key, would play the notated G's.

15. By observing carefully the variety in clefs and key-signatures at the beginning of each page of score, the student can soon learn to recognize the part written for each instrument. (Not all scores designate the instrumentation after the first page of the score.)

16. In general, the transpositions are given only on the first page. If the transpositions change within the movement, the composer writes the words, "Muta in——." This means "Change to——" (whatever the new transposition is). Such marking occurs most often in the French horn, trumpet, and timpani parts. Occasionally one sees it in the clarinet score.

In actual rehearsal, remember to specify "written" or "concert" pitch

Example 82. Rossini, *The Barber of Seville*. Overture (measures 1–9).

Example 82.   *(cont.)*

when discussing notes with a player of a transposing instrument. (See p. 145).

THE SCORE IN C

Some scores are written entirely in C scoring, that is, as if none of the instruments were transposing instruments. The exact pitches are notated throughout, just as they will sound. This makes it somewhat easier for the conductor. Prokofiev is the great modern exponent of this form of writing. The story goes that Prokofiev, in his student days, asked his teacher, Glazounov, "Why not write the score always in C and transpose only the parts for the players?" Glazounov is said to have looked the young man up and down rather coldly and then to have replied, "Young man, if it was good enough for Beethoven, it is good enough for you."

Nevertheless, today we find a fair number of Prokofiev's scores in C with the parts transposed for the players only. Recommended for perusal might be the *Lieutenant Kijé* Suite and the Fifth Symphony by this composer.

When the C scoring is used, the composer either specifies French horn in C, trumpet in C, and so on; or he writes, "Score in C, parts transposed." When the players read from C parts today, they must transpose to fit the instrument played upon. Either the player writes out his part in full in the transposition, or, if he is professionally efficient, he will read it correctly at sight.

A score in C is to be found in Example 83.

Example 83. Beethoven, *Leonore Overture No. 3*, Op. 72a (measures 378–389). Score in C.

Example 83.   *(cont.)*

Beethoven used the C scoring here for a reason different from Pro-kofiev's. In this case, the piece was in the key of C. Beethoven therefore specified that all instruments be in C and expected that C instruments would be used in the performance of the number. If the modern clarinetist is reading from the original C part, he will have to play each note *one whole tone higher* than written in order for it to sound correctly on his B♭ clarinet. (In studying this excerpt, remember that the French horns in C sound an octave lower than notated and that the trumpets sound as writ-ten.)

While we have this example in front of us, let us look at another phase of score-reading from the conducting standpoint. The page appears to be heavily scored. But look more carefully. Notice that in the first six measures there are actually only three rhythms going on: (1) the quarter-half-quarter-note rhythm of the first measure, prevalent at the top of the page, (2) the reiterated notes in the strings which correlate in pitch with the woodwinds, and (3) the rhythm of the trombones and timpani. Or, reducing still further the scoring, one might say that it is even simpler: only two parts, the melody in the woodwinds and strings doubling each other, and the distribution of the harmonizing notes among the brasses and second violins. Many of the greatest pages of orchestral music are as simple in construction as this when analyzed, so do not be afraid of many lines on a page. Take courage from this example and stop and see just what is going on.

THE SCORE NOT IN C

The more-often-encountered score is that in which all notes are written as fingered on the various transposing instruments. In such scores, the interpretation of just how these notes will sound is left to the conductor and his knowledge of the transpositions. The reader will quickly see that most of the scores quoted herein belong to this category. We are speaking at this time of the orchestra, but this manner of score-notation is well-nigh invariable in the full scores for band. Since these facts obtain, the future conductor will do well to acquire fluency in reading transpositions.

DEVELOPMENT OF THE ORCHESTRAL SCORE

The very early scores for orchestra are confined to the strings with or without the addition of a wind instrument or two. Among these early scores we find the *Brandenburg Concertos* by Bach. (See Example 84.)

The full wind-string orchestra as we know it today began to develop with the work of Haydn. Quite common in his day were the scores for oboes, bassoons, French horns, trumpets, timpani, and strings, with sometimes the addition of the flute. (See Example 85.)

The clarinet entered the orchestra symphonically about the middle of the eighteenth century. Examples of its use may be found in the works of some of the Mannheim composers and in Mozart's Opera, *Idomeneo* (1780), and his symphonies K. 297 in D major (Paris, 1778) and K. 543 in E flat major (Vienna, 1788). The composer himself added clarinets to his symphonies K. 385 ("Haffner") and K. 551 ("Jupiter"). His last concerto was written for clarinet and orchestra in 1791. The trombone was introduced for the first time symphonically by Beethoven in the Finale of

Example 84. J. S. Bach, *Brandenburg Concerto No. 2 in F.* First movement (measures 1–2).

* Cembalo and Violoncello are on a separate line from the Violone di ripieno in the original score. *Ripieno* is the tutti instruments as distinguished from the solo instruments (*concertino*), which appear on the four staves at the top of the score.

his Fifth Symphony, but the instrument had already established its place in church music performances and as a functional part of the opera orchestra. The timpani entered between 1670 and 1700 in the works of Locke, Lully, and Purcell. Under Berlioz, Wagner, and Tchaikovsky, the orchestra was still further enlarged in instrumentation, and in our day such novel effects as the recorded song of the nightingale,* the use of cow bells, and even the typewriter are accepted to add a bit of color to the performance.** Other "sound effects" have been also tried, but one hesitates to accept them as "music."

Some of today's rhythms are very complicated, and our harmonic structure encompasses the free use of all twelve tones of the chromatic scale, uninhibited by tonality. Instrumentation is whatever is needed to make the sound-effect desired.

The next excerpt, Example 86, is interesting from the standpoint of the syncopated accents and the articulation of the chords at odd moments.

**The Pines of Rome* by Ottorino Respighi.

**The Typewriter by Leroy Anderson.

Example 85. Mozart, *Symphony in D major ("Prague")*. First movement, beginning.

Example 86.   Rimsky-Korsakov, *Russian Easter Overture*, Op. 36. Allegro agitato (measures 58–65).

Obviously, the problems here are the chord articulations together with the accents in the oboes and clarinets. The conductor can momentarily disregard the violins and give his attention to the proper use of the gesture of syncopation for the after-beat chords.

As the instrumentation has expanded and the rhythms and harmonies have become more intricate, so has the job of the conductor grown in size. (See Example 87). (In the original of Example 87, cello II and bass each occupy a single line of the staff.)

Example 87 (a) shows a solo cadenza within the orchestra.

Example 87. Milhaud, *Concertino d'été* for Viola and nine instruments (measures 111–112.) © 1952 by Heugel & Cie. Editeurs, Paris. Reprinted by permission.

* The solo instrument in most orchestral scores is placed just above the strings and below the percussion.

Finally, let us quote a page from Stravinsky's *Rite of Spring*. "The Sacrificial Dance: The Chosen One." Here we see the very essence of modern orchestral problems. (See Example 88.)

For other types of twentieth-century scores see pp. 158, 189, and 213.

Example 87(a).   Rimsky-Korsakov, *Russian Easter Overture*, Op. 36. Lento mistico, (measures 6–8). The Solo Cadenza.

EXERCISES FOR PRACTICE: ACQUAINTANCE
WITH THE ORCHESTRAL SCORE

1. Memorize the order of instruments in a standard score such as the *Leonore No. 3 Overture*, Example 81.

2. Familiarize yourself with the order of instruments in the larger form of the score. See Appendix B, Part 1.

3. Study all of the full-page excerpts in this chapter, comparing format, transpositions, and so on.

4. Analyze each excerpt for the number of parts actually sounding. Notice where the scoring condenses to three or four parts.

5. Go through the score sheets and name each instrument when it enters after a few beats of rest.

6. Take the viola part (middle line is middle C) and play it through on the piano or on your own major instrument.

7. Practice the time-beating gestures for all of the excerpts given while either singing or thinking-in-pitches the melody line. Pay attention to the switching of the melodic outline from one instrument to another. If necessary, mark these changes lightly in colored pencil.

8. Refer to Appendix A. Study the seating charts for the standard grouping of instruments in the several types of orchestras given. Then practice the excerpts in this chapter, directing your attention to the place where this or that instrument is situated in the orchestral setup. The orchestral seating is more standardized than is the band.

RECOMMENDED REFERENCE READINGS
(SEE APPENDIX G)

BAMBERGER, CARL. *The Conductor's Art.* The section on "Conducting Revisited" by Gunther Schuller. Interesting ideas on contemporary music.

GÁL, HANS. *Directions for Score Reading.*

GREEN, ELIZABETH A. H. and NICOLAI MALKO. *The Conductor's Score* (formerly *The Conductor and His Score*). Many hints on score study, including marking the score.

JACOB, GORDON. *How to Read a Score.* Chapter VI, pp. 39–46, "Aural Imagination." Very fine examples stressing solo passages for the various instruments of the orchestra are to be found herein, as an aid to recognizing these instruments by ear.

READ, GARDNER. *Thesaurus of Orchestral Devices.* A large book containing hundreds of musical examples showing the various uses of the instruments in their many aspects.

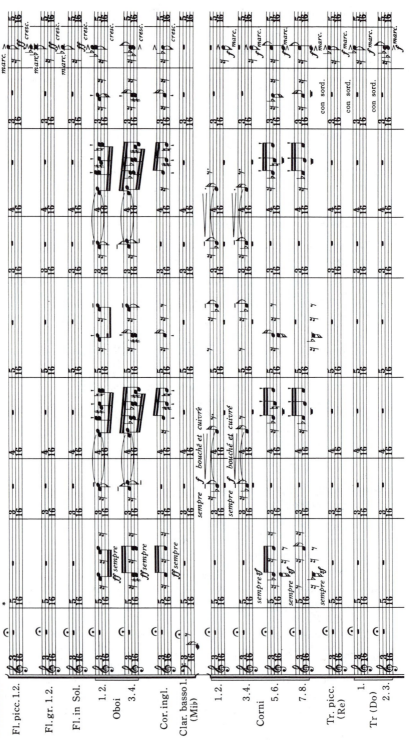

Example 88. Stravinsky, *The Rite of Spring.* Sacrificial Dance: The Chosen One (measures 1–10). Copyright 1921 by Edition Russe de Musique. Renewed 1958. Copyright and Renewal assigned to Boosey & Hawkes, Inc. Revised Edition Copyright 1948 by Boosey & Hawkes, Inc. Reprinted by Permission.

Example 88. *(cont.)*

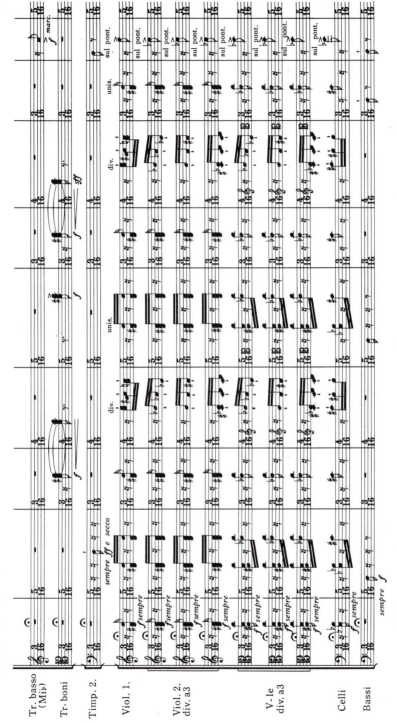

* The student will find editions in which the second and fifth measures of the passage quoted read 2/16, 3/16 instead of 5/16 shown here. NOTE: *Bouché et cuivré* in the French horn parts mean "muffled (stopped horn) and brassy."

177

12

Mechanics of the Band Score

The band score is largely a product of the twentieth century. During its emergence as such it has gone through many growing pains. An examination of the scores of the twenties and thirties will show great variation in the order of the instruments on the page. The size of the full score for band is necessarily larger than that for orchestra since the modern American symphonic band includes in its regular instrumentation many instruments which are used only upon occasion in the orchestra or are not used at all. These include the small E-flat clarinet, the saxophone, and the baritone horn (almost never seen in orchestral scores); the cornet, the English horn, and the alto and bass clarinets, used as desired by the orchestral composer but not constantly present. The sousaphones appear in the marching band and were used in the summer outdoor concerts under Glen Cliff Bainum of Northwestern University fame during the '30's.

Due to the pressure brought by the finest of the band conductors, full score for symphonic band has established itself with dignity, and has now settled down into a standard form with relatively little variation. There are also the many types of "condensed" scores. In general these latter are in C, giving an instant picture of the sound in concert pitch. They might be compared, in format, to the old theater-pianist scores (called the Piano-Conductor) rampant before the advent of the talking pictures.

THE PIANO-CONDUCTOR SCORE

The piano-conductor score is a C score of three lines. The top line carries the important melodies, annotated as to what instruments are playing the parts. Beneath appears a piano part that fills in the harmonies and strengthens the melody line wherever it may be thin. The two staves for the piano are bracketed as such. Many band scores of the present day use a comparable form.

The advantage that the piano-conductor score has is that it can be quickly and easily played on the piano, without transposition, and the conductor can thereby familiarize himself immediately with the sound of the music. Its great disadvantage is its lack of precise information as to which instrument is playing which note of the harmony. The conductor has only a general idea of what is transpiring when he uses this score.

In writing a condensed score, today's composer chooses the format (usually three to six lines) that best fits his material.

THE MODERN THREE-LINE BAND SCORE

The modern three-line band score is a derivation from this piano-conductor score-form. It may be played rather adequately on the piano since all parts are in C, but it is not written in a piano medium. The lowest line is devoted to the bass clef instruments and the upper lines are used as seems best for the other instruments of the ensemble.

Let us now examine the first page of a fine three-line condensed score for band. The Williams *Symphony in C minor* is a true band classic of the twentieth century. The full score is available, but for the purpose of presenting the various types of scoring, we have chosen this page in condensed form. (Example 89.)

We see here an excellent exemplification of what the condensed score deals with. Notice that when two lines will do instead of three (as shown on the bottom staves of the page) the composer has reduced the score accordingly and has clearly annotated the instrumentation.

The reader will further notice that at the beginning the *two* lowest lines of the three are used for the bass instruments, since the symphony opens with a heavier scoring in the low instruments. On the second set of staves this bass clef sign changes to treble clef for the horn entrance two measures before rehearsal number One. Such changes are typical of three-line scoring. Each line is used *as needed* with clef and instrumentation changing in the most functional way. The three-line score is used in edi-

Example 89. Ernest S. Williams, *Symphony in C minor* for band. First movement (measures 1–32). © 1938 by Ernest S. Williams. Copyright assigned by Edwin H. Morris Company to Charles Colin 1958. Reprinted by permission of Charles Colin, 315 West 53rd Street, New York, N.Y. 10019.

tions for school bands where much doubling of parts exists among the instruments of the several classifications.

In the fifth measure of the Williams work, notice the extra line for the percussion (Tam-tam). This writing of the percussion parts on a single added line is also typical of the condensed score. When the timpani part becomes prominent, it will usually be found on the bass clef scoreline with the other bass clef instruments. Observe its entrance on the third measure after number 1. The "plus" sign here means "add" the timpani to the instrumentation at this point.

Let us now refer to several measures of another work. Example 90 is taken from the *Bolero* of Moszkowski, arranged by Philip Lang. In this example, check the instrumentation as it skips from one scoreline to an-

Example 90. Moszkowski, *Bolero*, Op. 12, No. 5. Arranged for band by Philip J. Lang. (a) measure 1; (b) measure 5; (c) measure 37. © 1948 by Mills Music, Inc. Used by permission of Belwin-Mills Publishing Corporation.

other. Notice the abbreviation, *Cnts.*, designating the cornets, with *Hns.* for the French horns. In orchestral scores, *Cor.* invariably refers to the French horns when it is used. (Foreign terminology is given in Appendix B.)

A MODERN FOUR-LINE BAND SCORE

The four-line score is used when the disposition of the instrumentation and harmonic structure will not condense clearly into the three-line pattern. The four-line score can be a little more specific in the information it gives the conductor. Example 91 is taken from the transcription for band of the Coronation Scene from *Boris Godounov* by Moussorgsky, made by Erik Leidzén.*

Notice that Leidzén has devoted the second line of his score to the French horns, even though they are doubling the muted cornets in the first measure and the second and third clarinets and saxophones in the second measure of the example. Notice, too, the change in clef sign for the purpose of keeping the notes on the staff rather than on leger lines. This

Example 91. Moussorgsky, *Boris Godounov*. Coronation Scene, transcribed by Erik Leidzén (measures 3–4), condensed score. From *Boris Godounov* (Coronation Scene) by Moussorgsky/arr. Leidzén. Copyright © 1936 by Carl Fischer, Inc., New York. International Copyright Secured. All Rights Reserved. Reprinted by permission of the Publisher.

---

*Respectful tribute should be paid to two great arrangers for band, Leidzén and Lucien Cailliet. Their contribution to the recognition of the musical worth of the fine symphonic band has been of untold value, not only to the bandsmen themselves but also to the music profession as a whole.

fine notation makes for a clean-cut appearance on the page and an easy handling of the musical problems by the conductor.

THE SOLO INSTRUMENT IN THE SCORE

For the stand-up solo, many scores for band resort to the typical piano-conductor setup on the page. The solo instrument (or solo ensemble such as trumpet trio) is placed on the top line of the three-line score. The band accompaniment is written on the two lower lines, bracketed so that they look exactly like the former piano part, but marked "band" instead of "piano." Example 92 shows the first two measures of such an arrangement of scoring.

In the full score for band, the position of the solo line is still somewhat variable. Most commonly it appears between the woodwinds and the brasses, but sometimes it is found at the top of the score.

Example 92. Clifton Williams, *Dramatic Essay* for solo trumpet and band (measures 1–2). Copyright 1958, Summy-Birchard Music, Princeton, New Jersey. Used by permission. All rights reserved.

THE FULL SCORE FOR BAND

So now we turn to the full score for band. Example 93 gives an excerpt from the Fauchet *Symphony for Band*. This work is comprised of several movements and predates the Williams *Symphony* by a dozen years. The reader will notice the close resemblance to the orchestral score. The bar-lines break at the end of the small groups of instruments, just as they do for *families* of instruments in the orchestral score. Here Fauchet has grouped the clarinets together as a family. The bassoon appears as a maverick, at first glance, being placed with the flute and oboe. But this is not

Example 93. Fauchet, *Symphony in B-flat for Band*, arranged by Gillette. First movement (page 17 of the full score). © 1926 by Everett & Schaeffer. Copyright 1934 by WARNER BROTHERS INC. Copyright Renewed. All Rights Reserved. All rights for the United States and Canada controlled by WARNER BROS. Inc. Used by Permission.

184

Example 93. (cont.)

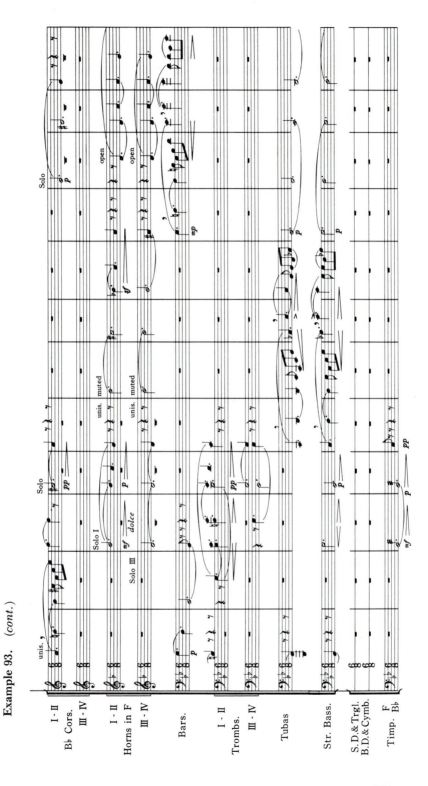

185

Example 94. Wagner: *Lohengrin*. Elsa's Procession to the Cathedral. Arranged for band by Lucien Cailliet, page 5 of the full score. © 1938 WARNER BROS. INC. Copyright Renewed. All Rights Reserved. Used by Permission.

186

Example 94. *(cont.)*

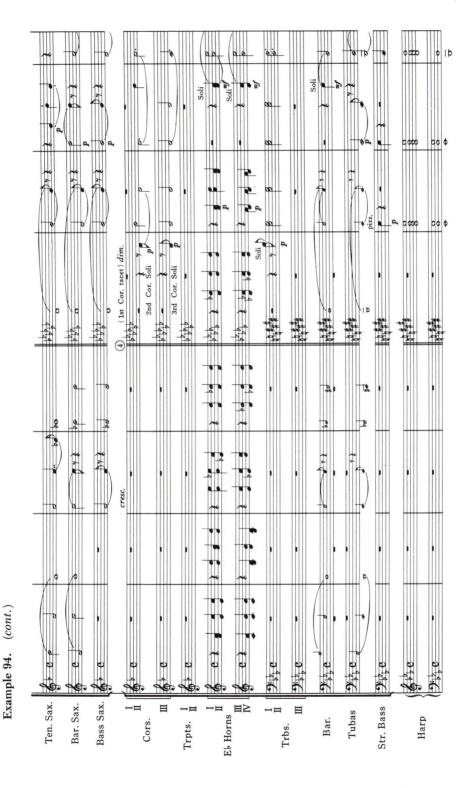

187

illogical, since oboe and bassoon together form the double-reed section of the band and the flute is often in octaves with the oboe. The upper middle section of the score is given over entirely to the single reeds, clarinets, and saxophones.

At the bottom of the score come the brasses. Notice the extra bracket grouping the staves occupied by instruments of identical name. The percussion is placed on the very lowest lines just as in many other types of scores for band.

A still larger score is presented in Example 94. We find that the number of lines has jumped from the 25 of the Fauchet score to a total of 31 in the Wagner-Cailliet work. (The timpani and percussion lines, tacet here, are omitted. They come just below the harp.) Notice that the positions of the baritones and trombones are reversed in the two scores. At the double-bar of the Wagner-Cailliet music, one sees the interesting enharmonic writing, sharps in the flutes, double reeds, and low brasses, but flats in the other instruments. A saxophone in E-flat, playing in a five-flat signature, *sounds* in the key of F-flat major, concert. This is, enharmonically, E major for the C instruments.

Note: The *full score in C* for symphonic band is now making its appearance, the parts only being transposed. Refer to p. 166, "Prokofiev."

INTRODUCTION TO THE ALEATORIC SCORE (BAND)

Finally, a sample of an aleatoric score is presented (Example 95). In this particular score, the standard instrumentation is called for. The figures above each measure signify "approximate seconds." Pitches are indicated in certain places, but left to the performer to choose his own in other places. The center line in each case represents the "approximate middle range for that instrument." Linear contour shows the direction in which the notes are to progress. Recurrent perpendicular lines state repetitions of the note or figure. Aleatoric scores explore the minds of the performers. Such scores are accompanied by a table of signs as the individual composer has used them. Here, crescendos and diminuendos are stated by words. In many scores, the broadening of a line or figure means crescendo; the diminution of size, diminuendo.

To conduct the aleatoric score, the technique of time-beating in ONE functions much of the time. Each written bar-line is clearly indicated by the baton. There is no metrical time-beating in many scores, but the conductor's hands show entrances, cut-offs, and dynamic changes. Players and conductor are "creating" in the process of realizing the score as written. See also pp. 213–14 and Example 104.

Example 95. Pennington, *Apollo*, Aleatoric Piece for Band. Page 2 of the full score. Copyright © 1971 by G. Schirmer, Inc. "Used by Permission."

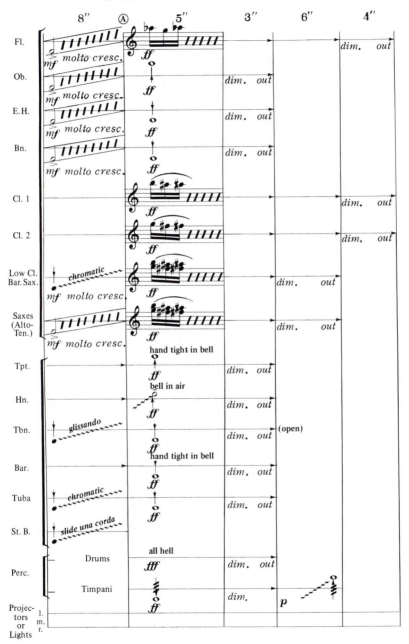

EXERCISES FOR PRACTICE: ACQUAINTANCE
WITH THE BAND SCORE

1. Study the band-score examples as given in this chapter. Acquaint yourself with the several types of scoring. Find other band scores in your music library or at a music store and compare their formats with those given here. Appendix B, Part 1.

2. Locate the melody line in the excerpts given here. Notice whether it is doubled and by what instruments. Imagine what tone color will come from such doubling. Study the accompanying rhythms. Look for the distribution of the chords among the accompanying instruments and notice how the individual notes are allotted within the particular group of instruments. Obviously, only a full score can tell you this.

3. Practice conducting the excerpts given.

4. Increase your ease with the transpositions by playing through the transposed parts on the piano.

RECOMMENDED REFERENCE READINGS
(SEE APPENDIX G)

Band

GALLO, STANISLAO. *The Modern Band.* This book introduces the reader to the European (Italian) approach to the band.

GOLDMAN, RICHARD FRANKO. *The Concert Band.* Chapters VI-VIII, pp. 147–211. Excellent material on band music, arrangements, and originals by the great composers.

GRIFFITHS, PAUL. *A Concise History of Avant-Garde Music.* Very readable; highly recommended.

LANG, PHILIP J. *Scoring for the Band.*

LEIDZÉN ERIK. *An Invitation to Band Arranging.*

SCHWARTZ, HARRY W. *Bands of America.* An excellent history of the band movement, exclusive of the public schools, 1853–1956.

WORRELL, J. W. "Music by the Masters," *The Instrumentalist*, XIV, 3 (1959), pp. 46–47, 92. A list of masterworks that have been arranged for the school band.

Orchestra

GREEN, ELIZABETH A. H. *The Dynamic Orchestra.* Information on the professional life and performance customs. Contemporary.

SCHERCHEN, HERMANN. *Handbook of Conducting.* Excellent information on handling the winds in the orchestra.

13

Interpreting the Vocal Score

Choral music has come through a number of stages in its historical development. Early music, largely church-oriented, was sung *a cappella*. There was no recurrent accentuation. The words themselves tied the music together and stress was laid on a level, continuous dynamic for all long tones. The conductor's hands, instead of time-beating, showed the entrances and exits of voices, the length of the sustained tones, the contours of the phrase, and the rise and fall of the several parts.

CHORAL STYLE

This style gradually succumbed to the idea that long notes should be made to "come alive." The *bel canto* school of singing took over. This was a style of great lyricism, stressing beauty of tone and the legato line. The sustained vowel sound, when interrupted by the articulation of a consonant, would be interrupted as little as possible. One should feel the legato line as continuous throughout, in spite of the consonant interruption. Instrumental accompaniment by stringed instruments became popular. Over the years the accompaniment emerged from its background position to become an active entity in its own right. Schubert's extraordinary talent for catching the spirit of the poem and transferring it to the music is given credit for this freeing of the accompaniment. Schumann continued this development and the *Lied* became a duet of sorts between the voice and the piano.

In choral music, the tangible emotion set by the words is heightened by the music. In instrumental music the emotional appeal relies upon the intangibility of the music itself. In both categories, however, the historical period in which the music was written shows its influence on our twentieth-century interpretations.

Let us examine for a moment the language aspect of style. A language such as Italian, which has many words ending in vowels, lends itself naturally to *bel canto*. In contrast, a language that bristles with consonants (as does German or Russian) will acquire a somewhat harsher type of articulation and therefore a different stylistic sound in making its musical contribution.

Dynamics in choral composition have an emotional basis. The emotion states the dynamic. (One does not sing a lullaby with either the same dynamic or the same emotional content one would use for an operatic cry of anguish.) In instrumental music the process is often reversed. The dynamic sounded induces the emotion in the listener. Emotions become tangible in choral music because the words demand it: they exist equally in instrumental music, but they are less tangible.

With this in mind, certain things of a practical nature may now be dealt with.

1. *Horizontal motion.* The horizontal or forward motion in each voice in a choral composition should have a certain inevitableness about it. Wide skips between notes in the horizontal line are always difficult and especially so in the inner voices. Notice these as they occur in the score and solve their problems before the rehearsal begins. Much valuable knowledge is gained through attention to the horizontal line of the choral score.

2. *Vertical relationship.* The vertical relationship of the parts is their harmonic relationship. Good ensemble is dependent upon the vertical synchronization of the parts. The best way to study this facet of the score is to sing each beat from the bottom upward, bass to soprano. This clarifies the harmonic outline in the conductor's mind.

3. *Difficult entrances.* There are times when the singers have difficulty in accurately locating their entry note following several beats of rest. Often the conductor can clarify such places by calling attention to the sounding of the same pitch a beat or two before by another voice. Example 96 is an excellent illustration of this. The entrance of the new part is made each time on the identical pitch as the *last sung note* in the preceding voice before the new voice enters. In the first measure of the example, the alto sings B on the eighth note just before the soprano enters on that same pitch. Each entrance is similar.

It is the conductor's job to clarify such difficulties for the singers. He

Example 96.   Galbraith, *Out of the Silence* (measures 12–15). 1919 by The Oliver Ditson Co. Reprinted by permission of Theodore Presser Company, Bryn Mawr, Pennsylvania.

will do well to search diligently during his score study for ways in which he can better these entrances after rests, should such help be needed in the rehearsal. Assurance on the part of the singers means confidence for the conductor. It works both ways!

4. *Breathing in long phrases.* When long phrases must be sustained, the conductor may suggest "staggered" breathing in which the singers do not breathe simultaneously, but each catches a quick breath as he needs it and then re-enters the music, thus preserving the sustained tone quality. A breath taken just after a strong beat is less noticeable than one taken before a strong beat. This principle may also be applied to slurred passages. When the breath is insufficent to carry through the slur, take a new breath *after* a note that falls *on* a beat and preferably on a strong beat of the measure.

5. *Tone quality.* The conductor of the vocal group is working with what might be termed the most *personal* type of music, namely, the instrument within man himself. In everyday life, subjective attitudes are usually apparent in the speaking voice. The choral conductor should face this fact and train his singers to set the mood of the song itself, regardless of their individual and personal feelings at the time.

Any spoken vowel, when sustained long enough, will take on the pitch of a musical sound. Beauty of vowel sound and clarity of consonant articulation are to be stressed. In score study, pay attention to the long vowels. When conducting, see that the singer's mouth is properly opened, without throat tension.

Many beautiful effects may be accomplished by giving the third of the chord special attention whenever the tone quality is weak or thin. Strengthening this note will add luster to the sound. The third of the chord

righe Vocal Score

is also one of the links in fine intonation. When a chorus begins to flat, it is frequently because the voices singing the third of the chord have been careless in perfecting the intonation. The seventh of the scale is also dangerous in this respect. Perfect intonation enhances tone quality.

6. Since the choral profession is apparently divided on the next point, we shall briefly state the two views without urging the acceptance of either. The problem concerns the vowel that is slurred over several notes. Example 97 is pertinent.

Example 97. Palestrina, *Tell Me, What Master Hand* (quoted in full in Example 78). By permission of Novello and Co., Ltd.

won - drous

One hears, at times, the articulation of a soft "h" attack in the slurred vowel as the pitch changes. Certain very fine teachers argue against the use of this device for two reasons: (1) It tends to interrupt the legato line which is the main reason for the writing of the slur; and (2) it tends to build breathiness into the tone. Other very fine teachers sanction its use to prevent the glissando which often mars slurred runs in vocal execution. Some opera singers use it, some do not. The young conductor of vocal groups is advised to talk with the finest vocal teachers he can contact on this point. Perhaps the use of this device may depend upon the size of the auditorium and the heft of the accompaniment.

7. *Final consonants.* The ending of most tones is given more special attention in choral music than in instrumental performance because of the fact that many English words end in a final consonant that must be articulated cleanly and together by the singers. This is especially true of *sustained* tones ending in a consonant. The cut-off should be shown in such cases, especially before rests.

Final S sounds cause much trouble. They should be spoken softly and placed late in the beat. Final D's and G's, when given clean-cut pronunciation, add immensely to the clarity of the words. There is a tendency for choruses to sustain final M's, N's and R's, instead of the vowel preceding them. These letters, too, should be delayed until the last possible moment.

The clean articulation of the consonant makes the speech understandable.* Since the words carry the story of the music, if they cannot

*There is the story of Chaliapin, the great Russian basso of the past, standing backstage in the opera house during rehearsal and singing over and over the Russian word for God (*Bog*), fighting out an articulation of both consonants that would freeze the blood of the audience when the dramatic moment should arrive.

be understood, there is no point to singing them. Their ultimate sense depends upon the distinctness of the consonant and the correctness of the vowels.*

The choral conductor should listen constantly and consciously to the words as his chorus sings them. Too often his own familiarity with the song gives him the illusion of good pronunciation on the part of his singers. Listen to *hear* what your chorus is saying.

A fine exercise for diction is that of having the whole chorus sing together one of the Gilbert and Sullivan "patter songs." It is great fun and an excellent exercise for the tongue.

CONDUCTING THE RECITATIVE

The recitative is, fundamentally, an insert, in a vocal composition, which is to be sung as if spoken. It is often relatively unrhythmic in structure, as speech is unrhythmic. Its purpose is to carry forward the story. It serves to brief the audience on what has transpired before the action continues.

Being of a spoken character, the recitative is usually not fully accompanied throughout. Either it is punctuated by single chords which state the harmonic structure or it is supported by sustained tones of a static character which change with the harmony as necessary. The conductor's biggest job in the recitative, therefore, is to see that these chords and changes in harmony occur at exactly the right instant, regardless of the unrhythmic character of the general takt. This requires finesse in the timing plus an understanding of the following points:

1. If a chord is to be articulated *on* a beat, it should be preceded by a secure and well-timed preparatory gesture which says clearly, "Here it comes."

2. If a chord is to be played *after* a beat, the gesture of syncopation will be used, preceded by a staccato preparatory beat.

The first two chords in Example 98 will be conducted as described in (1) above. The entrance at the end of the second measure will require the treatment given in (2), unless, perchance, the soloist keeps a steady takt throughout this measure, in which case simple time-beating may continue with the gesture of syncopation used on beat Three.

3. When the recitative is accompanied by sustained tones, the latter must be played softly and in good balance with each other. They must also be matched against the power of the singer's voice. Since the soloist

---

*The young choral conductor is urged to study diligently the Marshall book on English Diction. (See the Reference Readings at the end of this chapter.)

Example 98.   Handel, *Messiah*. No. 5: Recitative, Thus Saith the Lord (last five measures).

*Customarily, such closing chords are played *after* the singer finishes, starting on the last beat and ending on the first beat of an added measure.

will take whatever liberties are necessary with the rhythm, the conductor must often resort to a type of irregular time-beating.

Example 99 lends itself to a fairly regular time-beating, but sustained tones have a faculty for sounding a little late with the beat-point. Be doubly alert to anticipate the attacks.

4. The first beat of each measure must be clearly indicated by the baton as the measure passes. This is of utmost importance, since the takt within the measure may vary rhythmically. A simple dead gesture, from the wrist (down and immediately up) is all that is necessary. In the case of several measures of tutti rest, the conductor may make a series of several quick downbeats, each beat signifying one measure, and then just wait for the singer to finish those measures.

5. After the indication of the first beat of the measure, the baton may do one of several things in handling the rest of the measure. It may show nothing except this first beat, which is often done when the entire measure is a tutti rest for the accompanying instruments. Or it may design

orchestra each separately first; the chorus for words and action; the soloists, to know their parts thoroughly—the whole show depends on them when they are soloing; the orchestra to read through the music, to mark cuts, to check the parts for wrong notes, to indicate the number of verses, and sometimes "cue lines." Stage-exit repeats will have to wait for a stage rehearsal. Anything that can waste time in the full rehearsal should be taken care of beforehand. (2) Have the chorus and soloists on stage first without the orchestra. Get all stage-business working well before bringing in the orchestra. (3) At the first stage rehearsal (without orchestra) make sure that everyone on stage can see the conductor in the pit. Also assign certain leaders who must watch the conductor more intently (preferably strong singers). (4) After the speaking parts, it is better to "crash the last line" with the orchestra introduction than to have a wait. The wait kills the show. A good stage show must not be allowed to sag. Call the orchestra to attention before the last speech starts. Also, train it to *get the music ready for the next number as soon as the end of the previous number is played*. This saves fumbling when it is time to play. (5) Bring the orchestra "into the act." Their introductions and interludes (even one-measure interludes while the singers take a breath) "set the mood" and must be so played. Orchestra dynamics should *project on the interludes;* build them up for those single measures that are important. (6) One fine opera conductor told the author, "Always *one really slow number* somewhere in the performance. The change of pace sparks the rest of the performance." (7) One solo violin is more apparent dynamically than are two violins playing in unison. (8) Tell the soloists, "In general we shall follow you, so feel free to lead. However, there are certain places where you will have to follow the conductor or the orchestra will not be with you. These places concern entrances on a fraction of an up-beat (usually occurring after fermatas), when the orchestra must play either *with* the singer or on the following beat. In such cases the singer must take the cue for continuing from the conductor." (9) In school performances where the solo voices are weak (especially in junior high school), have the orchestra use the real "musical comedy style," very short notes articulating the beat but with little or no sustaining power. Strings: off-the-string bowings (spiccato), or using a position near the frog of the bow and lifting after all short notes (quarters or less). If the music calls for sustained tones, drop them back to double-piano immediately after the attack, to let the voices through. (10) Do *not* use the piano with the orchestra in performance if it is possible to avoid it. It usually leads out too loudly and the orchestra is blamed for the excessive dynamic. Warn the soloists on stage (and the chorus) that there will not be quite as emphatic an articulation from the orchestra as from the piano. Get them to listen intently to the orchestral sound during the rehearsals.

WHO CONDUCTS THE PERFORMANCE?

In the professional theater, opera, and musical comedy, it is always the orchestra conductor who does the performance. In school presentations, however, the choral conductor may take over with, perhaps, the orchestra conductor conducting the overture. Whichever conductor functions, there are facets of his conducting that will need special attention.

The **chorus conductor** has been through many rehearsals with the singers and pianist while teaching the operetta. When he stands in front of the orchestra, the first tendency will be to show the cut-off for the chorus (at the end of a song) and then to stop conducting—leaving the orchestra stranded. (An orchestra is not like a self-sufficient pianist.) The orchestral measures that continue after the singers have finished must be conducted. They are often written to give time for stage entrances and exits, and their interest has to be kept vital throughout.

Next, the choral conductor should see that he accounts for the *downbeat in every measure.* The orchestra players depend upon this to "keep the place" when they have a few measures of rest in their individual parts. The readable beat-pattern now assumes importance above and beyond what is needed for the chorus. Further, the conductor's hands must not be held so high that the orchestra players cannot see them.

When the **orchestra conductor** does the performance, he may tend to forget to make proper cut-offs for the stage performers, thus producing ragged endings. He will have to remember to lift his hands when his signals are directed to the singers on stage. Phrasings are important (for breathing), final consonants have to be given attention, and eye contact with the stage is imperative. The left hand can become invaluable in giving a warning gesture a measure or two before a chorus or solo entrance.

Both conductors, working in the pit, will be remote from the singers. The tone of the orchestra may reach the audience a fraction ahead of the singers' sound. Also the latter may miss the percussiveness of the piano, and may therefore lag a bit. Synchronization and balance should be checked from the back of the auditorium during rehearsals.

Dramatic timing becomes important. Variety of tempo spices the show. The conductor should guard against the unconscious habit of permitting his own natural pulse-beat to influence the tempo of the music. On stage, the performers have to be trained not to "crash a laugh," but to wait for the audience to "simmer down." The dramatic quality of a fermata and the intensity of a silence that may follow it, or the suddenness of surprise in a forte bass drum beat or a cymbal crash all come under the heading of dramatic timing.

The fine stage performance carries the audience with it by presenting clearly the literary content of the words and the beauty of the music. The excellent rendition of either should not be made the excuse for a poor rendition of the other. The words tell the story. The music heightens the emotional drive. Each must justify the existence of the other.

THE CHURCH ORGANIST-CONDUCTOR

Finally a word or two for the organist-conductor who directs the choir from his position at the organ. Here the development of the left-hand techniques become imperative. (Cuing gestures, p. 74.) Since the ear hears quickest the highest pitches, the audience will not miss omitted notes so obviously if they are in the bass (left-hand) part at the organ. Practice performing the accompaniments using the necessary conducting gestures. If this is not done, the rhythm may be momentarily upset by the functioning of the conducting hand. Sometimes mirrors have to be rigged so that the chorus members can see the organist's hand signals.

EXERCISES FOR PRACTICE: CHORAL INTERPRETATION

1. Take the assigned score for class performance and study it following the seven headings given in this chapter, pp. 192–94. Thereafter try to synthesize these various aspects into a single, total interpretation of the piece. Set the mood and see the composition in its entirety. The audience is not interested in details. It is interested in the *song*. Failure to synthesize brings with it the same result one gets in plucking the feathers from a bird one by one. In the end, most of the beauty is gone.

2. Prepare to conduct the song without looking at the score. Leave the speaking of the words to the singers who are reading the music and turn your attention to the mood and the sound of the final result.

RECOMMENDED REFERENCE READINGS (SEE APPENDIX G)

ADLER, SAMUEL. *Choral Conducting, An Anthology.* A fine selection of music classified according to conducting problems; includes contemporary works.

BALK, WESLEY. *The Complete Singer-Actor.* A method based on the brain research mentioned in Chapter 5 herein, p. 71.

BRAITHWAITE, WARWICK. *The Conductor's Art.* Chapter XIII, pp. 83–98, "The Conducting of Choral Works." Part III, pp. 101–176, devoted to the conducting of Opera.

COWARD, HENRY. *Choral Technique and Interpretation*, pp. 69–87, "Words, Articulation, Diction"; pp. 88–111, "Musical Expression"; pp. 203–248, "Analysis of the *Messiah.*"

CRIST, BAINBRIDGE. *The Art of Setting Words to Music.* Analysis of music plus discussion of specific works.

DAVISON, ARCHIBALD T. *Choral Conducting.* Chapter V, pp. 44–73, "Choral Technique." The instrumental conductor is urged to read this chapter.

DECKER, HAL A. and JULIUS HERFORD, eds. *Choral Conducting, A Symposium.* Chapter I, "The Development of a Choral Instrument" by Howard Swan. Don't miss this one! Also Chapter IV, "Choral Conducting and 20th Century Choral Music" by Daniel Moe.

FINN, WILLIAM J. *The Conductor Raises His Baton.* Chapters IV-VI, pp. 95–223, "Dynamics."

HOWERTON, GEORGE. *Technique and Style in Choral Singing.* Part II, pp. 79–187, deals with styles of the several historical periods of musical composition and of the various countries and geographical influences as applied to choral singing.

JONES, ARCHIE M. *Techniques of Choral Conducting.* Chapter III, pp. 37–45, "Diction" (Tables on the specific pronunciation of words, vowels and consonants in Chapter III); Chapter IV, pp. 46–56, "Choral Interpretation"; Appendix E, pp. 108–134, Interpretative Analyses.

MARSHALL, MADELEINE. *The Singer's Manual of English Diction.* A comprehensive and very complete manual of this important aspect of singing.

ROSS, ALLAN. *Techniques for Beginning Conductors.* This is a compendium of choral and orchestra music for conductors. Many examples reduced to two and three lines in addition to full scores.

14

Interpreting the Instrumental Score: Band and Orchestra

The conductor of the instrumental ensemble, regardless of whether his greatest interest lies in the band or the orchestra, will undoubtedly (especially if he is an outstanding musician) find himself standing in front of the opposite organization at some time in his career. He should know both sides of the coin.

The modern "symphonic band" is the outgrowth of long years of gradual development of the wind instruments and of their sequential entrance into the symphony orchestra. As need arose, new instruments were invented, some of which became permanent members only of the band. It is indeed a long road from the small strings-plus-one-wind scores of Bach and Telemann to the 32 lines of the Wagner-Cailliet score on p. 186.

Since 1961 when the first edition of this book appeared, many things have happened—new sounds and new ways of scoring. This is especially noticeable in current writing for instrumental ensembles. Let us now make certain comparisons between the band and the orchestra.

COMPARISONS AND CONTRASTS

There are many principles of musicianship that apply equally to both organizations. There are also fundamental differences between the band and orchestra of which the conductor should be cognizant.

Contrast of Basic Sound

The most basic difference between the symphony orchestra and the symphonic band has to do with the volume of sound. The wind instrument deals with an immediate force—wind is blown into the mouthpiece and sound waves as such emerge directly into the air, unhampered by the transference to and through the wood of the stringed instrument. In the latter, the vibrations initiated by the bow on the strings, pass through the bridge (wood) to the top of the instrument (wood) and finally to the air inside where the sound wave then forms. A certain loss of energy occurs in the process. Thus it is easy to see that a one hundred piece symphony band will have a greater volume than a one hundred member symphony orchestra where some sixty percent of the players are functioning on stringed instruments.

The orchestra relies greatly on its string tone for its basic sound. Each wind instrument now becomes a unique tone-color in its own right. Instead of a section of a dozen clarinets, two or four suffice; instead of six or eight flutes, two or three can handle the required scoring. In general, a solo wind will stand out more individually, as a color, against a string background than it will when accompanied by other wind instruments. The orchestra sound then, deals with the contrast of color between strings and winds—an effect that might be regarded as a type of transparency.

The wind player sitting in the orchestra will find himself using his finest solo tone with its obvious projection much of the time, whereas, in the band, he will, in addition, be more conscious of blending with his section in order that he not protrude unduly. (This is similar to the customary choral practices of blend of tone.) Balance and blend of sound among players in a single section and among instruments of different tone-color are fundamental problems in the band. Orchestrally, dynamic balance is also affected by color balance.*

The orchestra conductor, standing in front of the band for the first time, is likely to feel a bit overwhelmed by the sheer mass of the sound. Contrariwise, the band conductor in front of the orchestra may feel that the overall sound is a bit "thin." He will find himself working in a different medium wth a different type of resonance. The exciting *auditory* volume of the band is replaced in the orchestra by the *visual* excitement of the fast-moving bows, functioning in unison, and showing the same emotional drive.

*It was the consensus of opinion of a recent panel of Detroit Symphony winds that the orchestral musician has to have under control a wider dynamic range—softer pianos in the French horns, louder fortes in the flutes and bassoons. Concerning intonation: when playing with strings, infinitesimal pitch adjustments become paramount. As one panel member remarked, "D-sharp is not E-flat!"

Scoring

An important and recognizable change has been taking place in the scoring for symphonic band. One of the pivotal compositions was Persichetti's *Symphony for Band,** published in 1958. Here Persichetti began to experiment with emphasis on tonal colors rather than relying on the massive sectional sound. Witness, for example, the vastly empty pages: First movement, Measures 27–32, three clarinets and first horn only are playing; and later, in the last movement, Measures 92–97, solo oboe is accompanied only by the saxes (two altos, tenor, and baritone). The instruments are handled in a manner similar to the way the great masters of the past had used them in scoring for the symphony orchestra, thus bringing more transparency into the band sound.

The Melodic Line

In older band compositions, the clarinets assumed much of the melodic function that belonged to the first violins in the orchestra, both often doubled by the flutes. Cornet solos were frequent in band music but for the orchestra the trumpets were and are preferred. A melody performed by a solo wind still remains more prevalent in the orchestra, but not as much so today as in former years.

The Harmony

In the band, the three (or four) tones of the chordal harmony can be completed within one set of identical instruments (first, second, and third clarinets; three or four saxes; three trumpets; a set of trombones or horns). This similarity of tonal quality can help in balancing the tones of the chord. Since wind instruments more often come in pairs in the orchestra, the chordal harmony is likely to be scattered through the instruments of the family (woodwinds, brasses, or strings), thus requiring an adjustment that takes into consideration the tone-colors of the several instruments as well as their dynamic balance. The larger the orchestra, the more the harmonic distribution will resemble that of the band. A chord given to two violins, viola, and cello-bass will need attention for resonance.

The Percussion

Over the years, the percussion section has been used somewhat more sparingly in the orchestra than in the band with the exception of the timpani. Twentieth-century writing has brought a change here. A distinction should be made, in either organization, between the percussion as an addition to the general sound or as a solo section in its own right. In earlier

---

*Vincent Persichetti, *Symphony for Band* (Philadelphia, Elkan-Vogel, 1958).

works for band where the percussion becomes a rather constant rhythmic force, it has to be kept subservient to the pitched sounds—like a wonderful heartbeat that permeates the music but is not obviously apparent. Regardless of with which organization the percussionist performs, regardless of whether the music calls for a murmur, a simple statement, an unrelenting intensification of the emotional content, or a thunderous climax, the performer should be made aware of the fact that when pitched instruments are also sounding, the dynamic rendition of the percussion element should be in balance with them. (What a joy musicianly percussion playing is!)

MUSICIANSHIP FACTORS PERTINENT TO BOTH BAND AND ORCHESTRA

Tessitura of the Melody Line

The melody is clearest heard when it occupies a place in the score-range not cluttered up by accompanying instruments in the same octave. The closer in range the accompanying instruments are to the pitches sounded by the melodic line, the harder it is to project this line with the necessary clarity for the audience.* **Danger:** When the melody is written in octaves for flute and oboe, the tessitura lies in the oboe octave. When both instruments are played perfectly in tune, the oboe tends to blot out the flute.

Projecting the Melody

When the melody does not sound clearly, the first temptation is to ask the soloist to play louder—to project more. Far better, first, would be to temper down the accompaniment—a thing the conductor has every right to insist upon. If the melody cannot be heard, it is probably the conductor's fault. His ear must be the judge, not the composer's dynamic markings.

The Melody Accompanied by Sustained Tones

A soloist may be accorded certain expressive liberties when the accompaniment is in the form of sustained tones. A slight rubato in the phrasing will not upset anything. But when the reiterated-note accompaniment exists, the soloist must hew to the line rhythmically. Any lack

---

*One remembers a band competition where the melody disappeared for some eight measures in rendition after rendition. The melody was scored in the flutes on the five lines of the staff, undoubled, with thirteen instruments accompanying! An impossible situation! A bit of rewriting was warranted.

of total precision in the rhythmic accompaniment, to accomodate the soloist, will be instantly noticed by the audience. Composers know these things and write accordingly.

DYNAMICS IN THE LARGE ENSEMBLE—BALANCE

The interpretation of the dynamic markings in the score for the large ensemble is something quite different from their significance in solo music. In the latter, one can accept the dynamic at its face value. But in the orchestra or band the marked dynamics are only guide lines, open to all kinds of variations and interpretations in performance. The underlying reason for this is that no composer can predict beforehand the musical prowess of every organization that may play his music. Therefore, the marked dynamic becomes a variable quantity to be intelligently interpreted by the conductor and the performers. The conductor should have a mental concept of what he wants to hear in performance. Then he works with the instrumental balance to achieve the sound he has in mind.

The Two Systems of Marking Dynamics

There are two generally accepted systems of marking dynamics. The earliest one, historically, is the block dynamic where all instruments (or voices) in the score are marked forte at the same time; all are marked piano simultaneously. If a crescendo or diminuendo is desired, it is identically marked for all parts. The composer has given a general indication of his ideas. Today, however, many composers make an attempt to balance the score by marking varied dynamics among the several sections of the ensemble. This gives a clue as to what the composer considers important.

Interpretation of the Block Dynamic

A generally accepted principle in dealing with the block dynamic is to play the melody one degree louder than marked, the accompaniment one degree softer. There is also one other consideration: A forte played on a French horn will be much more powerful than it would be on an alto clarinet. This means that the instruments have to adjust until a uniform forte results. Further, it takes four violins to double the power of two and sixteen to double the power of four. Note that it proceeds by the square of the number in the violins. In studying score, try to imagine the sound as played by *your* ensemble.*

---

*Rimsky-Korsakov, in his *Principles of Orchestration*, pp. 33–35, has attempted to compare the relative strengths of the various instruments.

The Second Type of Dynamic Marking

The marking of a special dynamic for each section of the ensemble also has an historical basis. In Dvořák's orchestral score for the *Slavonic Dance*, Op. 46, No. 1, in C Major, at Measure 99, the violas and bassoons (melody line) are marked forte. The other strings together with the third and fourth horns are marked double-piano, while the first horn and clarinet have a piano indication. What a struggle it is for the conductor of the less-than-professional group to get the accompanying players to "shush down" when they hear the forte in the bassoons and violas!

Continuity of Dynamic

There are many places in the orchestral scores of Haydn, Mozart, Beethoven, and others where a small motif is played in succession by different instruments (for example, flute, oboe, clarinet, bassoon, or cello). Such places need careful dynamic rehearsing. The given dynamic should sound with equal loudness as the motif bounces around from instrument to instrument. If the dynamic continuity is not preserved, the musical result is ragged. Each player should temper his sound to preserve the overall line of the passage.

A second type of dynamic continuity has to do with crescendos and diminuendoes. These should progress smoothly, not by leaps and bounds. Beethoven particularly is fond of adding instruments to the ensemble as the crescendo builds. Instruments entering should do so softly and then gradually build up their own dynamic so that the crescendo does not suddenly take a great leap forward. In a long diminuendo, each instrument should soften before disappearing. Crescendos and diminuendos are smooth lines not interrupted by peaks and valleys.*

Customary Adjustments in Dynamic Markings

There are certain things that the fine professional musician does as a matter of course when performing in the large ensemble. The first of these concerns a passage where the whole ensemble arrives at a double-forte climax and then all instruments drop out except for one section, usually marked *piano*. (In the orchestra, the section that remains is often the violas.) In this circumstance the composer's marked piano does *not* apply to the remaining section. His piano dynamic has occurred automatically simply because most of the instruments have suddenly ceased to play. If the remaining section actually performs piano, the audience hears nothing

---

*The reader will find information from professional performers on the interpretation of marked dynamics in the first chapter of *The Dynamic Orchestra* (Green). See bibliography.

for a moment. There is a hole in the music. The section that continues should play forte for an extra beat or two, establishing itself, and then diminuendo rapidly to the required piano. In this way the continuity of the music is preserved. The remaining section has to have strength enough to carry the weight of the whole ensemble on its shoulders momentarily when the other instruments cease to play.

Another dynamic variation concerns passages where a certain note is repeated continuously, interrupted here and there by a single note of a different pitch. This odd note should be subtly projected above the surrounding reiterated notes. Such adjustments are too delicate for the composer to mark them himself.

Repeated notes (or sustained tones) leading into a melodic line should crescendo slightly just before taking over the melody. In this way the attention of the audience is guided to hear the *first* note of the melody.

To enrich the sound of a chord, strengthen the third of the chord. This effect can add greatly to a long diminuendo from sound to silence at the end of a piece, but it must be done with finesse.

When the brasses have a sustained double-forte chord, it is very easy for them to blot out the rest of the ensemble. In both band and orchestra such sustained fortes should be attacked at the marked dynamic and then immediately tempered down so that the moving voices are clearly heard. It is the moving voices that carry the music forward and they must not be covered up by the less interesting static chord. **Note:** This does not apply when the tutti ensemble has the sustained sound. In this latter case, a simple balancing of the harmony is all that is needed.

Sustained tones tend to drag. Be sure that they are synchronized precisely with the change of note in the florid or moving parts.

TWO PERFORMANCE CUSTOMS: BAND AND ORCHESTRA

In music of all periods, when a note is tied over, *in fast tempo*, to a sixteenth of the same pitch, and that sixteenth is the first of a group of sixteenths, it is customary to replace the tied sixteenth by a rest. (Examples 100 and 101.) Without the moment of rest, the following sixteenths usually

Example 100. Beethoven, *Symphony No. 3 ("Eroica") in Eb Major*, op. 55. Finale (measure 1).

Example 101.   Mozart, *Don Giovanni*. Overture (measure 56).

lack precision of ensemble. This custom is followed in both band and orchestra. In the orchestra, the bows must stop still for that instant, thus ensuring uniformity of attack as they continue.

The second custom concerns the eighth note followed by two sixteenths. Marked *allegro*, it is often notated thus: ♩ ♫ . Here we come to a discrepancy between band and orchestra. In the band, in fast tempo, the simple act of tonguing the sixteenths will ensure the staccatos. The discrepancy occurs in the orchestra. When each note is given its own bowstroke in fast tempo, obviously there is not time to stop the bow and start it again after each sixteenth note. Therefore the staccato dot does not mean staccato here. It means only separate bows. In performance, the spacing or separation comes after the eighth note. The sixteenths are played broadly, without stops.

Closely related is Example 102, (a), (b), and (c). In (a), the staccato dots again do not mean staccato. They are used only to show that the following notes are not slurred, but bowed separately, and on the string. When the tempo is fast enough to permit the use of the "staccato volante" (the bow coming off the string after each sixteenth note) then the bowing given in (b) and (c) becomes practical.

Example 102.

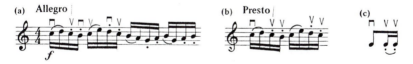

All of the facets of large-ensemble performance should be taught as young musicians are progressing through high school. When they know the "professional tricks," the end result is most gratifying. Train the players to recognize the visual difference on the page between a melody line and an accompanying passage. Sustained tones, repeated notes, recurrent rhythmic figures are probably accompaniment and should be played softer than marked. Measures filled with varied pitches, coupled to notes of differing values, are likely to be melodic. Project them. Musicians who are trained to make these dynamic adjustments automatically are worth their weight in gold in any musical organization. An infinite amount of rehearsal time can be saved.

A FEW WORDS ON "STYLE"

Style deals with three facets of score interpretation: the musical customs in vogue when the composition was created, the personal stamp of the artistic individuality of the composer, and the inner emotional drive of the composition itself. (Here brevity must be considered. We can only point the direction.)

The most obvious characteristics of the four basic historic periods are shown in Example 103.

A. The Early Classical Style (103 (a)): contrapuntal in nature, dealing with concomitant horizontal lines rather than vertical harmonies. Interpretatively, the faster, running notes (measure 1 in the example) are performed broadly and closely connected tonally. The shorter notes (measure 2) are spaced, but not staccato. The strings will use the broad détaché bowing. **NOTE:** Détaché is a French word. It does not mean "detached" in English. It simply means "unslurred." Winds might experiment with a ta or du tonguing seeking continuity.

Example 103.

EMBELLISHMENTS

Linking the Early Classical and the Later Classical periods we find the entire category of embellishments.

The appoggiatura. During Mozart's lifetime, the appoggiatura and the grace note were undergoing a change. The appoggiatura, written as a small note but showing exactly half the rhythmic value of the following note (Figure 59 (a)), is played *on* the beat and becomes the first (and accented) note of a group of notes of equal value (Figure 59 (b)). Notice that the slur is retained.

This type is known as the "long appoggiatura" and it usually indicates that the small note is not part of the prevailing harmony. The appoggiatura often appears as a link, melodically, in the interval of the third, thus producing a scalewise progression. In this case, it becomes the "short appoggiatura" and is played ahead of the beat.

The mordant. A single trill that starts and ends on the same pitch. It is accented and borrows its time from the preceding note. The mordant moves in a direction opposite to the melodic line. (Figure 60.)

The trill. In a stepwise progression, it starts on the upper note and ends on the lower note. In intervals of the third, its first note fills in the missing scale-tone. (Figure 61)

The turn. Follows the contour shown by the shape of the sign. Usually it proceeds upward first (Figure 62 (a)), but the upside-down form is used

Figure 59.

Figure 60.

Figure 61.

in performances of Wagner's *Rienzi* (b). When the turn is written in conjunction with a dotted note, it is performed so that it terminates on the dot (c). The main melody line is therefore re-established before the music proceeds. (Figure 62)

Figure 62.

B. The Later Classical Style (103 (b)): Haydn, Mozart. Here the big word is *clarity*. Every note sparkles. Crisp articulations are called for. Staccatos are functioning. Spiccato bowing has fully entered the picture, aided by the advent of the Tourte* bow. In slow compositions, beauty of melodic line and depth of emotion are maturing. Dynamics (block style) move immediately from loud to soft and soft to loud. All parts are marked the same but in performance the melody is played one degree louder than indicated, the accompaniment one degree soft than notated. Vertical harmony is apparent.

C. The Romantic Period (103 (c)): develops the long, steady crescendo leading to intense climaxes, as witness Beethoven's writings. Schubert—a link in lyricism. Beethoven marks his staccato dots carefully. During this period there is a constant expanding of brilliance and emotion leading to Berlioz and accompanied by the emergence of the Russian School: Glinka, Glazounov, Tchaikovsky, Rimsky-Korsakov.

D. The Contemporary Period (103 (d)): The twentieth century goes down in history as the time of the greatest scientific development since the world began. And music followed the same path. Here we have experimentation in harmonic relationships, rhythmic independence of voicing, beats that stutter instead of flow, requiring lopsided time-beating (the Russian revolutionary spirit bursting forth in Stravinsky!). All of this led finally to the exploration of the minds of the performers themselves through the "chance" or aleatoric score. The "Nationalistic" schools have fully emerged: Bartók with his irregular dance and folksong rhythms, Sibelius with his "northern" flavor, Debussy and Ravel presenting the French image, in Germany the stretching in length of everything that had gone before—Wagner, Mahler, Bruckner, and Richard Strauss—in Russia, Stravinsky, Prokofiev, and Shostakovich, all uniquely individual reflections of Rimsky-Korsakov's teaching.

To illustrate where music is right now, we add Example 104—a few

---

*François Tourte, (1747–1836), French, changed the shape of the bow from its early upward-curving stick to the modern shape known today.

Example 104. Bassett. *Echoes from an Invisible World.* First movement (measure 6 and following).

213

Example 104.   *(cont.)*

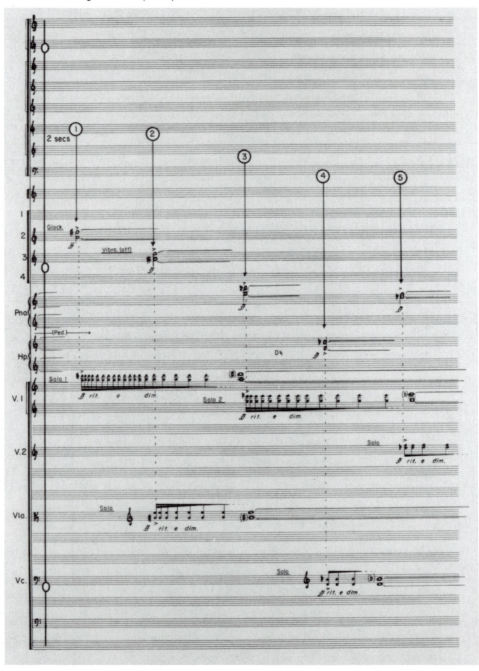

measures from Leslie Bassett's *Echoes from an Invisible World.* Here we see measures written in an unmetered notation, inserted into otherwise measured writing, with stated pitches throughout. The performer knows what to play instead of composing on the instant as in completely aleatoric music. Notice the unmetered time signature at the beginning of page 2 of Example 104—an invention of Mr. Bassett's.

Note: Leslie Bassett won the Prix de Rome, 1961–63, and a Pulitzer Prize in 1966. *Echoes from an Invisible World* was one of the six commission pieces by six composers, underwritten by six major orchestras, for the United States bicentennial celebration. *Echoes* was premiered by the Philadelphia Orchestra (who commissioned it) under Eugene Ormandy on February 26 and 27 and March 2, 1976. The most recent performances were September 26, 27, and 28, 1985 by the Detroit Symphony. The recording is CRI No. 429, with the Baltimore Symphony, Sergiu Commissiona conducting.

This chapter ends with the basic Bowing Principles in their simplest form. Complete discussions are found in *The Dynamic Orchestra* (Green, Prentice-Hall, Inc., 1987) and in *Orchestral Bowings and Routines.* (See Appendix G.)

Down-bow or Up-bow?

Uniformity of bowing deals with the *direction* of the bowing motions. In general, the down-bow synchronizes with the conductor's downbeat, but there are many exceptions to this principle.*

The Basic Bowing Principles in Their Simplest Form:**

1. The note on the first beat of a measure is taken down-bow. (Exceptions.)
2. The unslurred note before the bar-line is taken up-bow.
3. A note slurred over the bar-line is taken down-bow.
4. After a rest, the entrance is made on *up-bow* if an *odd number* of bows is needed before the bar-line is reached.
5. The entrance is made *down-bow* if an *even number* of bows is needed before the bar-line is reached.
6. In rhythmic figures, interspersed with rests, the note present with the greatest accent takes the down-bow:

---

*The exceptions to the basic bowing principles presented in this outline are to be found in Green, *Orchestral Bowings and Routines*, and in Green, *The Dynamic Orchestra*.

**Adapted from Green, *Orchestral Bowings*. Used by permission.

7. In passage work, four even, unslurred notes, starting ON the beat, take down-bow on the first note of the group. (Not always pertinent in Bach and polyphonic writing.)

8. Link the dotted-eighth and sixteeth:

9. In continuous passages of dotted-eighth-plus-sixteenth, marked piano, this bowing may be used at the point of the bow:

10. In 6/8 time, link the quarter and eighth:

11. Chords are played down-bow, all notes attacked simultaneously.

12. An ending note, preceded by a very short note, is played at the frog of the bow:

13. In 4/4 time, marked forte, an accented half-note on beat Two is taken on a *new* down-bow:

14. In continuous, unslurred, string-crossings, fast tempo: (a) Violins-violas, up-bow on upper string/(b) cellos-basses, down-bow on upper string:

15. The last note of a crescendo is up-bow, the climax note is down-bow.

EXERCISES FOR PRACTICE: SCORE INTERPRETATION (BAND/ORCHESTRA)

1. Compare recordings of the same composition, one played by the band, the other played by the orchestra: Bernstein *Candide;* Shostakovich, *Festival Overture;* Wagner, *"Liebestod"* (from *Tristan and Isolde*); J. Strauss, *"Die Fledermaus Overture;"* etc. Listen particularly for balance problems.

2. Look through the scores in Chapters 11 and 12. Decide what clues are present to help you place them in their correct setting and style historically.

3. In soft pencil, mark the bowings in Chapter 11, applying the principles given in this chapter.

4. Study the scores in Chapter 11 and 12. Apply to them the knowledge you have gained thus far regarding building your own interpretation.

RECOMMENDED REFERENCE READINGS (SEE APPENDIX G)

AUSTIN, WILLIAM A. *Music in the Twentieth Century, Debussy through Stravinsky.* The music of each composer is dealt with individually and at some length. Contains 110 pages of bibliography!

BERRY, WALLACE. *Form in Music.* The whole book is applicable.

CHRISTIANI, ADOLF F. *Principles of Expression in Pianoforte Playing.* This book is probably the greatest treatise available to the English-speaking student on expression in music. Starting with the section on "Melodic Accents" (p. 138) and reading to the end of the book, one can pick up information not obtainable from other sources. In reading the book for uses other than pianoforte playing, the word "accent" may be interpreted simply as "stress" or "swell" in the tone.

COPE, DAVID. *New Directions in Music.* Information on twentieth-century writing.

CROCKER, RICHARD L. *A History of Musical Style.* A very complete history of music approached through the music itself; pp. 355–526, the development of the orchestra via composition.

FARKAS, PHILIP. *The Art of Musicianship.* Farkas (for many years solo French horn of the Chicago Symphony) gives an authoritative analysis of the many facets of musicianship. Highly recommended.

GALAMIAN, IVAN. *Principles of Violin Playing and Teaching.* Bowing styles dealt with in detail.

NEIDIG, KENNETH L. *The Band Director's Guide.* A compendium of articles by various authors covering all phases of band performance.

RABIN, MARVIN and PRISCILLA SMITH. *Guide to Orchestral Bowings Through Musical Styles.*

VAN ESS, DONALD H. *The Heritage of Musical Styles.*

WENNERSTROM, MARY H. *Anthology of Musical Structure and Style.*

15

Memorizing the Score: Performing the Score

There is no set rule, universally recognized, for memorizing a score; no sure-fire, cut-and-dried method guaranteeing foolproof results. Charles Munch stated in his book (see Appendix G) that he did not require his students in conducting classes in Paris to work from memory at the outset of their training. He felt that the security of having the score present helped the young conductor. Hermann Scherchen, on the other hand, required absolute memorization and intense mental concentration before he permitted the student to conduct the work. However, Scherchen may have geared this approach to those who had had some previous experience.

Perhaps the most often asked question is, "Just what is meant by 'memorizing the score'? Does the conductor who uses no score at the concert really know every note of every instrument?"

The answer is interesting. It varies with the convictions of the conductor. Many of the greatest conductors do "know every note of every instrument." But in the actual performance there is no time to think of each note any more than there is time to think, "My notes in this run are A, C, F, G, A, E, G, B, D, C," and so on, when one is playing a solo from memory in public performance. The player may know these notes and be able to write them out perfectly. He may have assimilated the run completely and absolutely. But to put conscious thought such as "A, C, F, G, etc.," before each played note would slow down the performance unbearably. Music moves too fast for this.

The mind should be actively alerted during the formation of the habit, but once the habit has been perfected it will run itself, thus releasing the mind for a genuinely creative expression. The mind *as a conscious force* works hard during the learning process, namely, during the sightreading of the music and during the first stages of the practicing. But as the music is gradually assimilated, the mental effort gives way to the habitual action. A certain type of "memorization" has taken place.

The performing from memory might be described as a "free-wheel-ing" of the mind, the auditory apparatus, and the necessary physical motions. As a musician, one mentally listens for the sounds he wants to produce and these sounds come out of his instrument. The response of the skilled hands is so closely linked to the mental concept of the desired music that they seem to be part of the mind itself. This is an uncanny attribute with which man is endowed. We are, by nature, wonderfully made to be self-contained units of efficiency.

The brain specialists in the medical profession tell us that every repeated action makes a deeper and deeper impression on the brain centers involved until eventually the settling into activity of the motivating force for the certain action will cause the action to take place as a matter of course, an instantaneous and uninhibited "circuit" occurring in the brain.

There are many ways to remember many things. We remember how a loved one *looks* (Visual memory). We remember how the wind sounded in the pine trees during a northern vacation, or we remember the sound of a plane going over on a still night (Auditory memory). We think of a certain fenced field in the country and we immediately remember the dangerous bull that was confined therein (Memory by association of ideas). We do delicate piecework in a factory. At first intense concentration is needed to turn out a perfect unit, for the hands are clumsy in the beginning. Later the mind can go off on other thoughts and the hands will continue to turn out perfect work without conscious effort (Memory by habit-forming, repeated action). We find out that we cannot remember how to make a certain little gadget of folded paper. Someone shows us that this fold comes first, then this one and so on. We find that we now know how to make it perfectly (Memory by stepwise sequence, logical analysis, and synthesis).

We remember some things by visualizing a geometric design. A child wants to play hopscotch. He remembers how to draw the correct set of elongated rectangles.

We remember certain things by a principle of contrast. This twin always wears the ring with the blue stones in it while that one wears the red stone. We know which is which by contrasting the one thing that is different.

There is also a memory for timing. The teacher whose life is spent in the 50-minute classroom, or the radio engineer whose day is divided into half-hour periods, soon acquires the *feeling* that the time has elapsed without looking at the clock. This is a memory for the duration of time.

So when we memorize a score, we have many ways, too, to remember things. If the memory balks at conquering a certain passage, perhaps the wrong approach is being used. We must analyze the difficulty and try to decide which of our many ways to remember things is needed for that particular spot in the music, just which memory ability will unlock it for us.

Let us see how this can work out. It may be a place in the score where remembering how those two quarter rests look between those two quarter notes in the middle of the passage will straighten us out (Visual memory). It may be that we can remeeber what is going on if we play it several times very slowly so that the ear can really hear exactly what it should be (Auditory memory). Or perhaps it is a passage where we have to be forewarned. "When that high C is heard, remember that the fermata on the F comes in the very next measure" (Association of ideas).

Perhaps the baton balks at performing a certain succession of legato and staccato gestures. We do them many times slowly and correctly, letting the mind have time to think each one precisely, and after a while the habit comes, through repeated action, until finally the baton will move perfectly with scarely any thought at all (Habit formation through repeated action).

We come to a long passage with many changes in it. We start to pick it apart to see what it really does. It is, upon analysis, a sequence, repeated every four measures. Each repetition is one whole tone higher than the one before. The fact that it had so many accidentals in it made us overlook this simple solution until we could go at it systematically with real thought. So now we have used logical analysis and synthesis. The passage is firmly fixed in the mind.

We have some cues in a score which come so fast that the mind can scarely think "flute, clarinet, bassoon, oboe." So we notice how these instruments are seated in the orchestra (Figure 63).

Almost instantly, through geometric design, we can give a perfect rendition of the cues with the necessary speed of execution. The troublesome spot is solved by performing a simple clockwise square.

We have a nasty passage: 2/4, 3/4, 1/4, 3/8, one measure of each. The conducting must show only quarter notes throughout. We acquire a complicated set of memories to handle this one. We set the upper numbers in our mind just as we would a telephone number: two, three, one, one-and-a-half. We practice performing the passage with the baton, repeating it many times until the hand seems to acquire a "feel" for it. We listen to it time and again, until the lopsided rhythm is compensated for by a sort

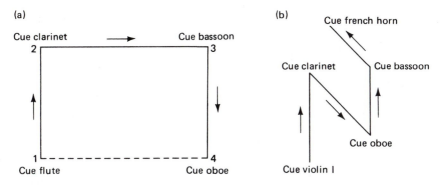

Figure 63. Geometric *design* for cues.

of melodic sound which gradually emerges. And so, by working at it in several ways, we eventually conquer it.

Here is a melody that comes in twice. The first time the low C is followed by D, a quarter note, and the melody goes off into the oboe solo passage. The second time the low C is followed by F, a half note and this leads directly into the French horn quartet section. Thus, by clarifying the contrast of the changing note (the note that acts like a switch in the track) we can conduct convincingly and securely what is to come (Memory by contrast).

Now we find a clarinet run. Four measures later the same run is played by the flute. We have weighty problems in the intervening measures and cannot concentrate on counting measures, yet we invariably bring the flute in at the right time. The duration of time memory is partly helping us here.

So, in the overall memorization of the score, many means are employed. Since we are meant to be efficient machines, we have only to replace fear with confidence and to go ahead and work it out. Memory often is just the good result of real mental alertness, of noticing what is going on when it happens.

WHAT IS MEANT BY A "MEMORIZED SCORE"?

There are several schools of thought on what is necessary to call a score "memorized." Some say, "One must know every single note of every single part, and be able to write out every part from memory." Others contend that it is sufficient to know "how the melody sounds and the sequence throughout; to know the harmony and what the accompanying instruments do; but not necessarily how each note of each accompanying chord is distributed among the various instruments." This latter definition is akin to memorizing a solo with piano accompaniment. The player knows how the parts fit together and whether they sound right or whether wrong notes are being played by the accompanist, but he has not learned the piano part so that he could perform it alone. There are still other "conductors" who contend that it is "sufficient to know the number of measures and conduct accordingly." Obviously this last definition is the product of the "time-beater" who is doing only that. (One wonders about the emotional appeal of his performances!)

Toscanini, when asked, said that he did not know how he memorized. Chotzinoff (see Appendix G) tells that Toscanini remarked that he had always had a facility for knowing how a score would sound by looking at it. "Sometimes I tell myself a story about a beautiful girl. This melody depicts the forest. This melody is an evil man. . . . ," and so on. One can see why his performances were so often described as having great imagination and great appeal for the audiences. He lived them in his mind.

The author has been told that Guido Cantelli* memorized the part for each instrument *in toto* first, starting with the first flute and working right down through the score. When he finished an individual part he would ask his wife to give him an examination on it. She would ask such questions as, "What note is played by the second clarinet on the first beat of the second measure after A?" After memorizing the several parts Cantelli would group them by families, working with the four or five lines of the family in the score. Then, lastly, he would correlate the whole score.

It is probably safe to say that a score is memorized when one can "think it through" accurately from beginning to end without recourse to the printed page or to audible sound.

SOME PRACTICAL HINTS ON MEMORIZING

It would be advisable now to check back to the Introduction to Score Study, pp. 136–37, paying particular attention to points 5, 6, and 8. Read the score through, as you would a novel. Then proceed with the following suggestions for memorizing.

1. *Chart the composition.* Write out, in your own variety of musical shorthand, an outline of the composition. For example: "Initial fermata, f and dim. Theme A, violins, repeated forte. Theme B, flutes-oboes, piano; repeated with violins mf. Theme A returns, strings tutti, forte, dim-

---

*Guido Cantelli, a protégé of Toscanini, had begun to make a name for himself when he was killed in a plane crash in the 1950s.

inuendo to piano fermata, etc." Once having charted the entire work in outline, including where necessary the number of measures for certain sections, think it through, humming the melodies, the connecting links, and so on. When this becomes easy, you will find that you can begin to make condensations in the outline: "Section I, A - B - A to Fermata," and so on. Work all of this with pencil in hand. When the mind has assimilated the music thus, you will find that you can write the outline-synopsis rapidly from memory, carrying the music in your head throughout. Still later, discard the pencil and work through the piece entirely in your mind. *Allow no interruptions when working through in this way.* What you are doing is training your mind to concentrate intensely over the necessary span of time. When all of this has been accomplished you should be safe in performance.

2. There are certain *safety checks* of which you should also be conscious that will ensure mental alertness at the dangerous places. The first of these is the *audible clue*. *Before* a difficult passage, mark a distinctive note, rhythm, or instrument-motif that will instantly inform you that the danger approaches. When you hear it, you react as if a red light had flashed on. Associate the clue with the coming problem.

3. For *fast cues*, distributed among several instruments, check on the *geometric design* that would form on paper if you drew a line to each instrument in turn as the cues are made (Figure 63, p. 221). This is an added safety check.

4. When *two sections of the music are identical* for a number of measures, check on the one note that acts as a switch in the tracks—the first note where they part company. Compare the note in the first rendition with the different note in the second rendition. Know which note leads where.

5. *Count the measures* in the dangerous places where the phrasing is irregular. Count such places even when you are conducting.

6. Notice *interlocking phrases* where the new phrase starts on the same beat that ends the old phrase. Be ready to conduct the *new* phrase.

7. Sometimes it helps to have *certain words* in mind such as: "After the trumpets . . . " or "Oboe leads to cellos. . . ."

8. Practice the dangerous piano-subitos so that the hands respond instantly when the passage occurs. Train the *muscular habits* to react confidently in the difficult irregular time-beating changes.

9. **Important:** Find places in the music where everything is so safe that the mind can snatch a few measures of rest from its intense concentration. Have an audible clue, as described in No. 2 above, that will re-alert the mind in plenty of time. These *moments of rest* are very precious and very necessary.

10. Let *your ear* guide you, supported by the knowledge that has been gained through the study outlined in these ten steps. After all, music is sound. You are memorizing sound. Trust your ear and let the music speak to you. It will tell you what is about to happen if you listen as you conduct.

You ask, "Is all of this really *necessary?*" The answer is "No!" But the resultant musical performance is never as effective as it would be if you freed yourself from dependence on the score. Do not be afraid to try. You will probably find that you already have much of the piece memorized unconsciously. This has been proven many times in the classes. **Caution:** If you are mentally tired, use the score in rehearsals.

EXERCISES FOR PRACTICE: MEMORIZATION

1. Memorize a chosen movement (symphony, band score, long chorus). Get it so that you can chart it as given under point 1 above. Be ready to conduct it without benefit of score.

2. During this process decide what your own natural approach to the memorization process is. Are you leaning more on your auditory memory or on your visual memory?

3. Practice the actual conducting of the work, using the gestures you will later on perform before the ensemble. Mark any places which bother you. Give these special attention. Check on your fairness to the composer. Are you yourself enjoying the sound of the performance? Does it inspire you to deliver your very best? (This, incidentally, is a pretty good test of the real musical value of the work and of your own musicianship in relation to it.)

4. *Write out* the shorthand analysis of the work from memory, if you have not already done so. Follow the suggestions given under step 1.

PERFORMING THE SCORE

The rehearsal is the first "performance" for the conductor. When he steps before his musicians, he is ready for the final public presentation. The rehearsal gives him time to help the musicians understand what he is trying to produce musically. But he must be secure in his own mind as to his interpretation and how to produce it. Every rehearsal is a performance for the conductor.

The conductor's attitude in rehearsal has a potent effect on the final performance. Poise is a requisite. His authority is respected if he is organized and ready to achieve certain set goals in each rehearsal. No orchestra in the world wants to sit through a rehearsal where the conductor is apparently wasting time.

The public performance is the final test. During the short interval, after the orchestra is on stage and tuned, take time to relax and collect your thoughts. They cannot start without you. You are in control.

Walk onto the stage with confidence and authority. Create a feeling of friendliness, within yourself, toward the audience and their welcoming applause. Smile when you make your bow, stage front. Bow, preferably before stepping on the podium. The act of ascending the podium is a command for attention, addressed both to the musicians and to the audience. During all of this, be thinking your tempo and the first notes of the music you are about to conduct. Do not pick up the baton until you feel that you yourself are ready to begin. *You* are in control.

Be patient if the audience is restless and not yet settled down. Almost any audience will eventually quiet itself if you just wait. (Moments can seem very long.) There is no point in starting before the audience is ready to listen. A "piano" gesture in the left hand—fingers together, pointing upward, palm facing the players—can help.

Rehearsal vs. Performance

The first difference between rehearsal and performance is that one does not stop for repairs in performance. Muddle through somehow if things go wrong. But DON'T STOP! The unforgivable is to stop. Remember, too, that everything exaggerates its importance in your mind when you are performing. Things that seem completely tragic may not even be noticed by the audience—unless you stop!

The second difference in performance is that your own musical intensity is felt vitally by players and listeners. The professional performer recognizes this magic of the theater, be he actor or musician. One "feels" the intensity of the audience response.

Stage Etiquette

There is a formalized stage etiquette that should be observed. Before stepping onto the podium, it is always permissible at the beginning of the concert to shake hands with the concertmaster. This is almost invariably done in "guest" performances.

The conductor's handshake at the end of the concert is his formal *thank-you to the entire membership of the orchestra.* It should not be interpreted as a "pat on the back" for the concertmaster alone. (In the band, the solo clarinet becomes the concertmaster,—first chair to the conductor's left as he faces the band.)

When you leave the stage, do not delay your re-entrance *after your first exit.* Return almost immediately. A hesitation may kill the applause. Modesty at this time is not good showmanship. And applause is "money in the pocket" for your musicians as well as yourself.

When the conductor motions the orchestra to rise, they stand up simultaneously with the concertmaster. When the conductor leaves the stage, the players again watch the concertmaster, and resume their chairs as he sits down.

Soloists precede the conductor going on and off stage. If the conductor is a woman, a male soloist may step aside for her to precede him going offstage—or he can lead the way and step aside at the exit, permitting her to go out first. This applies only to going off stage.

At the end of a solo rendition, the soloist thanks the conductor (and through him, the orchestra) by shaking hands with him. The soloist, not the conductor, makes the first move toward the handshake. If the soloist is unhappy with the accompaniment, the handshake may be omitted—and may leave the conductor stranded with outstretched paw and no response.

The soloist may also shake hands with the concertmaster if desiring to do so. But under no circumstances does the soloist motion for the orchestra to stand. The soloist has no authority over the players. They obey only the conductor. The soloist can ask the conductor to have the players stand.

Building the Program

Think "interest" when setting up the concert program. Think "contrast" to guard against monotony. One slow number following another slow number is usually not effective.

Consider "sequence"—how one composition leads to the next. Some conductors are key-conscious, taking key relationship into consideration for continuity. Too great a difference between key sequences may have a disruptive effect. Live the concert in your mind. Imagine yourself as a member of the audience. Will you be interested throughout the concert, or will you fall asleep? Careful planning can "sell" the program regardless of the maturity of the players.

See that your performers keep the vitality going through to the very end of the very last note of a composition. There is nothing worse than a final note that sags. The rendition is not finished until *after* the applause starts.

And so the final words arrive.

Be sincere and honest in your musicianship. Work to describe, with the tip of the stick, the music and the spirit underlying it. In this way the conducting can become as varied as the music itself.

Feel the texture of the tone as you call it forth. Sense that the hands and baton are molding, shaping, sculpturing a living thing, for Music is an Art that exists and breathes only while it is being performed.

Remember that certain gestures in conducting are for the purpose of guiding the listeners to what you want them to hear. The audience itself is the ultimate reason for your public performance. Respond to their intensity as they respond to yours. Listen to the music yourself and be not unmindful that *it* is speaking to *you*.

Finally, above all, be sincere and honest in your approach to the creative element in conducting. Keep modest, work hard, and do not forget the composer. "After all," as Efrem Zimbalist, Senior, the magnificent violinist, so beautifully remarked on one occasion, "the greater genius is the one who put the notes on paper in the first place. All we, as interpretive artists, can do, is do the best we can."

RECOMMENDED REFERENCE READING (SEE APPENDIX G)

Memorizing

BERRY, WALLACE. *Form in Music.*

GREEN, ELIZABETH & NICOLAI MALKO. *The Conductor's Score.* Phrasal analysis for memorizing.

WENNERSTROM, MARY. *Anthology of Musical Structure and Style.*

Rehearsing vs Performance

BARRA, DONALD. *The Dynamic Performance.*

GREEN, ELIZABETH A. H. *The Dynamic Orchestra.*

LEINSDORF, ERICH. *The Composer's Advocate.*

PETERS, THOMAS J. & ROBERT H. WATERMAN. *In Search of Excellence.* Advice on handling people, Chapter 8, and on leadership, Chapter 9.

appendix

A

Seating Charts

Figure A-1. This arrangement is good when the tenors and basses are strong and the sopranos and altos fully adequate.

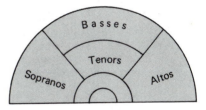

Figure 1-2. A highly recommended setup is given here. Unified strength is given to the sopranos and altos in their joining behind the men's voices. This setup is also good when boys' voices are timid in school groups. The centering of tenors and basses together in front gives them confidence through proximity to the conductor.

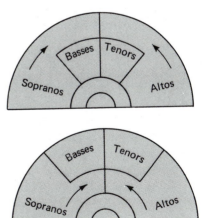

Figure A-3. A good arrangement for unity between sopranos and altos, since their voices are not split by the intervention of the men's voices.

Figure A-4.   This is good when tenors and basses are strong. Note that it shows the tenors on the same side as the sopranos, which is preferred by some conductors. This placement of the tenors is feasible in the preceding chart, also, if desired.

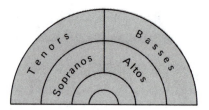

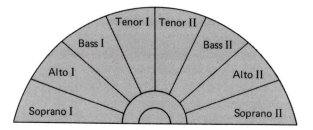

Figure A-5.   The large double choir is shown here in one of the standard setups. This formation is often used in large auditoriums where the strength of the soprano sound needs to come from both sides of the stage. Otherwise, the setups of Figures A-1 through A-4 may be used with each section split into first and second parts.

Note: In all of the foregoing arrangements the sopranos are located at the conductor's left, comparable in position to the first violins in the orchestra or to the leading clarinets in the band. Customarily, the lead melodies come from the conductor's left. However, there are instances in which conductors have experimented with the sopranos on the right, and a few prefer that setup.

SPECIAL CHORAL GROUPS

Figure A-6. Three Women's Voices. This is the standard setup for this type of vocal ensemble, owing to the usual close correlation between the first and second sopranos in vocal composition. The other choice would be with the altos in the middle.

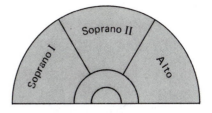

Figure A-7. Men's Chorus. The most common arrangement is given here.

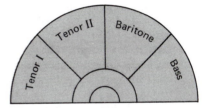

Figure A-8. Men's Chorus. This formation is also standard and may be used if desired or whenever it is necessary for acoustical purposes.

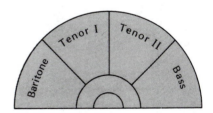

ORCHESTRA

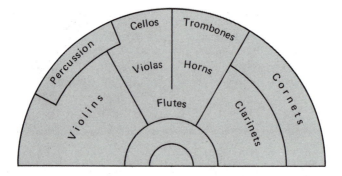

Figure A-9. Grade School Ensemble. The present trend is to use only one violin part in the young orchestra, that is, "first" violins only. It is not wise to split a weak section into two parts. When all children play first violin, strength is confidently adequate. Most grade school orchestras have a surplus of clarinets and cornets. These should be seated at the right, blowing *toward* the strings. This helps to soften their tone for the audience and to hold the group together. The location of the percussion behind the strings also helps to produce good rhythm in the ensemble. Furthermore, when the percussion is too close to the young brass section, the latter usually plays much too loudly. The violins must *always* be seated at the conductor's left so that their *ff*-holes face the audience for maximum sound.

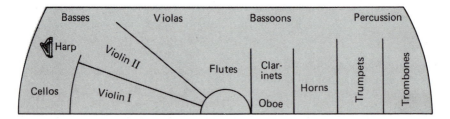

Figure A-10. Pit Orchestra. Customarily, the pit orchestra also groups the strings on the conductor's left with the winds in the center and on the right, blowing toward the strings. This helps the balance against the stage voices. The shape of the pit has to be considered in any setup of this type. In school performances, if the pit is shallow (from audience to stage) and very extended (left and right), it helps to seat the trumpets near the front on the conductor's right. Their strength holds the group together.

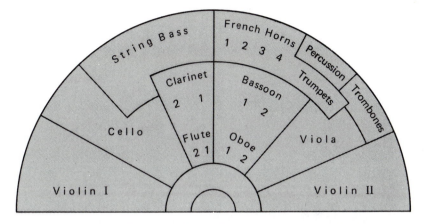

Figure A-11. Traditional Symphony Arrangement. The difference between traditional and modern arrangements for symphony orchestras lies in the positions of the second violins, the cellos, and the basses. Compare this setup with that in Figure A-12. Four things must be observed in all orchestral setups: (1) The first violins must be on the conductor's left; (2) The first chairs in the woodwinds are grouped in the center with the sections spreading outward from them; this is for efficiency when only solo winds are called for in the score. (3) The trumpets are usually seated so that they blow somewhat across the orchestra, not directly toward the audience. (4) The basses should stand behind the cellos, since they double the cello line an octave lower almost constantly. A unified bass line results.

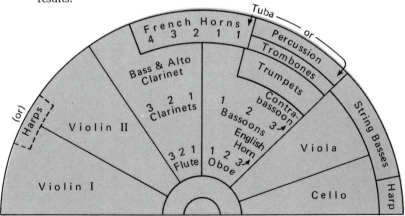

Figure A-12. Modern Symphony Arrangement. This arrangement has evolved largely during the twentieth century, and many orchestras use it as standard now. Sometimes violas are on the outside.

BAND

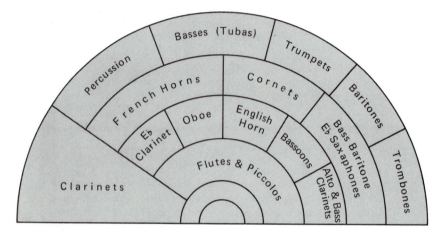

Figure A-13.   School Bands, General Setup. As in the orchestra, the instruments that play the lead melody line (the clarinets) are placed on the conductor's left as he faces the band. The trumpets and cornets are generally located so that they do not blow directly toward the audience. Sometimes two rows of clarinets replace the flutes at the conductor's right. In this case the flutes and piccolos are grouped in the center, the alto and bass clarinets are moved back a row, and the saxophones slide to their own right or are placed behind the English horn. When there are too many trombones, the baritones may be moved ahead a row, between the saxophones and the cornets. Within the clarinet section, the first clarinets are grouped near the front with the seconds and thirds filling the back part of the section—a decided difference from the seating of the second violin section in the orchestra.

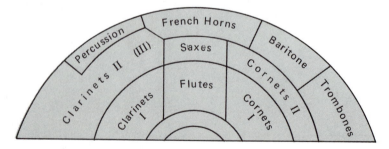

Figure A-14.   Young Band, Incomplete Instrumentation. This is a typical adaptation of the larger band setup for a grade school band.

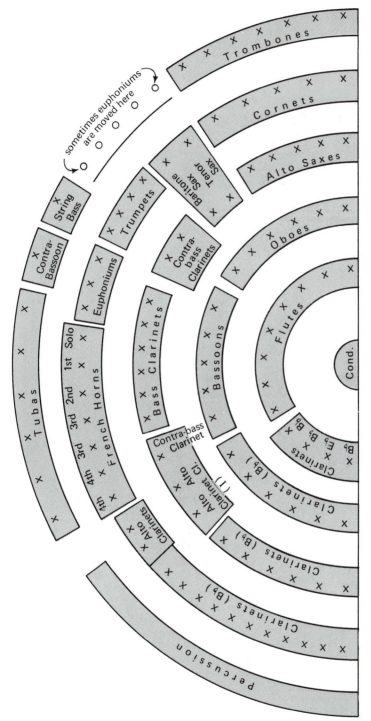

Figure A-15. Symphony Band. The setup given here is subject to variations, among which are: bassoons move from row two, center, to row three, outside right; bass clarinets and saxophones move to row four, outside right; cornets move toward the center; baritones move to back row as indicated in the figure; flutes in front of clarinets on conductor's left, completing their circle or adding oboes. Many variations exist.

235

appendix

B

Instrumentation

ORDER OF INSTRUMENTS IN THE SCORE

Orchestra	Band
Piccolo	Piccolo in C (and/or Db)
Flutes I, II	Flutes I, II
Flute III (sometimes plus Piccolo)	Oboes, I, II
Oboes I, II	Eb Clarinet
English horn	Clarinets I
Clarinets I, II	Clarinets II
Alto Clarinet	Clarinets III
Bass Clarinet	Eb Alto Clarinet
Bassoons I, II	Bb Bass Clarinet
Contrabassoon	Eb Alto Saxophones I, II
French horns I, II	Bb Tenor Saxophone
French horns III, IV	Eb Baritone Saxophone
Trumpets I, II, III	Bassoons I, II
(Cornets)	Cornets I
Trombones I, II	Cornets II, III
Trombone III and Tuba	Trumpets I, II
Timpani	French horns I, III
Percussion	French horns II, IV
Harp	Trombones I, II
Violins I	Trombones III
Violins II	Bb Baritone horns (treble clef)
Violas	Euphoniums (bass clef)
Cellos	Basses (Tubas)

Basses
To balance such an orchestra the
strings would number, from violins to basses, respectively, ap-
proximately 20, 18, 12, 10, 8.

String Basses
Timpani
Percussion

LANGUAGE CHART: GENERAL TERMS

English	German	French	Italian
Major	Dur	Majeur	Maggiore
Minor	Moll	Mineur	Minore
B sharp	Bis, His (Kreuz)	si dièse	si diesis
B natural (ti)	H	si	si
B flat	B (Be)	si bémol	si bémolle
A sharp	Ais	la dièse	la diesis
A natural	A	la	la
A flat	As	la bémol	la bémolle
G sharp	Gis	sol dièse	sol diesis
G natural	G	sol	sol
G flat	Ges	sol bémol	sol bémolle
F sharp	Fis	fa dièse	fa diesis
F natural	F	fa	fa
F flat	Fes	fa bémol	fa bémolle
E sharp	Eis	mi dièse	mi diesis
E natural	E	mi	mi
E flat	Es	mi bémol	mi bémolle
D sharp	Dis	re dièse	re diesis
D natural	D	re	re
D flat	Des	re bémol	re bémolle
C sharp	Cis	ut dièse	do diesis
C natural	C	ut	do
C flat	Ces	ut bémol	do bémolle

NOTATION TERMINOLOGY

United States	British
double whole note (eight counts)	breve
whole note	semi-breve
half note	minim
quarter note	crotchet
eighth note	quaver
sixteenth note	semi-quaver
thirty-second note	demi-semi-quaver
sixty-fourth note	hemi-demi-semi-quaver

LANGUAGE CHART ORCHESTRAL INSTRUMENTS

Abbreviation	English	German
Fl.	Flute(s)	Flöte, Flöten
Ob., Hb.	Oboe(s)	(H) oboe, (H) oboen
E. H.	English horn	Englisch Horn
Cl., Kl.	Clarinet(s)	Klarinette(n)
B. Cl., Bkl.	Bass clarinet	Bassklarinette(n)
Bn., Fg.	Bassoon(s)	Fagott(e)
C. Bssn., Con. Bn., C. Fag., C. Bon.	Contrabassoon	Kontrafagott(e)
Hn., Cor.	French horn(s)	Horn, Hörner
Tr., Tbe. (pl.)	Trumpet(s)	Trompete(n)
Crnt., Kor.	Cornet(s)	Kornett(e)
Trb., Tbn., Tbni. (pl.) Pos.	Trombone(s)	Posaune(n)
Tuba, Btb.	Bass Tuba	Basstuba
Timp., Pk.	Timpani (pl.)	Pauke(n)
*Sn. Dr., Tr., C. C.,	Snare (side) Drum	Trommel
B. Dr., Gr. Tr., C., Gr. Cassa	Bass Drum	Grosse Trommel
Cymb., Bck., Ptti.	Cymbals (pl.)	Becken (pl.)
Trgl.	Triangle	Triangel
Tmbn., Tamb.	Tambourine	Tamburin, Schellen Trommel
Ch., Glk., Cloch., Camp.	Chimes	Glocken
Harp, Hpe., Arp.	Harp(s)	Harfe(n)
V., Vn.	Violin(s)	Violine(n)
Vla., Va., Br.	Viola(s)	Bratsche(n)
Vlc., Vc.	Cello(s)	Violoncello(-e)
Cb., Kb.	Double bass(es)	Kontrabass(-bässe)

The following instruments are occasionally used in the orchestra:

Sax.	Saxophone(s)	Saxophon(e)
Bar., Eph.	Baritone horn(s)	Euphonion
	Euphonium(s)	Baryton
Xyl.	Xylophone	Strohfiedel (Holz und Strohinstrument)
Cas., Kas.	Castanettes	Kastagnetten
Glck., Glsp.	Orchestra bells	Glockenspiel

Note: Cel., Celesta; Caisse sourde, tom-tom;

The term tamburo is a general term meaning *drum;* tabor, small drum. For complete and detailed percussion information the reader is referred to: *Modern School for Snare Drum,* Morris Goldenberg, Chappell & Co., New York, 1955 ©

French	Italian
Flûte(s)	Flauto(-i)
Hautbois	Oboe, Oboi
Cor anglais	Corno Inglese
Clarinette(s)	Clarinetto(-i)
Clarinette-basse	Clarione, Clarinetto basso
Basson(s)	Fagotto(-i)
Contre-basson(s)	Contrafagotto(-i)
Cor(s)	Corno(-i)
Trompette(s)	Tromba, Trombe
Cornet(s)	Cornetto(-i)
Trombone(s)	Trombone(-i)
Tuba basse	Tuba di basso
Timbale(s)	Timpano(-i)
Caisse claire	Piccola Cassa Tamburo
Grosse caisse	Gran cassa
	Tamburone
Cymbales (pl.)	Piatti (pl.) (Cinelli)
Triangle	Triangolo
Tambour de Basque	Tamburin
Cloches	Campane
Harpe(s)	Arpa, Arpe
Violon(s)	Violino(-i)
Alto(s)	Viola, Viole
Violoncelle(s)	Violoncello(-i)
Contrebasse(s)	Contrabasso(i)
Saxophone(s)	Sassofono(-i)
Baryton	Bombarda
Claquebois	Gigelira (Silofono)
Castagnettes	Castagnette, Nacchere
Jeu de timbre(s)	Campanelli
Jeu di clochette	Strumento d'acciaio
	Carillon

See also: *Dictionary of Percussion Terms* by Morris Lang and Harry Spivack. (New York: Lang Percussion Company, © 1977).

Name of Bowing	Section of Bow Used	How Performed	Notation	Typical Use
		ON-THE-STRING BOWINGS—LEGATO		
Whole bow Smoothly	Entire length of bow from frog to point ⊓ ∨ or any part thereof.	Bow must remain parallel with the bridge throughout its length of stroke. Requires bow-arm to reach forward as bow moves from middle to tip, and pull inward as motion goes from tip to middle.	Adagio	Any slow passages where breadth or length of tone is important
Slurs	May be performed in any section of the bow ⊓ and ∨	The bow moves smoothly in one direction while the fingers change the notes on the string or strings.		Used wherever the slur-line indicates in the music. Used in legato melodic passages, in short motifs, and in scales and arpeggios where indicated.

	Bow location	Description	Notation	Usage
Détaché	Middle or middle to point ⊓ ∨	Short separate bows played smoothly: *not* slurred, *not* staccato.	(fast tempo)	In passage work where the notes are of equal length and are *not* marked with staccato dots. Also used in broad figures of this type on the eighth notes. Used in fast *fortes* for notes with staccato dots among slurred notes.
Louré	Any section of the bow is feasible ⊓ and ∨	The bow *continues its motion* as in any slur, but releases pressure slightly between notes so that the notes become somewhat articulated.		Used for expressiveness in slurs where the notes need emotional individuality and in slurred bowings on the *same pitch* to distinguish rhythm.
Tremolo (Bowed)	Middle and middle to point ⊓ ∨	Very short separate bows, very fast. Actually a speeded-up détaché bowing. Motion centers in flexibility of the wrist. Not necessary to count the number of notes per beat. Usually indefinite.	(Adagio) trem.	For the excitement of a fast shimmering effect in chordal accompaniments or in melodic playing. Softer effects are played near the point of the bow. Louder at the middle. If very loud, inside players on each stand broaden to détaché instead of tremolo.
Tremolo (Fingered)	Any section of the bow is practical ⊓ and ∨	The bow plays smoothly as in a slurred bowing. Fingers alternate rapidly on a pair of notes on *one string*—as rapidly as a trill.		Wherever a trill-effect is desired on notes more than the interval of a second apart.

241

ON-THE-STRING BOWINGS—STACCATO

"Staccatos"	Any section of the bow ⊓ and ⌄	Any note with a stop at the end of it may fall under the generic term "staccato" on the stringed instruments.	Invariably printed with a dot above or below the note, but not all dots mean on-the-string staccatos. See Spiccato, Sautillé, Staccto volante, Ricochet below.	Anywhere a stop is desired after a note. The note may be long or short, but if followed by a momentary stop it is some variety of Staccato.
Martelé	Any section of the bow is practical from whole bow to half an inch of bow ⊓ ⌄	The bow applies pressure to the string while standing still before moving. The pressure is sufficiently released, at the instant the bow starts to move, to produce a good sound. The bow stops still at the end of the stroke, and again sets pressure preparatory to the next stroke. This bowing is the underlying foundation on which ultimate clarity of style is built.	Sometimes: Sometimes:	This bowing cannot be used in fast passage work. The tempo must be slow enough to provide time for the stopping and the setting of the bow between notes. It is used for all types of on-the-string staccatos from *pp* to *ff*. Used wherever heavy ictus is needed in the sound. Also for accents.
Slurred Staccatos	Any section of the bow is good. ⊓ and ⌄. Most often ⌄. Not used in orchestra	A series of martelé strokes moving in one direction of the bow. The bow does not leave the strings between notes.		Most often written, when written, on long runs. is practical. in Moderato or slower, and *f* or heavy.

OFF-THE-STRING BOWINGS

Spiccato (Controlled)	Anywhere between frog and middle including middle ⊓ ∨	The bow is dropped on the strings and rebounds of its own accord. Must be held very lightly by hand and allowed to recoil of its own volition.	Molto allegro	From *pp* to *f* in passage-work where lightness and sparkling character is desired.
"Chopped"	At the frog ⊓ ∨	Similar to Spiccato, but heavier, with less finesse.	*ff*	When a spiccato effect is called for but the dynamic is too loud for a real spiccato.
Sautillé (Uncontrolled Spiccato)	Middle, and very slightly above and below the middle ⊓ ∨	A very fast détaché which is so rapid that it flies off the string each time the bow changes its direction from ⊓ to ∨, and ∨ to ⊓. The hand moves in a more perpendicular swing in the wrist joint than for tremolo.	Presto and Prestissimo	In very fast, continuous passage work where lightness and speed are the requisite.
Staccato volante (Flying staccato)	A series of spiccatos in one direction of bow, ∨-bow only	The bow is dropped on the strings, rebounds and drops again without changing its direction, continuing in this manner.	(volante)	For lightness on scale passages usually. For the two-note-bow slurred-staccato in very fast passages.

OFF-THE-STRONG BOWINGS (cont.)

Ricochet	A series of spiccatos in one direction of the bow, ⊓ -bow only	The bow is dropped on the strings going down-bow and allowed to bounce the requisite number of times.	Short, light, sputtering runs and "galloping" rhythms as in the William Tell Overture.
Ricochet tremolo	Middle ⊓ ∨	Two down-bow bounces followed by 2 up-bow bounces (spiccato).	To replace the single spiccato on repeated notes, especially in fast tremolos of long duration.

From *Orchestral Bowings and Routines* by Elizabeth A. H. Green. Used by permission. (See Appendix G.)

appendix
D
Synopsis of Musical Form

Musical Form deals with the patterns underlying the construction of our many types of musical composition. A composer, desiring to write a simple Minuet, will use a small two-part song-form. If his Minuet is to have an added Trio, he will build around the pattern of the three-part song-form. If his aim is to write the first movement of a symphony, the form adopted will usually be the Large Sonata Form. Such forms are subject to variation just as patterns for clothing are subject to variation. There is, therefore, a certain amount of flexibility to be found in the application of these forms to individual compositions.

The experienced conductor knows that one of his greatest aids to score memorization is a thorough acquaintance with the form of the particular composition being studied. Many conductors make this a point of departure. Since Musical Form is quickest grasped through the medium of the worked-out example, the following very simple development may be of assistance to the student who has not yet had formalized instruction in this branch of music theory.

The **Germ** of the musical thought is a basic rhythmic figure or a simple grouping of several notes:

(a) Monometer: one major accent

(b) Bimeter: two major accents

It is important to recognize the Germ in Beethoven's works especially. It helps in balancing the parts dynamically. Perhaps the best-known Germ in all of music is the opening notes of Beethoven's Fifth Symphony:

The Germ may be *developed* in many ways to lend variety and interest, while preserving the feeling of unity within the work. The conductor should be alert to recognize the composer's cleverness in the handling of his motifs. Development may take place through the following means:

1. Transposition of the notes:

2. Expansion of the intervals between the notes:

3. Contraction of the intervals between the notes:

4. Diminution of the note time-values:

5. Repetition of the members of the motif:

6. Omission of members of the motif:

7. Irregular changes in the order of the notes, rhythm unchanged:

8. Retrograde motion, rhythm unchanged:

9. Combinations of members of the Germ:

10. Inversion: turning the intervals upside-down:

11. Various combinations of the foregoing, used simultaneously; as Inversion and Repetition:

The development of the Germ often results in the **Motif**, the basic thought of the composition. In the case of our example, it might be stated as follows:

The next example presents (1) the Motif (first two measures), (2) the Phrase (second two measures), (3) the Period, ending on the eighth measure, (4) the second theme of a Two-part Song-form, ending on the sixteenth measure. This simple form may be enlarged greatly by the composer by doubling the length of each section as given here in the small form:

THE TWO-PART SONG-FORM

When the second theme of a Two-part Song-form is followed by the first theme again, then the Three-part Song-form results. Retain similarity of style in conducting parts I and III. This is shown in the next example.

THE COMPLETED THREE-PART SONG-FORM

In a real musical composition, the length could be doubled by marking repeat dots at the double bars. The composition may further be lengthened by the addition of Introduction and Coda, each of which may assume quite some proportion in the larger compositions.

The gradual expansion of Form proceeds as follows: (Refer to the preceding examples.)

The **Phrase**: four or eight measures ending with a cadence or a half cadence. Mark phrases not from the up-beat but from the first full measure following the up-beat.

The **Period**: eight or sixteen measures. If it is eight measures, it is then four plus four, with a cadence separating it from the next section; or if sixteen, then eight measures ending on the Dominant, plus another eight measures ending on the Tonic. (The shorter form was used in the tune developed herein.) Vary size and speed of gestures to show these divisions.

The **Two part Song-form** (A–B): eight measures ending on the Dominant (Section A) and eight measures ending on the Tonic (Section B). In the long form, each section is sixteen measures instead of eight.

The **Three-part Song-form** (A–B–A): Short form, eight measures (A), eight measures (B), eight measures of (A) used as a D.C. Long form, sixteen measures each.

The **Rondo** forms: A Rondo is like a layer cake where the cake is always the same but the filling between each layer is different. Technical names are Theme and Episode. The Theme, either in its original form or embellished, occurs more than twice in the Rondo form. For specialized details, the reader is referred to one of the books on Musical Form in Appendix G. Retain similar conducting style for the theme.

The **Theme and Variations**: the theme usually consists of four or more measures. It can be followed by any number of variations the composer may wish to write. These variations may take the form of embellishments of the melody, changing meters and rhythms, changes in mode, developments of germs drawn from the principal theme, and clever adaptations of the various devices numbered 1 to 11 in the forepart of this discussion. In the classical period, these transformations adhered rather closely to the original harmonic structure, but this is not true in the subsequent writings. Classed as types of Theme and Variation are the often-encountered **Chaconne** and **Passacaglia**. Vary the conducting style for the variations.

The **Fugue** concerns itself with a principal theme called the subject. As each instrument enters, it plays the subject, previously stated in another instrument. Once having stated the subject, the instrument continues with counterpoint to the subject, which counterpoint may be called the countersubject when it has an individual character of its own and recurs repeatedly. The first instrument states the subject in the Tonic key; the second instrument renders the subject either a fifth higher or a fourth lower than the original instrument. Such a statement is called the *answer*. The third instrument usually states the theme an octave higher or lower than the original instrument, and it, in turn, is followed by a fourth instrument on the subject—this in the case of a four-voice fugue. The conductor's job is to see that each statement of the theme is clearly heard as such. When the third voice enters, balance requires the two voices already playing to be toned down. Most fugues have a stretto section where the subject and answer are brought as close together as possible. Many fugues include a coda.

The (early) **Classical Sonata Form:** Part I is usually somewhat in excess of a sixteen-measure unit. It starts in the Tonic key and modulates to the Dominant, in which key the first part ends at the double bar. Part II starts again with the first theme, but this time in the key of the Dominant and gradually moves back into the Tonic for the ending of the movement. If the first part is in a minor key, then the modulation before the double bar may go to the Major with the section following the bar in the Major.

The **Large Sonata Form** is used almost invariably for the first movement of the multiple-movement works such as symphonies, quartets, solo sonatas of the romantic and post-romantic periods, and solo concertos after the early classic period. (In the latter, a lengthy orchestral exposition precedes that of the solo instrument.) Part I of this form is called the *Exposition*. It is comprised of two themes of contrasting character, the first in the Tonic key, the second in the Dominant. Part II, the *Development*, is to be found after the double bar in the classic and romantic symphonies. This concerns itself with the rather exhaustive treatment or "development" of motifs drawn from the first two themes. Part III is called the *Recapitulation*. It brings in the material of the Exposition once again. In the classical use of this form, the second theme is in the Tonic key in the Recapitulation. This form is often expanded by a lengthy introduction (usually slow) and a closing theme or codetta which is present (if not of major importance) in Mozart and Haydn symphonies and sometimes assumes the proportions of another major theme in the works of the romantic period (Brahms symphonies, for example). A facile recognition of form aids memorization.

The **Modern Sonata Form** in use today is far freer than its predecessors in its motion, in its key relationships, and its general structure. The double bar, which is an almost ever-present adjunct of the Large Sonata Form, is most often missing in the modern version.

Let us emphasize again that this short summary gives only the obvious and most generalized structures. In actual composition, each work has its own idiosyncrasies and the work states its form rather than the form stating the work.

Any of the forms discussed herein, except the Fugue and the Modern Sonata Form, may be found lengthened by the composer through the addition of repeat dots at the double bars.

appendix
E

Terminology for the Conductor

The following list of one hundred terms is comprised of foreign language designations which the young conductor should know. Common words such as legato, allegro, etc., are not included in the list. It is taken for granted that the college student in music will know such customary markings. The terms given here are frequently encountered in conducting the standard repertoire and the school music of a training nature. A lack of knowledge of these words can cause the conductor to make bad mistakes, rhythmically, musically, and in handling the instrumentation and routines generally. Since the lists are limited to the more common terms, the student will have to resort to the large musical dictionary for further help when needed.

Classification is made alphabetically under three headings: (1) Terms of a general nature, (2) Terms affecting the tempo and time-beating, (3) Terms affecting the handling of the instruments themselves.

TERMS OF A GENERAL NATURE

A DUE (*a 2*). To be played by both, as by first and second flute.

COLLA PARTE. With the other part; often refers to accommodating the soloist at that place in the score.

COME PRIMA. Like the first time.

COME STA. Exactly as written; do not change anything.

CON. With; seen in other forms as a contraction with the article in Italian, thus: *col, coi, colle, cogli, colla* (depending upon the gender and number).

EN DEHORS. Out in front of; means the part so marked should be projected through the ensemble; it must be heard.

ERSTES MAL. The first time.

ETWAS. Somewhat.

FORTE POSSIBILE. As loud as possible.

FRAPPE; FRAPPER. The downbeat; to beat time.

GLEICH. Quickly.

GLISSEZ; GLISSER. Slide; to slide.

IMMER. Always.

L'ISTESSO (LO STESSO). The same; used usually with the word *tempo*, meaning that the new part should be in the same tempo as the preceding part.

MARCATO. Marked, accented.

MENO. Less.

MEZZO. Half; usually *mezza voce*, softly, as if whispered.

MODO. Style, manner.

MORENDO. Dying away.

MOTO. Motion.

MURKEY BASS. Broken octaves, lower note coming first.

MUTA. Change; usually reads *muta in* _____, meaning change the instrument to the pitch designated. Most often seen in timpani and French horn parts.

OHNE. Without; usually *ohne Dämpfer*, without mute.

OSSIA. Otherwise; often refers to a simplified part—otherwise do it so.

PARTITUR. The score.

PETIT. Little.

PEU. A little.

PIACERE, A PIACERE. At pleasure.

PIENO. Full.

PIÙ. *More;* most often seen with *mosso*, meaning more motion, slightly quicken the tempo. Also, PLUS.

PULT. Desk, a music stand. Usually refers to number of stands which are to play the part.

RIPIENO. Similar to *tutti*, it distinguishes the accompanying instruments from the soloist.

RUHIG. Tranquil.

SANS. Without.

SCHNELL. Quick, rapid, *presto*.

SCIOLTO. Fluently.

SCORDATURA. Tuning contrary to the normal, addressed to the strings.

SEC, SECCO. Dry, very short, no after-ring.

SEGUE. Follow, continue in the same manner.

SEHR. Very.

SENZA. Without; usually *senza sordini*, without mutes.

SMORZANDO. Suddenly dying away.

SOTTO VOCE. In an undertone, soft voice.

SPIANAR LA VOCE. With smooth voice.

STENTATO. Labored.

STIMME. A single voice or part in the score.

STREPITOSO. Noisily.

STRISCIANDO, STRISCIATO. Legato motion, smooth.

SUBITO. Suddenly; usually with a *piano* marking.

TROPPO. Too much.

TUTTI. The whole ensemble, everybody.

UNISONI. In unison; as *violini unisoni*, all violins in unison.

VIDE. A cut; VI is printed where the cut starts and DE is shown at the end of the cut, thus: VI . . . DE.

VIRGULA. The old terminology for the baton.

VOCI PARI. Equal voices.

TERMS AFFECTING THE TEMPO AND TIME-BEATING

A PUNTO. Exactly in rhythm.

ACCELERANDO. Gradually increasing the tempo.

AD LIBITUM. At liberty; take time, permit liberties here.

AFFRETTANDO. Excitedly, increasing the tempo.

CON ALCUNA LICENZA. With some license; not perfectly rhythmic.

ETWAS LANGSAMER. Somewhat slower.

IM TAKT. In tempo.

LANGSAM, LANGSAMER. Slow, slower.

MÄSSIG. Moderato.

PRESSANDO. Hurrying, pressing forward.

RHYTHMÉ. Rhythmic feeling emphasized.

RUBATO. Varying the note values within the rhythm, not strictly as written.

STRETTO. Condensing, accelerating the tempo. (Do not confuse with the stretto of the fugue form, which is only a condensing of the distance between subject and answer.)

STRINGENDO. Accelerating the tempo.

SUIVEZ. Follow; usually refers to following the soloist who may take some liberties with the tempo for expression.

TACET. Silent; usually means the particular instrument does not play in that movement of the work.

TAGLIO. A cut.

TAKT. The time, the measure, rhythmically; sometimes, an accenting of the first beat in the measure.

TEMPO PERDITO. Unsteady tempo.

TEMPO REGGIATO. Regulate the tempo, usually to accommodate the soloist.

TEMPO RUBATO. Not strictly on the beat.

ZURÜCKHALTEN. Ritard.

Note: the term *Agogic* is a general classification for the modifying of the tempo in favor of the expression.

TERMS AFFECTING THE HANDLING OF THE INSTRUMENTS THEMSELVES

A PUNTA D'ARCO. At the point of the bow.

AM STEG. Played with a light bow stroke very close to the bridge so that the quality of the tone is shimmering, sounding the component harmonics of the fundamental tone (*Ponticello*).

ARCHET. Bow, with the bow.

ARCO. Bow, with the bow.

COL LEGNO. With the stick of the bow; usually performed by striking the strings with the stick of the bow.

CON SORDINI. With mutes.

DÄMPFER. Mute; usually *mit Dämpfer*, with mute, or *ohne Dämpfer*, without mute. Often seen as *gedämpft* (stopped) in horn parts. Also means without snares.

FIRST TREBLE; SECOND TREBLE. First soprano; second soprano.

LEGNO. Wood (of the bow).

OTEZ. Remove (the mute).

PAUKENSCHLÄGEL. The timpani stick.

PONTICELLO. Light tone near the bridge so upper partials sound in the tone.

SORDINO. Mute; also *sourdine*.

SPITZE. Point of the bow.

STEG. Bridge.

STIMMUNG. The tuning.

SULLA TASTIERA; SUL TASTO. On the fingerboard; a command to bow the string just over the end of the fingerboard for a light, flute-like tone.

SUR LA TOUCHE. On the fingerboard, same as *sulla tastiera*.

SUR LE CHEVALET. Literally, "on the little (wooden) horse," bowed very close to the bridge, *ponticello*.

SUR UNE CORDE. On one string; the melody to be played entirely on one string. The German word for string is *Saite*.

TON BOUCHÉ. Stopped tone in French horn playing.

+. Refers to plucking the string with the *left* hand when used in string music, and to playing the notes so marked as stopped tones on the French horns when given in their parts.

Regarding abbreviated writing:

One bar on the stem = play eighths:

Two bars on the stem = play sixteenths:

Three bars on the stem usually means tremolo, free, fast reiteration:

But in adagio and largo, it may mean play thirty-second notes, rhythmically.

SOME SPECIALIZED PERCUSSION TERMS

COPERTI. Covered, muffled.

ÉTOUFFÉ. Dampened.

LAISSER VIBRER; LASCIARE VIBRARE. To let it ring.

NADEL. Mit dem = played with a knitting needle.

SCHWAM. Aus = made of sponge, soft stick.

SCORDATE. Tuned, no snares.

SECOUÉ. Rubbed, struck.

SKIN. Membrana, peau, fell, parche.

SNARES. With = con, mit, avec. Without = sans, ohne, senza. Snares = timbres, cordes, Schnarren.

WIRE BRUSH. Spazzole, brosso, scavolo di ferro, spazzola di ferro, balais, ballai mettalique, cepillos metal, rute, and verga or verghe (as in *Peter and the Wolf*).

PLAYED WHERE:

> *On the rim:* au ribord, al cerchio.
> *On the edge:* au bord, am Rand.
> *Close to the rim:* près du rebord.
> *At the center:* au centre, au milieu.

PLAYED HOW:

> *With the thumb:* Avec la pouce, mit dem Daumen.
> *With the knuckles:* colla nocce, mit dem Knöcheln.
> *With the fist:* mit der Faust.
> *On the knee* (tambourine): Sur la genou.

CYMBALS:

> *Antique:* crotales.
> *Attached:* befestigt.
> *Crash:* tellern, platos.
> *Suspended:* cymbale sospendue, frei, hangend, sospeso.

Caution: SCHLITTEN means tuned sleighbells, as in Mozart's *Sleighride*.

TAMBOURINE DI BASQUE, as in the *Farandole* by Bizet, is played on drum without snares.

appendix
F

The Physical Exercises in Sequence

THE PHYSICAL EXERCISES IN SEQUENTIAL ORDER: COMPLETE SERIES

1. Relaxation study: arms hanging relaxed at the sides; body twists left and right; arms allowed to swing freely where they will. Stop body motion, allow arms to continue their free, uncontrolled swing until they come to a stop of their own accord.
2. Horizontal and perpendicular arm-hand motions, pp. 10–11.
3. Left fist exercise, activate and de-activate, p. 72.
4. Cues with and without preparation, p. 73.
5. Long crescendo-diminuendo gesture in left hand, p. 73.
6. The *perpendicular* motions of No. 2, the two arms moving in opposite directions, simultaneously.
7. Horizontal arm-hand motions, one arm tenuto, other arm staccato. Let the tenuto arm depend upon habit. Look at the staccato arm to see that it stands still while the tenuto arm completes its motion. Both arms should *start* at the same instant. Then reverse arms' style.
8. Perpendicular gestures, arm-hand, staccato in one arm, tenuto in the other, simultaneously. Reverse. Also combine perpendicular (one arm) against horizontal (other arm).
9. No. 6, staccato vs. tenuto.
10. Wrist circles, outward, inward, arm static.
11. Arms tight to sides, down to the wrists. Arms do not move. Flip hands forward and backward rapidly in wrist joint. Keep wrists relaxed. Next:

Arm tight as far as elbows. Swing arms freely from elbows only. Hands may hit shoulders. Then: Relax arm fully and swing from the shoulders, even to the complete circle up and around. This exercise links the mind to the several sections of the arm. Helps you to use only that part of the arm needed for the given dynamic.

12. Bend arms at elbows and hold them tight to the sides. Perform the tenuto down-up with just the hands in the wrist joint, both hands moving in the same direction.

13. Same as No. 12, both hands staccato.

14. Now, staccato in one hand, tenuto in the other.

15. Nos. 12, 13, and 14, with the hands moving in opposite directions.

16. The perpendicular gestures of No. 2, but performed from the elbows only, the arms tight to the sides as far as the elbows.

17. No. 16, staccato. In both excercises, see that the angle of the hands is correct as in the first study, No. 2.

18. Nos. 16 and 17, moving in opposite directions.

19. Drill Study from page 129, variation of speed of motion.

20. Arm is extended forward or to the side. Tension travels from the shoulder to the fingertips gradually. Try to feel the muscles tense throughout the length of the arm.

21. Same as No. 20, but tension traveling from fingertips to shoulder.

22. Same as Nos. 20 and 21, but starting with tension and letting relaxation travel through the arm.

Note: In all of the exercises, see that the angle of the hand, relative to the motion of the arm, is always in the opposite direction, as given in the initial Exercise 2 on p. 11.

appendix

G

Bibliography

The following works are specifically mentioned in the Recommended Reference Readings at the ends of the chapters.

ADLER, SAMUEL. *Choral Conducting, An Anthology.* New York: Holt, Rinehart and Winston, 1971.

ADKINS, LIEUT. COL. H. E. *Treatise on the Military Band.* London: Boosey and Hawkes, Ltd. New York: Boosey & Co. Ltd. 1931.

AUSTIN, WILLIAM A. *Music in the Twentieth Century.* New York: W. W. Norton and Co., 1966.

BALK, WESLEY. *The Complete Singer-Actor.* Minneapolis, Minn., University of Minnesota Press, 1977.

BAMBERGER, CARL. *The Conductor's Art.* New York: McGraw-Hill Book Co., 1965.

BARRA, DONALD. *The Dynamic Performance: A Performer's Guide to Musical Expression and Interpretation.* Englewood Cliffs, N.J.: Prentice-Hall, 1983.

BERRY, WALLACE. *Form in Music,* 2nd ed. Englewood Cliffs, N.J.: Prentice-Hall, 1986.

BLACKMAN, CHARLES. *Behind the Baton.* New York: Charos Enterprises, 1964.

BOULT, ADRIAN C. *A Handbook of Conducting.* Oxford: Hall the Printer, 1936.

BOWLES, MICHAEL. *The Art of Conducting.* Garden City, N.Y.: Doubleday and Co., 1959.

BRAITHWAITE, WARWICK. *The Conductor's Art.* London: Williams and Norgate, 1952.

CHRISTIANI, ADOLF F. *Principles of Expression in Pianoforte Playing.* New York: Harper Brothers, 1886.

CLYNES, MANFRED. *Music, Mind and Brain.* ("Sentics.") New York: Plenum Publishing Co., 1982.

COOPER, G. W., and L. B. MEYER. *The Rhythmic Structure of Music.* Chicago: The University of Chicago Press, 1960.

COPE, DAVID. *New Music Notation.* Dubuque, Iowa: Kendall, Hunt Publishing Company, 1976.

COWARD, HENRY. *Choral Technique and Interpretation.* London: Novello and Co., n.d.

CRIST, BAINBRIDGE. *The Art of Setting Words to Music.* New York: Carl Fisher, 1944.

CROCKER, RICHARD L. *A History of Musical Style.* New York: McGraw-Hill Book Co., 1966.

DANNREUTHER, EDWARD. *Musical Ornamentation.* London: Novello and Company, n.d.

DAVISON, ARCHIBALD T. *Choral Conducting.* Cambridge, Mass.: Harvard University Press, 1940.

DECKER, HAROLD A., and JULIUS HERFORD. *Choral Conducting, A Symposium.* Englewood Cliffs, N.J.: Prentice-Hall, 1973.

EARHART, WILL. *The Eloquent Baton.* New York: M. Witmark and Sons, 1931.

FARKAS, PHILIP. *The Art of French Horn Playing.* Evanston, Ill.: Summy-Birchard Co., 1956.

————. *The Art of Musicianship.* Bloomington, Ind.: Musical Publications, 1976.

FINN, WILLIAM JOSEPH. *The Conductor Raises His Baton.* New York: Harper Brothers, 1944.

FUCHS, PETER PAUL. *The Psychology of Conducting.* New York: MCA Publications, A Division of MCA, Inc., 1969.

GALAMIAN, IVAN. *Principles of Violin Playing and Teaching.* Englewood Cliffs, N.J.: Prentice-Hall, 1985.

GALLO, STANISLAO. *The Modern Band.* Boston: C. C. Birchard and Co., 1935.

GOLDMAN, RICHARD FRANKO. *The Concert Band.* New York: Rinehart and Co., 1946.

————. *The Wind Band, Its Literature and Technique.* Boston: Allyn and Bacon, 1962.

GREEN, ELIZABETH A. H. *The Dynamic Orchestra: Principles of Orchestral Performance for Instrumentalists, Conductors, and Audiences.* Englewood Cliffs, N.J.: Prentice-Hall, 1987.

————. *Orchestral Bowings and Routines.* Ann Arbor, Mich.: Campus Publishers, Ed.2, 1957, renewed, 1985.

————, and NICOLAI MALKO. *The Conductor's Score.* (Formerly *The Conductor and His Score.*) Englewood Cliffs, N.J.: Prentice-Hall, 1985.

GRIFFITHS, PAUL. *A Concise History of Avant-Garde Music.* New York: Oxford University Press, 1978.

GROSBAYNE, BENJAMIN. *Techniques of Modern Orchestral Conducting.* Cambridge, Mass.: Harvard University Press, 1956.

HANSEN, PETER. *An Introduction to Twentieth-Century Music,* Third Edition. Boston: Allyn & Bacon, 1971.

HOWERTON, GEORGE. *Technique and Style in Choral Singing.* New York: Carl Fisher, 1957.

HUNSBERGER, DONALD, and ROXY ERNST. *The Art of Conducting.* New York: Alfred Knopf, 1983.

JACOB, GORDON. *How to Read A Score.* London: Hawkes and Son, 1944.

JACOBSON, BERNARD. *Conductors on Conducting.* Frenchtown, New Jersey: Columbia Publishing Co., Inc., 1979.

JONES, ARCHIE M. *Techniques of Choral Conducting.* New York: Carl Fisher, 1948.

KAHN, EMIL. *Conducting.* New York: Macmillian Co., 1965.

KELLER, HERMAN. *Phrasing and Articulation.* New York: W. W. Norton and Co., 1965.

KENNAN, KENT. *The Technique of Orchestration.* 3rd ed. New York: Prentice-Hall, 1983.

KJELSON, LEE, and JAMES MCCRAY. *The Conductor's Manual of Choral Music Literature.* Melville, N.Y.: Belwin-Mills, 1973.

KOHUT, DANIEL L. *Instrumental Music Pedagogy, Teaching Techniques for School Band and Orchestra.* Englewood Cliffs, N.J.: Prentice-Hall, 1973.

LABUTA, JOSEPH. *Teaching Musicianship in the High School Band.* West Nyack, N.Y.: Parker Publishing Co., 1972.

LANG, PHILIP J. *Scoring for the Band.* New York: Mills Music, 1950.

LEIDZÉN, ERIK. *An Invitation to Band Arranging.* Philadelphia: Oliver Ditson Co., 1950.

LEINSDORF, ERICH. *The Composer's Advocate.* New Haven, Conn.: Yale University Press, 1981.

LOEBEL, KURT. "A Symphony Player Looks at Conductors," *The Instrumentalist,* vol. 29, No. 7. Feb. 1975, pp. 30–34.

LONG, R. GERRY. *The Conductor's Workshop.* Dubuque, Ia.: Wm. C. Brown Co., 1971.

MALKO, NICOLAI. *The Conductor and His Baton.* Copenhagen: Wilhelm Hansen, 1950.

MARSHALL, MADELEINE. *The Singer's Manual of English Diction.* New York: G. Schirmer, 1951, 1953, 1956, 1957.

MARTIN, WILLIAM A. and JULIUS DROSSIN. *Music of the Twentieth Century.* Englewood Cliffs, N.J.: Prentice-Hall, Inc., 1980.

MATTHAY, TOBIAS. *Musical Interpretation.* Boston: Boston Music Co., 1913.

MCELHERAN, BROCK. *Conducting Technique, for Beginners and Professionals.* New York: Oxford University Press, 1966.

MOZART, LEOPOLD. *A Treatise on the Fundamental Principles of Violin Playing*, trans., Edith Knocker. London: Oxford University Press, 1948.

MUNCH, CHARLES. *I Am a Conductor*. New York: Oxford University Press, 1955.

NEIDIG, KENNETH L. *The Band Director's Guide*. Englewood Cliffs, N.J.: Prentice-Hall, 1964.

PETERS, GORDON B. *The Drummer: Man*. Wilmette, Ill.: Kemper-Peters Publications, 1975.

PETERS, THOMAS J., and ROBERT H. WATERMAN, JR. *In Search of Excellence*. New York: Warner Books, Inc., Harper and Row, 1982.

PIETZSCH, HERMANN. *Die Trompete*, edited by Clifford Lillya and Renold Schilke. Ann Arbor, Mich.: University Music Press, n.d.

PRAUSNITZ, FREDERIK. *Score and Podium*. New York: W. W. Norton, 1983.

RABIN, MARVIN, and PRISCILLA SMITH. *Guide to Orchestral Bowings Through Musical Styles*. Madison, Wis.: University of Wisconsin Press, Extension Arts, 1984.

READ, GARDNER. *Thesaurus of Orchestral Devices*. New York: Pitman Publishing Co., 1953.

──────. *Modern Rhythmic Notation*. Bloomington, Ind.: Indiana University Press, 1979.

RESTAK, RICHARD M. *The Brain: The Last Frontier*. Garden City, N.Y.: Doubleday and Co., 1979.

RIMSKY-KORSAKOV, NICOLAI. *Principles of Orchestration*. London: Russian Music Agency, n.d.

ROOD, LOUISE. *How to Read a Score*. New York: Edwin Kalmus, 1948.

ROSS, ALLAN. *Techniques for Beginning Conductors*. Belmont, Calif.: Wadsworth Publishing Co., 1976.

RUDOLF, MAX. *The Grammar of Conducting*. New York: G. Schirmer, 1980.

SALZMAN, ERIC. *Twentieth Century Music: An Introduction*, Second Edition. Englewood Cliffs, N.J.: Prentice-Hall, 1980.

SCHERCHEN, HERMANN. *Handbook of Conducting*. London: Oxford University Press, 1933.

SCHONBERG, HAROLD C. *The Great Conductors*. New York: Simon and Schuster, 1967.

SCHWARTZ, HARRY W. *Bands of America*. New York: Doubleday and Co., 1957.

SELF, GEORGE. *New Sounds in the Classroom*. London: Universal Edition, n.d.

VAN ESS, DONALD H. *The Heritage of Musical Styles*. New York: Holt, Reinhart and Winston, 1970.

WAGNER, JOSEPH. *Band Scoring*. New York: McGraw-Hill Book Co., 1960.

──────. *Orchestration: A Practical Handbook*. New York: McGraw-Hill Book Co., 1959.

WAGNER, RICHARD. *On Conducting*. London: William Reeves, 1897.

WEERTS, RICHARD K. *Developing Individual Skills for the High School Band*. West Nyack, N.Y.: Parker Publishing Co., 1969.

WEINGARTNER, FELIX. *On the Performance of the Beethoven Symphonies*, trans., Jessie Crosland. New York: Edwin F. Kalmus. N.D.

WENNERSTROM, MARY H. *Anthology of Musical Structure and Style*. Englewood Cliffs, N. J.: Prentice-Hall, 1983.

REFERENCE WORKS

Index of New Music Notation. New York Public Library at Lincoln Center. 111 Amsterdam Avenue, New York, N. Y. 10023.

Music Industry Directory, Seventh Edition, 1983. Marquis Professional Publications, Marquis Who's Who, 200 Ohio Street, Chicago, IL. 60611.

Prospectus of New Music. Box 270, Yardley, PA., 19067.

Terminorum Musicae Index Septum Linguis Redactus (Polyglot Dictionary of Musical Terms). Akademiai Kiado-Budapest.//Bärenreiter Kassel-Basel Tours—London, 1978.

Topical Index

Index of Musical Examples

Index of Figures